The Free Church in the Andes

Scottish missionaries in the mountains of 20th century Peru

Edited & Introduced by

Iain Fraser Grigor

Published in 2020 by
Iain Fraser Grigor

Book design by Lumphanan Press
www.lumphananpress.co.uk

Printed & bound by Imprint Digital, UK.

ISBN: 978-1-5272-6768-8

for
Hugh Fraser
Rheindown

Nurse Netta Fraser, standing, with her sister, mother and brother, shortly before her departure for the Andes.

Contents

Introduction

THE DISRUPTION OF THE CHURCH OF SCOTLAND IN 1843 WAS A landmark event in the religious life of 19th century Scotland. Its origins were clear: did, or did not, a landowner have the power to appoint the minister of a Church of Scotland parish within the boundaries of his estates? The dispute reached back to the previous decade (though its roots can be traced to the century before). In 1834 the "evangelicals" – those opposed to the patronage of land-lords – won their case with a Veto Act at the General Assembly of the Church of Scotland. The opposition "moderates" took the matter to the civil courts, and in 1838 they won. And so five years later, under the leadership of the 63-year old Thomas Chalmers, some 450 ministers (out of a total of 1,200) marched out of the old church and into the "new" one, the Free Church of Scotland. (The Free Church believed that it stood in direct line of succession to the Reformed Church of the 16th century: and in that sense was not "new" at all).

Those who followed Chalmers – he had just four more years to live – included nearly all of the overseas missionaries, as well as the Gaelic-speaking and Highland congregations. The Church of Scotland kept everything in terms of property, and the new church began with nothing in the way of stipends or manses or churches. There was open obstruction from some, too: in Strontian, famously, the landlord refused land for a new church, and services were conducted on a purpose-built iron barge – an eaglais iaruinn – anchored just off the beach.

But the new church did have ambition, vision, energy and an unlimited quantity of what might be called spiritual capital. Within just one year, it had organised 500 churches, and by the time of Chalmers' death in 1847, it had no less than 700 (along with 650 schools, catering to nearly 50,000 pupils). And its overseas mission work was perhaps the largest of any church in the world – in India, Africa, the Orient and the Near East (but not – not yet – in South America).

Nor did the small secession of 1893, which led to the formation of the Free Presbyterian Church, have any significant effect on affairs, although it did produce the future Free Church missionary and later Princeton Theological Seminary professor, the spectacularly talented John Alexander Mackay. His Free Presbyterian father Duncan was a Gaelic speaker from Kishorn, at the foot of the bealach, and his mother Isabella, a MacGregor from a MacDonald mother, from the same locality. Mackay spent four year at Inverness Royal Academy, where he was taught Latin and Greek by William J. Watson. (Watson, whose father was a blacksmith, was a Gaelic speaker from Easter Ross, and he studied at the universities of Aberdeen and Oxford. His wife was the daughter of the Lismore-born Gaelic folklorist Alexander Carmichael). Later, Watson was the professor of Celtic at Edinburgh University for more than 20 years, and wrote The Celtic Place Names of Scotland.

John Alexander Mackay also studied (philosophy) at Aberdeen University. A scholarship next took him to Princeton Seminary in the United States and another scholarship took him to Spain. There he met the celebrated Basque poet and philosopher Miguel de Unamuno, who had once taught himself Danish in order to be able to read Kierkegaard in the original and whose library, Mackay later observed, contained books in 15 languages. (Mackay's brother, William Roderick, was Moderator of the Free Church General Assembly in 1958).

But the Free Church would shortly encounter, in 1900, some-thing close to disaster when the huge bulk of its membership joined with the United Presbyterian Church to form the United Free Church of Scotland. (In turn, the vast majority of this short-lived church would merge in 1929 with the Church of Scotland). All of the Free Church's pre-1900 missionaries, about 160 in total, had gone to the new church. At the 1901 General Assembly of the Free Church, there were just 27 ministers left, and perhaps 60 congregations. This post-1900 Free Church was overwhelmingly Highland in character – of its 11 presbyteries, 9 were in the Highlands, while the Glasgow presbytery actually included Inveraray and Arran. The new church was also very Gaelic in character, as shown by the large amounts of Gaelic material carried in its periodical, the Monthly Record.

The production of that monthly paper was in itself, given the circumstances, something of a major achievement. Within just seven months of the 1900 division, the new paper was being printed and distributed: 16 pages of dense bi-lingual text, produced in hot-metal type to impeccable standards of accuracy, under the editorship of Archibald MacNeilage in Glasgow: he would edit it for 18 years.

Foreign mission work was an immediate aspiration of the new church. In February 1906, the Monthly Record could report that, "Miss Elizabeth MacLeod has docked in Bombay, and embarks on a 36-hour train journey to Seoni". And by July 1908, the Monthly Record could note that, "the needs of South Africa will not absorb all the Foreign Mission revenue of the Free Church". By the autumn of that year, "the Free Church has now her missionary on his way to South Africa. The Rev. Alexander Dewar has wide experience in missionary work among native races in Africa". (Dewar was the uncle of the Scottish Labour politician, Donald Dewar).

In August 1909, there is a prophetic editorial in the Monthly Record referring to Peru and suggesting, inter alia, that the native people of the Peruvian Andes, "had been better off under the Inca than the Spanish": while the following May there is notice of the World Missionary Conference to be opened in Edinburgh in a matter of weeks. This conference would be of critical importance to the forthcoming missionary operations of the Free Church in Peru. Three missionary agencies were already at work in South America – the Regions Beyond Missionary Union, the South America Evangelical Mission and the Help for Brazil Mission.

(One of these early missionaries was the Baptist James "Diego" Thomson, from Scotland. As early as the summer of 1822, he arrived in Peru and spent two and a half years there, and in that short period contrived to have the New Testament translated into Quechua, the language, along with Aymará, of many of the mountain Indians).

The missionaries of these agencies objected when they learned that the continent was not to be discussed at the Edinburgh conference, because Anglicans (or some of them) did not like the idea that predominantly Roman Catholic lands be considered legitimate areas for Protestant missionary work. A year later, then, at the Keswick Convention in Liverpool, the Evangelical Union of South America was inaugurated, and it allocated to the Free Church of Scotland a huge area in the north of Peru for missionary work. And in the Monthly Record for August 1914 – as the lamps were indeed going out all over Europe – there was a five-column editorial on mission work in South America, where there were, "six million Indians to be baptised".

By this stage, then, the die was irrevocably cast: and so the Free Church of Scotland began its mission to the continent of South America. John Alexander Mackay had volunteered to work somewhere in South America for the Free Church. While still at Princeton, he was invited by the Church to make an exploratory tour of some countries throughout the southern continent. His tour (he left just three days short of his 26th birthday!) took four months, and included Peru, Bolivia, Chile, Uruguay and Argentina.

From Chile, he had intended to cross to Buenos Aires in Argentina by train, but the line across the continent was blocked, so Mackay took the coal-fired Orita for Montevideo in Uruguay via the stormy Magellan Straits, to the immediate north of Tierra del Fuego. (Some relations of his mother were farmers there, and his brother Duncan was also farming in that vast region: but he was unable to visit any of them). After visiting Buenos Aires, he returned to Montevideo, and in September embarked for Plymouth, on the Ruahine: for the Foreign Missions' Committee of the Free Church was urgently awaiting his report. He proposed that the Church start with educational work in Lima, but added: "we must have a medical mission in Peru". The Church agreed.

And so in the autumn of 1916, Mackay and his new wife Jane Logan Wells embarked (they sailed on Friday the 13th of October) from London on the Kanuta, a coal-powered cargo-ship on which they were the only passengers. In the western Channel, Mackay recalled many years later, they passed a full-rigged sailing ship working her way out into the U-boat infested Atlantic. The Kanuta coaled on the American coast at Virginia, and arrived in Peru after a lengthy passage via the Panama Canal. The Mackays took over an existing missionary school in Lima and began educational work at once in the Peruvian capital.

But while the history of the Free Church educational work in Lima has been written, Free Church missionary work in the mountains of Peru has received no attention. No doctoral theses appear to have been written on the subject at any of the Scottish universities.

Nor is anything to be found in the Scottish history journals. There is nothing in the Records of the Scottish Church History Society. There is nothing in the Transactions of the Gaelic Society of Inverness, nothing in the Scottish Historical Review and nothing in Northern Scotland. Nor is there anything in either the (Canadian) International Review of Scottish Studies or the (French) études écossaises (although there is much of Highland interest to be found in its pages). Nor is anything to be found in the journals which concern themselves with religious affairs. There is nothing in either the Journal of Ecclesiastical History or the venerable and prestigious Revue d' Histoire Ecclésiastique: nor in Mission Studies, the International Review of Missions or the International Bulletin of Mission Research.

There is, then, no secondary printed material on the extra-ordinary challenges that confronted the early Free Church missionaries in the Andes. And these challenges certainly were immense. Encouragement could hardly be expected from the long-established Roman Catholic church (and it was certainly not forthcoming). Other Protestant missionaries were also active throughout South America at one point or another during the 20th century: among them Baptists, Methodists, Seventh Day Adventists, Pentecostalists, Anglicans and Presbyterians: and some of these were immensely well resourced compared to the Free Church of Scotland. Lima itself must have been something of a surprise to newcomers largely from the Highlands of Scotland: the capital of a one-time Spanish colony from the sixteenth century, with the oldest university in the Americas, San Marcos, which easily pre-dated the likes of Harvard and Yale and Princeton. (Of course, Aberdeen, St. Andrews and Glasgow – which have produced many a worthy Free Church graduate – are older than any of them). The size of Peru must also have been something of a surprise, its length equivalent roughly to the distance from the Faroes to the south of France. The Andes themselves presented an immense challenge in terms of movement and communications. And what would the Indians of these mountains make of these Scottish missionaries (and vice versa)?

The natural ruling elites of the Indians had been largely exterminated during and after the Conquest. In the words of one writer, John Savage of the Evangelical Union of South America: "In 70 years, the population of Tahuatinsuyo [the Inca empire] decreased from 10 million to 3 million people. For over 400 years, they have eked out a miserable existence in poverty, ignorance and superstition, living in fear of the land-owner, lawyer and priest. They have built themselves a stronghold of suspicion and prejudice, and resistance to change which defies all approach. Their minds have been stupified by the addiction to aguardiente and coca. Long distances must be traversed and high mountain ranges crossed to reach them. These Quechua-speaking Indians of the high Andes constitute one of the largest unevangelised groups in South America today".

And in the words of the celebrated Peruvian Leftist, José Carlos

Mariátegui, (who would send at least one son to be a pupil at the Free Church school in Lima), "the population of the Inca empire, according to conservative estimates, was at least ten million. Some people place it at twelve or even fifteen million. The Conquest was, more than anything, a terrible carnage. The Spanish conquerors, with their small numbers, could not impose their domination, but only managed to terrorise the Indigenous population. The invaders' guns and horses, which were regarded as supernatural beings, created a superstitious impression. The political and economic organisation of the colony, which came after the conquest, continued the extermination of the Indigenous race. The viceroyalty established a system of brutal exploitation. Spanish greed for precious metals led to an economic activity directed towards mines that, under the Incas, had been worked on a very small scale because the Indians, who were largely an agricultural people, did not use iron and only used gold and silver as ornaments. In order to work the mines and obrajes (sweatshops) where weaving was done, the Spanish established a system of forced labour that decimated the population. This was not only a state of servitude, as might have been the case had the Spanish limited the exploitation to the use of land and retained the agricultural character of the country, but was in large part a state of slavery".

As for language: Quechua itself was for the missionaries a huge challenge – little material was published in the language, and it was spoken in many mutually unintelligible varieties. Most of its speakers were in any case illiterate in any language, which made the distribution of evangelical texts somewhat problematic. And languages are part of any people's cosmology – their world-view, their weltanschauung: and world-views can differ very radically indeed between different languages and cultures.

In the early twentieth century, too, before the development of civilian aviation services, travel in Peru was a matter of very considerable difficulty. In 1922, it took missionaries five weeks to travel from Lima to Moyobamba on the far slopes of the eastern Andean cordillera, beyond which stretched the jungles of Amazonia. "It was not until after they had waved goodbye to the Free Church of Scotland missionary, the Rev. J. Calvin Mackay, manning the last mission station on the eastern slopes of the Andes, that the realisation of what was involved in such a journey as they were undertaking began to dawn on them": which was travelling by foot or on mule-back, in mud so deep that it could reach the bellies of the mules, often in torrential rains, staying at night in caves or tents or tambos, proceeding on desperate mountain tracks so narrow that a rider was unable to mount or dismount a mule, often in freezing high-altitude winds, and crossing fearsome gorges and tempestuous rivers on primitive footbridges largely lashed together with home-made rope.

In June 1916, an editorial in the Monthly Record proclaimed, however: "the South American Mission – the Church is now fairly committed to prosecute this work which Providence seems plainly to have put in hand. With regard to the proposed medical side of the work, the committee was in the fortunate position of having an offer for service from Dr. Helen MacDougall. They have accordingly agreed to recommend to the Assembly that a medical mission on a small scale to begin with should be established on the Peruvian Sierra. Miss Sarah MacDougall, a highly trained nurse, [and sister of Dr. Helen] will also be available for the work of this mission".

Five months later, John Alexander Mackay sailed for Peru. In June 1918, he reported, "several months ago I told of the allocation to us of a large region in Northern Peru. One of the most vital and distressing problems in Peru today is the condition of the more than two million Indians who inhabit the Sierra and forest regions of the country". The following spring, Mackay spent a month visiting these areas himself, going up to 13,000 feet: and a month later Miss Sarah MacDougall arrived in Peru, aboard the Mexico, and in Lima met with Annie Soper.

By June 1919, progress was clearly under way. The General Assembly of the previous month had been told, "the missionary party who are leaving in a week for Lima – the Rev. J. Calvin Mackay, M.A., late of Nairn, and Mrs. [Rachel] Mackay [a farmer's daughter from near Tain], who is also a graduate of Arts of Edinburgh University, Miss Catherine Mackay, M.A., who is accompanying her brother to the mission field, and Dr. Helen MacDougall – came forward. The Assembly then listened to a moving address from the Rev. Angus Mackay, the father of the two young missionaries who are proceeding to Lima". As John Alexander Mackay reported to the same Assembly, "now is the moment for an advance into the interior. Our hearts swell with joy at the prospect of the reinforcements that are soon to reach us".

A year later, the newcomers were still in Lima, perfecting their command of Spanish. But they were preparing to move to Cajamarca at 9,000 feet, up on the Sierra and, "on the direct route leading far into the interior" – by which was meant Moyobamba in the tropical jungle region, beyond the far side of the eastern cordillera, and bordering with Amazonia to the east.

At mid-summer, 1920, the Free Church sent two men out to report on the situation in Peru. One was Professor J. Kennedy Cameron, and the other was the Rev. Finlay MacRae, minister in Plockton. (MacRae had been Moderator of the General Assembly of the Free Church in 1914 and, as a Gaelic speaker, had preached to Gaelic-speaking servicemen during World War One). It took them a month to get to Peru, and they spent five weeks in the country. They left Edinburgh on the overnight train for Liverpool, and the following afternoon embarked aboard the Oriana, an 8,000 ton coal-fired vessel of the Pacific Steam Navigation Company. They called at La Pallice on the French coast for mail and passengers, and then sailed for La Coruña. "After leaving Coruña, the Oriana next rounded Cape Finnisterre and entered the Bay of Vigo in the north-west of Spain. This is reputed as the largest and best of all the Spanish harbours. It reminded us of the beautiful bay of Lamlash on the island of Arran – though in respect of extent comparison utterly fails". Twelve days' steaming followed, at fifteen knots, for Havana on Cuba, where seven hundred passengers from Spain were put ashore. Next came Colon, at the eastern end of the Panama Canal, where they coaled at night (all doors and portholes closed against the dense clouds of coal-dust), and then made their way out into the Pacific. "After leaving Panama, the Oriana drew out well to sea. Consequently Colombia and Ecuador were not in view. The first time we saw the South American coast was when the ship called at Payta, a port in the north of Peru. We had never seen anything so utterly destitute of vegetation. On reaching Callao, however, on the morning of 22nd July, we were glad to have reached the end of our voyage, and we looked forward to the pleasure of meeting the friends ashore who were waiting to greet us".

In the August of the following year, J. Kennedy Cameron published a 70-page booklet on missionary conditions in Peru. And the following month, the Rev. J. Calvin Mackay (he would be Moderator of the General Assembly in 1942), his wife and their two very young children, finally left Lima for Cajamarca. It took them four days by boat, one day by railway, and another two days on horse-back. "In that old historic city", he noted with a shadow of pride, "where the Spanish adventurer Pizarro [the one-time pig-herd from Estremadura] defeated and murdered the last of the Incas, Atahualpa, the Free Church of Scotland will soon have a mission station".

And there was more: this time, perhaps, in tones of even greater pride – although it does show the astounding ambition of the Free Church during its early days in Peru. "It is an extraordinary coincidence that the Free Church mission should be delivering the first real attack in its evangelistic conquest of Peru at the same point from which Pizarro led his Castilian knights to the conquest for Rome and the Papacy of the old Incan Empire". (And the ambition was not entirely without historic foundation. After all, within a single lifetime from Luther's Theses of 1517, Protestantism had swept across much of Europe. And the very rapid growth of the Free Church after 1900 must also have inspired her Peruvian missionaries).

Sixty five years later, the Rev. J. Calvin Mackay recalled: "from the commencement of our church's work in Peru, it was envisaged that our efforts would not be confined to the undoubtedly great and important institution established in Lima. The Committee on Co-operation in Latin America allocated to the Free Church a large section of northern Peru, extending from the Pacific coast to the Brazilian border. In response to an appeal for help at the school, a year or two following its founding, after prayerful consideration of the words "Behold, I have set before thee an open door", I felt impelled to offer my services. Accompanied by my wife and our first child, and by my sister Catherine, we proceeded to Lima in July 1919. To begin with, I became a member of the school staff, while acquiring facility with the Spanish language, in preparation for commencing evangelistic work at a point within the territory of northern Peru. Peru consists of three distinct regions. The narrow strip of land between the Pacific coast and the Andes is the coastal region – the Coast. The Sierra embraces the three parallel mountain ranges, with intervening valleys, extensive plains, and elevated plateaux. From the eastern slopes of the Andes, to the Brazilian border, is the Montaña – a forest region, through which flow large rivers, tributaries of the Amazon. Dr. Mackay had founded the school in Lima, the capital of Peru, on the coast. It was decided that our work in the Interior should commence in Cajamarca, the first Sierra town on the route from the Pacific port of Pacasmayo to Iquitos on the Amazon. Cajamarca is of strategic importance, being the capital of the department of the same name, with roads leading to many distant points. It is of historic importance as it was here that the Spanish adventurers in the 16th century had succeeded in capturing the last Inca ruler, Atahualpa. Later, breaking the terms of a ransom agreement, they put him to death on 29th August 1533, and they became the dominant power. Part of the aim of their conquest was to bring their religion to the native Indians, but what they succeeded in doing was to impose on those Sun Worshippers the outward signs only of their religion".

In January 1922, Nurse Sarah MacDougall (who was from Glenurquhart), joined the party in Cajamarca – she would die there in 1955 – and together they embarked on a programme of missionary activity: medical work, church services, Bible classes, a bookroom, and the distribution of texts such as Bibles, New Testaments, Gospels and Shorter Catechisms (for a well-wisher had sent a large bundle of such materials in Spanish from a printing works in Stirling). Later in the year, Nurse MacDougall could report, "medicines and dressings are very expensive indeed as the distance from the coast is so great. Mr. Mackay has given me two rooms, one as a surgery – on all sides is felt the great need for a hospital".

And in April 1922, the Monthly Record could note, "thus a beginning has been made. More workers will soon be wanted for northern Peru, which is the area we have received in trust for aggressive evangelism. Is the Free Church at home sufficient to carry on this new enterprise? Has she sufficient resources in spirituality, men and money for the task?" (That autumn, there was an immediate setback: Dr. Helen MacDougall would resign, reportedly on account of ill-health, and go to Canada).

But in the Monthly Record for February 1924, it is reported that Annie Soper and Rhoda Gould, late of Lima, were now working, independently of the Free Church but under the auspices of its Foreign Missions' Committee, in Moyobamba, "more than a hundred miles and many days journey north of Cajamarca". Meanwhile, at the end of the year, Miss Christina Mackay, a teacher from Easter Logie, near Tain, had travelled up to Cajamarca from Lima, to take over the running of the school, and the Rev. J. Calvin Mackay had himself visited Moyobamba.

His report on that visit runs to two columns in the Monthly Record. "Between Moyobamba and Yurimaguas the path is impossible even for a mule and the traveller must accomplish the twelve days on this section either by foot or on an Indian's back. There is certainly in Moyobamba a favourable and promising field, not only for a hospital and nurses but also for an ordained man to establish and work up a Protestant church".

By the end of 1925, Miss Christina Mackay could report that there were 73 children on her school roll in Cajamarca: while a year later Annie Soper could write from Moyobamba, "we are sending two of our people to the Bible Institute in Costa Rica. They have sold all of their possessions. They will leave on foot – barefoot – on a journey of sixteen days over the mountains. They will pass through Cajamarca, and will see the Rev. J. Calvin Mackay and Mrs Mackay".

In ten years, in other words, Free Church missionary activity in Peru was able to claim some significant success. The school in Lima was flourishing. Affairs in Cajamarca had gone well too, with direct evangelical work under way, along with a primary school and medical services. There was also the semi-independent hospital, and an incipient orphanage, run by Annie Soper and Rhoda Gould in Moyobamba.

At the end of 1926, Dr. Kenneth Mackay arrived in Moyobamba. He was soon reporting in the Monthly Record that, "I have found Miss Soper and Miss Gould well, but tired. The hospital is simply one large ward with 20 beds. There is a very good church building where at a meeting last night I saw 70 people present". That same month, the missions' committee of the Free Church was able to note that, "it had accepted an offer of immediate service by Miss Annabella MacLeod, a native of Lewis, who is a fully qualified nurse. She will sail for Peru in company with Miss Margaret Fraser, from Achiltibuie. Miss Fraser, who is a qualified teacher, will go straight through to Moyobamba, halting only at Cajamarca. There will be an interesting gathering in the church in Cajamarca when the Rev. J. Calvin Mackay unites Dr. Mackay and Miss Fraser in marriage".

Sixty years later, Margaret Fraser recalled that her husband had gone out to Peru a year before she went, while she was still a primary teacher in Balmacara, near Kyle of Lochalsh. Her family were Gaelic-speaking but, "at that time you didn't advertise that you had it". There were nine in the family, and five of them became teachers (though the boys, apart from looking after the sheep and fishing, "played shinty all the time"). She and Annabella MacLeod conversed in Gaelic throughout the six-week trip to Peru. She had said her farewells to her family in Achiltibuie, and then made her long way to Liverpool. She clearly recalled that in her luggage was, "a hat suitable for church" and "a cream chiffon wedding dress, with veil, bought in Sauchiehall Street". On arrival, they were met by the Rev. J. Calvin Mackay and Dr. Kenneth Mackay. Travel over the mountains was by mule-train (along with wedding dress and hat suitable for church), and when Calvin Mackay conducted the wedding service, it was done in Spanish. She also recalled that Dr. Kenneth, on his arrival in Peru, had had to retake all his medical exams in total (as would David Milnes, a later missionary, on his arrival). At the time, Peruvian doctors were only willing to work in coastal cities, and the existing medical facility in Moyobamba was run by nuns. "It had not even a supply of water, and they were medically unqualified, but they were decent people". She ran a Sunday School in Moyobamba, and had 100 children at it within three weeks. And she also recalled that, "the priests were very nice as a rule. Some were rascals, but you get that anywhere". After twelve years in Peru she had seen a revolution in medical provision in the Andes with many Peruvian doctors coming to the mountains, and she and her husband (a piper, although in Peru he only had an organ to make music with) returned to Scotland via Iquitos, and down the Amazon to the open Atlantic.

By the autumn of 1927, Nurse MacLeod was reporting, "the sea voyage was exceptionally fine – in fact, we came to the conclusion that the Atlantic is preferable to the Minch any day!" And the following May the Rev. J. Calvin Mackay could note that the old days of missionary difficulty in Peru were on the brink of change, for a new road meant that Cajamarca was now just 5 hours from the nearest railhead: rather than a whole day and a whole night on the back of a mule.

And in October 1928, two new missionaries arrived in Cajamarca: The Rev. James Turnbull, and his wife, a nurse (although they were actually Baptists). They joined the Rev. J. Calvin Mackay, Nurse Sarah MacDougall, and Christina Mackay at the school, which by now had 108 pupils on the roll. That autumn, the Rev. Mackay had bought himself a mule, for £30; which allowed him, in the words of the Monthly Record report, to "rush around" his patients during an epidemic of dysentery. Soon, Miss Soper (who had been on furlough in England) was embarking from Liverpool for distant Peru: Christina Mackay the teacher was leaving Peru (although she certainly would be back), and in January 1931 the editor of the Monthly Record, Archibald MacNeilage, died.

At the end of the 'twenties, Misses Soper and Gould left Moyobamba to head deeper into the interior of Peru, at Lamas: and the Free Church missions' committee was appealing for nurses to replace Misses Soper and Gould. And again, the nature of the missionary challenge in Peru was about to undergo revolutionary change: and this time, in a shape more profound – or elevated – than any mere road.

In October 1930, Nurse MacDougall could report with some amazement that, "we have had great excitement in Cajamarca during the last week when we witnessed the arrival from Lima of two aeroplanes. From Lima to Cajamarca – five hours. From Cajamarca to Moyobamba – two hours, instead of 16 days overland!" And a month later another Christina Mackay, Nurse Christina Mackay of Moyobamba (and Shawbost) could write, somewhat plaintively, "soon we expect to have aeroplane services from Lima via Pachamayo, Cajamarca and Chachapoyas, and when these are established we shall not feel so far away".

But older forms of transport and communication still prevailed. In February 1931, Dr. Kenneth Mackay could report the arrival of, "our beautiful Communion set": it had come over the Atlantic and up the Amazon by ocean-going ship to Manaus, and thereafter by river-boat to Iquitos (though it was still a very long way from Cajamarca or Moyobamba). Meanwhile, Nurse MacLeod was back in Scotland on furlough, and had headed for home in Lewis. In Peru, more furloughs were coming up – two in Moyobamba and one in Cajamarca. In April 1932, two new missionaries arrived: Nurse Marion MacMillan of Minard in Argyll for Cajamarca, and Nurse MacDonald, from Edinburgh, for Moyobamba. That same month, Dr. Kenneth Mackay was off on furlough: "I have chosen to go by Iquitos. I plan to take the way by Bapapuerto, five days foot journey, the children on bearers, and there we are on navigable river, three days in canoe to Yurimaguas, whence river steamer to Iquitos and

Booth Line boat to Liverpool. The five days' walk is hard, because there are no habitations, but our camp-kit is well proved".

Dr. Kenneth Mackay spent his furlough touring Scotland in the cause of missionary work. He was scarcely home but he had addressed meetings in Lewis – Kinloch, Ness, Bernera and Stornoway – along with one in Achiltibuie and another in Glasgow's Partick district. But by June 1933, he was off again, on the liner Laguna from Liverpool, in the company of his wife and children, along with Nurses Sarah MacDougall and Annnabella MacLeod. A year later they were joined by Flora Matheson, a 24-year old teacher and graduate of Edinburgh University (whose father Norman, originally from Kilmaluag at the north end of Skye, was Free Church minister in Beauly). Miss Matheson was headed for Moyobamba.

(Lore recalls that at one point during her service in Peru, Flora Matheson went high into the mountains on the back of a mule, with an Indian to guide her. The party came at length to a stupendous chasm at right angles to the narrow and precipitous track. The Indian slapped the mule on the rump and ordered it to leap. The mule backed off. Quick as a flash, the Indian hooked Flora off the mule – and just as quickly the mule jumped across the haughty gulf. It now studied them with a quizzical eye. The Indian ordered Flora to jump. Flora backed off – and quick as a flash the Indian hooked her over his shoulder, and jumped with her. The chasm-problem thus resolved, the party continued on its lawful way).

In the autumn of that year, 1934, Miss MacDonald was touring her area. "On the second day's journey from Moyobamba, the road is something terrible. The mud is so deep at places that animals sink so far as to make it almost impossible to get out. It was with a desperate struggle the mule I rode got through, and he was a fine, strong animal. The return journey was not so tiring. From Pachiza – a village about a week's journey from Moyobamba – I went a day and a half journey down the river Huallaga on a raft. It was a pleasant change from the saddle".

In September 1935, the Rev. Murdo Nicolson (from Raasay) was preparing to leave for Cajamarca, while six months later the new church there opened. By then, the Rev. Nicolson was on a Dutch ship out of Amsterdam. (Most of the passengers were Jewish refugees from the land of Goethe and Beethoven: and, of course, Martin Luther). The Rev. Nicolson was headed for Panama and then the Peruvian coast. In April 1937, a scheduled air-service opened between Cajamarca and Moyobamba. It was to run once every three weeks, and cut journey-time to less than two hours compared to an overland trip of between 12 and 16 days. And that December, Dr. Kenneth Mackay visited Cajamarca to hear the Rev. Murdo Nicolson preach in the new church. "Mr. Nicolson is a fine preacher and his command of Spanish is something to marvel at. I have not known any man acquire such a vocabulary and use it as fluently as he has done in his short time".

But new air-services or not, conditions were still very challenging for the Peruvian traveller in the 1930s. In that decade Alexander Renwick took four weeks to get overland from Lima to Cajamarca and Moyobamba. He was headed for Iquitos, and then down the Amazon to Manaus, and a ship for Britain. A former minister of the Free Church in Dumbarton, and a Gaelic-speaker with roots in Kintail, he had been in charge of the Free Church school in Lima and had completed a doctoral thesis (written in Spanish, of course) at the university of San Marcos on the relationship between altitude and the nature of religious belief.

John Alexander Mackay had already been given an honorary doctorate at San Marcos on account of his ability as a lecturer in philosophy. Four other teachers at the Free Church school in Lima also took doctorates at San Marcos. The first of these was Herbert Money (whose wife Netta Kemp was from Culbokie). He wrote his thesis on the sociology of Peruvian Amazonia. The second was V. R. Browne. The third was Neil A. R. Mackay, a Gaelic-speaking polymath, born in Breasclete, Lewis, who for a time held the chair of English literature at the university of San Marcos, and who was deemed by his contemporaries to be at least as intellectually gifted as John Alexander Mackay. Mackay's thesis was on the mathematician-philosopher-theologian A. N. Whitehead (whose son Eric had died at 19 as a fighter-pilot in World War One). The fourth was W. Stanley Rycroft. He too had been a fighter-pilot in World War One. Shot down twice, he was later involved in a mid-air collision and crash which nearly killed him. As World War Two came to a close in Europe, Rycroft led a high-powered commission to study conditions in the mountains of Peru: its report was subsequently published as Indians of the High Andes.

Even the early stages of Renwick's journey give a sense of the difficulty of travel in Peru in the late 1930s. He was just some miles north of Lima when, "the ascent and descent of the steep Huachoc Hill was a revelation of what Peruvian chauffeurs could do. Neither sudden turnings nor terrible declivities could make our driver slow on any account". Later, following the coast northwards, the car took to the beach. "Finally we came to the straggling village of Huarmey. I remember the delightful ride along the beach at Grita Lobos ("the place where the seals cry") for in those days the chauffeurs were glad to leave the shifting desert sands and run for some miles along the beach, even when the wheels were at times half covered with water. At Chimbote we had covered 102 miles since we left Pativilca twelve hours previously. It looks like poor travelling but it was, in reality, a record for the roadless deserts, and we considered ourselves singularly fortunate". Later, driving very slowly at night in mountainous terrain, the problem was, "the fierce bellowing of its wild bulls at the eerie hour of 1am. A great landowner hereabouts rears these animals for bull-fighting purposes. They are allowed to run wild on the outskirts of his estate and are exceedingly fierce. They have been known repeatedly to chase cars for good distances". Later still, Renwick was joined by James Turnbull of Cajamarca. Soon, they were at 13,000 feet, and, "time and again the car sank in the mud, and had to be heaved out by sheer strength. On such occasions the grim determination and ready resource of his ancestors from the Scottish Borders shone out in Mr. Turnbull, and he proved simply invaluable. To arrive at Huamachuco on a cold rainy evening at that height of over 10,500 feet was a dreary experience. I have seldom seen a more woebegone place. It looked as if the channels of life were being frozen in both man and beast. It had taken us fourteen hours to cover the 124 miles from Trujillo".

About the same time – in March, 1938 – another medical missionary was on the way to Moyobamba. Dr. Harold Lindsay, from Belfast, was aboard the Royal Mail Ship the Oropesa, which would call at Bermuda, Cuba and Jamaica before transiting the Panama Canal. Dr. Kenneth Mackay was leaving after 11 years in Moyobamba: and by Christmas the following year, Dr. Lindsay could report that there was a radio receiving set (just one, it seems) in Moyobamba, which allowed missionaries to listen to English-language reports about the new war which had recently broken out in distant Europe. Within months, he was married to Flora Matheson: the service was conducted, in Spanish, by the Rev. Murdo Nicolson. In May, 1940, the General Assembly of the Free Church was told that a fourth mission station (in addition to Lima, Cajamarca and Moyobamba) had been opened in Peru, at Chachapoyas; and that autumn the Rev. Malcolm MacRae was, "inducted to the mission field in northern Peru".

In January 1942 a new church was opened in Moyobamba: 400 people were seated inside (with as many again crowded outside). Some people had walked for three days to be at the opening ceremony. By that summer, the Rev. Malcolm MacRae was in service in Cajamarca (and was also married to Nurse Annabella MacLeod). Towards the end of the war in Europe, it was reported that the Rev. J. Calvin Mackay and his wife were to return to Peru; although, "he had come home a physical wreck", and had since served as minister of Kincardine and Croick. And to mark the end of that war, perhaps, there was in the autumn of 1945 a serious earthquake in Moyobamba. Dr. Harold Lindsay reported that there was no significant damage to Free Church property – the hospital, the new church, the old church, and the mission house. The only serious damage, he noted without further comment, had been to the town's Catholic church.

In the autumn of 1946, Mrs. Rachel Mackay was revisiting Cajamarca by air (the name of her pilot, she notes with some delight, was MacKenzie). And that same month, Nurse Rebecca (Netta) Fraser was coming to Peru – by air – to serve in Moyobamba. Nurse Fraser was from the Braes above Beauly (and had gone to primary school there with Flora Matheson). She was brought-up in a Free Church house in which there were but four books – a Gaelic Bible, an English Bible, a volume of Spurgeon's sermons, and a copy of John Bunyan's Pilgrim's Progress. After the Royal Academy in Inverness, she trained as a nurse in Aberdeen, and then as a midwife in Perth. In the late summer of 1946, aged 30, she headed for Peru. She flew from a London still heavily-scarred from the German Blitz on an Arvo York civilian airliner (though it was very closely modelled on the wartime Lancaster heavy bomber) via France, Spain, Dakar in west Africa and Natal on the coast of Brazil. A series of flights on small aircraft took her to the Amazonian port of Iquitos – and then on to Moyobamba. As a missionary, she would at times travel by mule to visit distant patients; keep as pets variously a marmoset, a parrot and a puma; and add to her nursing skills on an informal basis the skills of anaesthesia and minor surgery – the latter at times with the immediate aid of a copy of Gray's Anatomy.

Her son, John Milnes, recalls that the puma grew quickly, "and when meat was brought into the house it would snarl in a blood-curdling way. Sometimes my mother would take it for a walk on a chain leash. It didn't like the local dogs at all. If one came within reach, the puma would kill it instantly with a casual side-swipe of a paw. After a few such incidents, my mother decided that the time had come for her pet to be re-homed."

On arrival in Moyobamba, she was to "hold the fort" until the return of Dr. Harold Lindsay: who had indeed returned by March 1949. Others were soon to follow Nurse Fraser. At the end of 1949, Nurse Mary I. MacLeod, from Partick Highland Church, was on her way to Moyobamba. And a year later, Miss Christina Mackay, the former teacher in Cajamarca, ("who has already given long service in Peru") was preparing to sail from Liverpool on the Reina del Pacífico. Miss Florence Donaldson, from Northern Ireland, headed for Moyobamba, was to accompany her. And in the autumn of 1950, the Rev. Malcolm MacRae was reported to be going out to Cajamarca "shortly".

In October, 1950, however, it was announced that Dr. Harold Lindsay was to leave Moyobamba: and Nurse Rebecca Fraser did not stay there for very long. In January 1948, in Lima, she had married a missionary of the Evangelical Union of South America, Dr. David Milnes, and they would soon move to another mission area, in southern Peru, where Dr. Milnes's fluency in Quechua could be put to good use, and where conditions were very primitive indeed.

"We had another good Bible school there, and did quite a lot of medical work. We were staying in a house situated at the foot of a huge natural fortress, which towered more than two thousand feet above us. At the end of the Bible school we had a day off and climbed this in easy stages and saw how expertly it had been fortified. While we were on top of this fortress, a condor circled us. It had been watching over a new-born calf at the foot of the mountain and one of our party had disturbed it with a stone. As we sat on the fortress, they told us a little of the ways of the condor and of its tremendous strength. It is well-known how these birds will gather together from over a wide area whenever there is carrion to be had. Just from how wide an area, and how many birds come together, would seem to depend on the food available, for it is said that during the Crimean War, the whole of North Africa was bereft of its vultures. However, it is not the first bird which arrives which begins the feast. All have to wait for one to whom deference is made as leader".

And the Milnses were to confront very profound issues of modern versus traditional approaches to medical treatments and healing processes. "Once, when I was out at a Rural Bible School with Cirilo Quispe, he described to me in graphic terms how they used to treat sickness in the old days. His father had been sick and household herbs had been of no avail, so his mother decided to send for the spirit-doctor, who is called the paqo. When this most important visitor arrived, all the family were there to greet him and all had to be present during the ceremony, the object of which was to summon the spirits to find out what was wrong with the father. First the doctor examined his patient, his eyes, his pulse, his head, his urine. Then he made an offering to the earth and the neighbouring hills with the crude rum which they had provided for him and which, with the coca leaves, plays such an important part in the ceremony. The drink-offering he pours on the floor and flicks towards the hills, and the coca leaves he allows to fall to the ground and then he reads them to find out where the disease has come from. It may be due to witchcraft on the part of an enemy or because the patient has been affected by a wind or has taken liberties with the rainbow or has been careless when going to the spring for water. According to his diagnosis he would then send the old wife to the town to buy what was necessary to make ready his table and meanwhile he gets his spirits up by drinking steadily of the rum. There is no doubt that much of this procedure is often nothing more than trickery and ventriloquism. For instance, when the spirit is supposed to be entering through the roof, the paqo will throw up a handful of gravel to simulate the noise that it makes. Also, after such an awesome experience, the patient will almost always feel some alleviation of his pains. Nevertheless, there is no doubt that there are men who are in touch with evil spirits and that remarkable 'cures' occur just often enough to keep the whole system going. After the Bible school, to which about thirty came, we went for our convention to another more isolated part, called Anchapara. Here they have a nice church with a corrugated iron roof and glass in the windows. At these extreme heights this is much appreciated. As there was only one meeting room, Netta had the women's meeting out in the [open] patio while snow was falling".

In January, 1951, the Monthly Record was reporting a missionary farewell meeting in Glasgow's Partick; Miss Florence Donaldson was headed for Moyobamba; and the Rev. and Mrs. MacRae were on their way to Cajamarca. That summer, Alexander Renwick was addressing the Women's Foreign Missionary Association of the Free Church. "In 1900 the little Free Church had no missions and in the stress of her fight for life no mission work was possible for some years. But in 1906, £388 was contributed. Contributions at intervals of ten years were: 1916 – £1020: 1926 – £2573: 1936 – £3069: 1946 – £6599: 1950 – £8508".

The following year, the Rev. Malcolm MacRae was reporting in confident tones from Cajamarca, and while Nurse MacDougall would be home soon on furlough, news from Moyobamba indicated that after 10 years, Dr. Harold Lindsay would not be returning after his next furlough. An urgent search for a replacement doctor began at once. And that August old Norman Matheson, father to Dr. Lindsay's wife Flora and nine other offspring, and Free Church minister in Beauly for 20 years, died at Inverness.

In October, 1952, Alexander Renwick authored in the Monthly Record an obituary for John Ritchie of Greenock, who had been a missionary in Peru for an astonishing 46 years. Ritchie had been born in 1878 and had left school at the age of eleven to train as a printer. He sailed to Peru in 1906 via the Magellan Straits. As well as a publisher of religious literature, he founded a school – which he handed over to John Alexander Mackay in 1916. "It is now called the Colegio San Andrés and is still going strong under our own Rev. James Macintosh. It was the fostering and nurturing of the indigenous church, Iglesia Evangélica Peruana, that Mr. Ritchie saw as his greatest work".

The 1954 General Assembly of the Free Church heard that, "in Cajamarca, a native church was being formed. A replacement for Dr. Lindsay in Moyobamba has not yet been found and this was today our most desperate area. It would be a tragedy if we had to close the hospital down". That same summer, Nurse Agnes Gunn was preparing to head for Moyobamba: and the annual meeting of the Women's Foreign Missionary Association was addressed by Mrs. Milnes (Nurse Rebecca Fraser), then home on furlough. (By now, the Moyobamba hospital had 35 beds, and "an exceptionally busy" out-patient department).

From the middle of the 1950s, however, the question began to be asked, with growing insistence, of when and how the Free Church would progressively devolve its evangelical work in Peru to native pastors and a native church. This would not be without some debate, and indeed dispute. In 1955, the General Assembly heard that, "a policy for the new native church in Cajamarca" was under way. In Moyobamba, meanwhile, a Dr. Merriman had replaced Dr. Harold Lindsay (though Dr. Merriman did not stay for long, as increasing deafness forced him to return to Britain). And at that year's annual meeting of the Women's Foreign Missionary Association, Mrs. MacRae of Cajamarca recalled that she had been in Peru for no less than 25 years.

At the following year's Assembly, "the convenor made sympathetic reference to the death of Miss Sarah MacDougall. There was illness among missionaries. Miss Elizabeth MacLeod was still very ill. Miss Mary MacLeod, newly home from Peru, had been very ill, but was recovering. Miss Sarah MacKenzie [of the school in Lima] had taken ill and was not able to proceed overseas at present. Miss Margaret Buchanan, Glasgow, was going out soon to Moyobamba. Meantime, Miss Agnes Gunn was left in that lonely outpost to hold the fort alone in Moyobamba". The Assembly also received an appeal for funds for a new church in Rioja, "less than a day's journey from Moyobamba": it was signed by Alexander Renwick, J. Calvin Mackay, Kenneth Mackay and Harold Lindsay.

A year later, the Assembly heard that the hospital in Moyobamba had been closed because of a lack of a doctor, though nursing work still seems to have been conducted there by Nurses Margaret Buchanan and Agnes Gunn. And there was continuing uncertainty over the speed and direction of the development of a fully native church in Peru. A deputation was to be sent from Edinburgh to review affairs which could not be managed solely via correspondence. That autumn the new church did open in Rioja. The members of the deputation were at the opening: the Rev. W. R. Mackay (minister in Kingussie), and Alexander Renwick. They had flown up from the coast – a journey of one hour, forty minutes, rather than 14 days by mule. Miss Florence Donaldson had come from Chachapoyas and Nurses Buchanan and Gunn had come from Moyobamba on foot, having left at 4.30 that morning. In January 1958, the Monthly Record reported that, "by now the Rev. and Mrs. H. B. Sutherland and the Rev. and Mrs. George T. Thomson will be nearing the end of their long journey to Peru": and in March came a "call from the Mission field" from the Rev. Malcolm MacRae in Cajamarca.

Still, the question of the native church exercised attention. The 1959 Assembly heard that, "the native church question, particularly in Cajamarca, is not easy of solution": and a year later, Nurse Agnes Gunn told the Assembly that, "for a long time yet they must continue to depend very much on the home Church for workers, for money and for prayer". A year later, the Rev. Fergus MacDonald and the Rev. W. M. Mackay were preparing to leave for Peru, and in 1962 the Assembly heard from Miss Florence Donaldson and the Rev. MacRae, home on furlough.

Miss Donaldson, "spoke of the work in Moyobamba, where the Rev. George Thomson had recently seen some fruit for his labours". She added that Chachapoyas, "had been a very neglected field until the Rev. and Mrs. Hugh Sutherland had arrived there". The Rev. MacRae reported that, "the growing native church must be adapted to local needs while in everything that was basic it remained the same in doctrine and aim with the parent church".

The following year, the Assembly was told that, "the concept of the indigenous church was the goal of every mission" – the Assembly was being asked to authorise the official designation of the native church as the Iglesia Evangélica Presbiteriana. And the 1964 Assembly was told that the proposals for the church, approved by the last General Assembly, were now being implemented. The Church had come into being as a legal entity the previous August, "and it was being organised on sound Reformed and Presbyterian lines". The Assembly also heard that, "the medical work in Moyobamba has now virtually come to an end. The whole future of medical work in Peru has been under discussion by the Board and they have decided that for the present they must abandon it. The Board has accepted Nurse Agnes Gunn's resignation with deep regret".

A number of factors underlay these developments. One was money. The funds of the Free Church, after all, came from its members. These members' pockets were not bottomless: although these members, nevertheless, were strikingly generous. In just the one month of February 1964, for instance, monies donated for Moyobamba alone came from Edinburgh, Glasgow, Kilwinning, Partick, North Knapdale, Croy, Inverness, Kiltarlity, Kingussie, Nairn, Killearnan, Knockbain, Kilmorack, Edderton and Tain, Lochbroom, Clyne, Dornoch, Tongue, Reay and Wick.

Another factor was that of people. The school in Lima was often short of Free Church teachers from Scotland. And the mission stations in the Sierra and the jungle to the east were often short of skilled people too.

At the 1965 General Assembly, disagreement had become open dispute, between the previous missionary in Cajamarca, the Rev. MacRae, and the present one, the Rev. Angus R. Beaton (who was from Australia); the somewhat arcane, if important, subject of the row including, "the status of the missionary in relation to local Church Councils". As a result, the former was being recalled from Peru. Meanwhile, the Rev. W. M. Mackay told the Assembly, "the Evangelical Church in Peru had a profound respect for the judgement of the Church at home. Its sense of independence, however, would assert itself more and more as the years passed, and the life and growth of this Church must be nourished. The future lay with the Native Church, but it would be years yet before they [the Elders] could take full responsibility for the work".

The same debates dominated the rest of the 'sixties, and still there were those willing to head for Peru. While the Rev. Angus Beaton would be, "returning from the field next summer", the Rev. Ronald C. Christie and his wife, "would shortly be going out". Mr. Hugh Varnes, meantime, had left the Free Church school in Lima for Cajamarca (where he would run an evangelical bookroom and an English academy). The 1968 General Assembly heard from the Rev. George T. Thomson, home on furlough from Moyobamba, and Miss Donaldson, home from Lima.

In 1970, the Rev. Thomson was moving from Moyobamba to Lima, and was to be replaced by Tim Donachie, who would spend four year in Peru: while the Rev. William Mackay could tell the General Assembly that, "working with the Evangelical Presbyterian

Church in Peru there now existed some fifty congregations and groups who were the fruits of the missionaries of the Free Church of Scotland some 50 years ago".

Broader movements, however, were also under way in Peru and throughout the continent. As one speaker told the following year's General Assembly in Edinburgh, "there is arising now in Peru, as throughout South America, a new generation and a new sense of revolution – the new left, backing its campaign with violence, often led by highly-educated men springing often from upper middle class families". Within a decade, these developments would engulf Peru in great violence throughout the central Sierra.

Meantime, missionaries continued to arrive: and depart. Hugh Varnes was to leave Cajamarca and return to his native Australia, to study for ordination. Miss Florence Donaldson and the Rev. George Thomson, home on furlough, spoke to the 1973 Assembly. A year later, the Rev. Christie was still in Cajamarca, and the Rev. William B. Scott (who would spend five years in Peru) in Moyobamba. A few years later, Dr. David Ford and his wife were headed for Peru, and in the autumn of 1978 the Rev. Donald Smith was writing from Cajamarca about the serious drought and danger of famine in the area: the Free Church had already sent £1,500 from its Disaster Fund. In November, 1979, there was a farewell meeting in Edinburgh for the Rev. Andrew Fraser and wife, who were headed to Peru for a second term of missionary work. In March 1980, however, there was an ominous and unsigned report in the Focus diary-column of the Monthly Record: "Rumour has it that the Foreign Board is under severe pressure to cut back expenditure. But surely, of all areas of the Church's life, this is the last in which to apply the axe".

By now, at the dawn of the 1980s, new developments were under way in Peru. For years, the Free Church had been troubled in Cajamarca by competition from Seventh Day Adventist missionaries. But there was competition from other denominational quarters too. As early as October, 1964, the Monthly Record could report a speech by John Alexander Mackay, delivered in Minnesota. In fifty years, he said, the number of Protestants had grown in Latin America from

200,000 to ten million. But the lion's share of these recruits was being taken by the Pentecostalists, whose numbers were beginning to grow quickly throughout the continent.

Secondly, by the dawn of the 1980s, Peru was on the brink of the bloody revolutionary upheavals associated with the Sendero Luminoso (Shining Path) insurrection. (The name derived from the writings of Mariátegui, with whom John Alexander Mackay had been an acquaintance in Lima). The movement, led by an academic philosopher, aspired to seize military control of the Sierra and its impoverished and marginalised Indians, and from that "Red Base" take control at length of Lima and the country itself.

Sendero Luminoso derived from what it saw as the exploitative relationship between the United States and the countries of central and southern America, the legacy of colonial occupation, the historic exploitation of the Peruvian Indian, and of the huge class and income differentials in Peru. Its principal focus as the agent of change, under its revolutionary leadership, was the Indian population of the high Sierra. The strategy might even have worked too (and introduced catastrophe to Peru). After all, it had worked in China and Cuba; and indeed, at times, the movement came close to seizing complete power in Peru.

But Sendero Luminoso, though it murdered Evangelicals (and many others) in the central Sierra, did not trouble the north of Peru. In the north, the problem from Leftist insurrectionaries came from the Tupac Amaru Revolutionary Movement, named after the leader of an anti-Spanish rebellion in the late 18th century.

Older difficulties were still present in the early 1980s. The matter of a "moratorium on missions" was raised in the missionary magazine From the Frontiers in February 1981. But still new volunteers presented themselves for service in Peru. That same month, Dr. David and Mrs. Olwen Ford came to Cajamarca, while that summer the care of the church in Moyobamba was taken-over by Dutch missionaries. In the February 1982 issue of From the Frontiers, there was a two-page report from Dr. David Ford in Celendín, four hours from Cajamarca over 68 miles of road. Mr. and Mrs. Charles Douglas were also due to return to Cajamarca in the spring of 1982. (Mrs. Douglas's father had been the Rev. Duncan Beaton, with family roots in Lochcarron). Two delegates from Scotland were mandated to visit Peru, "to discuss how best to cooperate with the sister church". The visitors would also, "assess the two mission ventures which for the present still remain under ultimate Board control, namely Colegio San Andrés and the Cajamarca bookshop".

In 1982, the General Assembly heard that the Rev. Donald Smith was masterminding a Community Health and Development Project in Cajamarca, known as PROESA: and in the June 1983 issue of From the Frontiers, the Rev. Fergus MacDonald was reporting at length on his recent visit to northern Peru. By October 1984, From the Frontiers could report that, "Shining Path violence was engulfing central Peru. Evangelical Christians are suffering greatly". A Pentecostal church had been attacked, with six killed, and the pastor was still in hospital. Within a year, between ten and eighteen refugee families from central Peru had been re-settled in Moyobamba.

But by the early months of 1986, it was being reported that Dr. David Ford and his wife Olwen, and Charles and Daphne Douglas were leaving Peru for good. From the Frontiers reported in February that, "it must surely be glaringly obvious that from mid-1986 the Free Church presence in Peru will have been whittled down to its lowest ever level"; with just the Rev. Donnie Smith and his wife in Cajamarca (not on wholly evangelical work) assisted by a Belgian, Marie-Christine Lux.

In the May issue, John O. Sutherland was reporting on his recent visit to the north of Peru, which took him to Celendín. It also took him to Moyobamba, where he was shown round by a sprightly 84 year old – once, one of the boys who had left barefoot for the Bible Institute in Costa Rica back in the 1920s!

By the winter of 1986-1987, however, Free Church presence in the Andes was reduced even further, with the Rev. Donnie Smith and his family moving to Lima (where he was to lecture at the Lima Evangelical Seminary). And a year later, Tupac Amaru militants were attacking police stations in the area of Moyobamba, while the

Free Church ceased to have any direct involvement in Cajamarca, as Marie-Christine Lux was leaving. There were still links, however. In the spring of 1990, the Evangelical Presbyterian Church of Peru was asking the Free Church to help recruit an ordained missionary for work in Chiclayo: while that autumn there was a very severe earthquake in the area of Moyobamba. This one did not spare Presbyterian property, and the church, manse and school were either destroyed or severely damaged.

In 1991 David MacPherson, at the time a self-supporting volunteer in Moyobamba for a Peruvian relief-agency, noted that, "the young folk of the Free Church were supporting a small church school begun last year". (MacPherson would return to the mountains of Peru in 1998 as an ordained minister of the Free Church). Economic problems were mounting, he said: inflation in Peru was now running at 7000 per cent per annum, and the production of cocaine was flourishing in the northern regions of the country. But the local church, MacPherson reported, attracted 300 people each Sunday and between 150 to 200 at Sunday School, while an anonymous donor had gifted £760 for the reconstruction of the Annie Soper School in Moyobamba. Still, the 1991 General Assembly heard that, in Cajamarca, "the work of PROESA has been scaled-down and the whole project is being re-assessed".

By 1994, there was talk of a union between the Evangelical Presbyterian Church of Peru (strongest in the north) and the National Presbyterian Church of Peru (mainly Quechua speaking, and strongest in the south). That year, the Foreign Missions' night at the General Assembly heard that the Evangelical Presbyterian Church, "is a truly Peruvian church and at present no Free Church missionary serves as a pastor in the church". And the next year, the General Assembly was told that the churches had now merged, in the Evangelical Presbyterian and Reformed Church of Peru. It had 15 presbyteries and 15,000 members. "It adheres to the Westminster Confession and has requested the continuing co-operation of the Free Church of Scotland".

By 1996, the editor of the Monthly Record had been the Rev.

Ronald C. Christie for 6 years (and before that, he had been editor of The Instructor for 6 years). That summer, it was reported that Marie-Christine Lux had been at the General Assembly, back from Moyobamba, where she was training community health-care workers. (She would not remain there for long, however). And the following year, £6,000 had been sent to the Annie Soper school, while the annual meeting of the Women's Foreign Mission Association heard that £3,000 had been sent to Moyobamba, where there had been serious flooding, as aid. At the end of 1997, another £4,000 was going to the Annie Soper school in Moyobamba. The following spring, another £5,000 was sent to Peru as aid, and in 1998 the Rev. David MacPherson and family arrived in Moyobamba. (The Rev. Angus Lamont and family had also gone to Peru, but he was not to serve in the mountains). In Moyobamba, the Rev. MacPherson would set-up Bible Institutes to provide training for elders, deacons, Sunday School teachers and youth leaders". The Rev. Angus Lamont would return to be minister in Dornoch in 2001, while the Rev. David MacPherson's work in Moyobamba would continue into the new millennium.

But by the start of that new millennium, the pioneers of the early days were beginning to leave the stage of earthly endeavour. Annie Soper had died in 1980. (In that same year, in distant Scotland, there was a reception for guests which included an elder of the Evangelical Presbyterian Church of Peru, "founded by the Free Church of Scotland. He spoke in Spanish, with translation by the Rev. John MacPherson of Dornoch. Psalm 121 was then sung, in Spanish").

In March 1982, an obituary appeared for Dr. Harold Lindsay, by then of Dornoch, in the Monthly Record. He had gone to Peru in 1938 and came home in 1954 with his wife Flora (who had predeceased him), in the cause of their children's education. In September 1983, there was an obituary for John Alexander Mackay, now of Princeton, who had died at the age of 94. In December 1986, there appeared an obituary for the Rev. J. Calvin Mackay, who had died the previous October, aged 95. "Mr. Mackay's death marked the end of an era of missionary endeavour – but not the end of the endeavour".

In October 1987, there appeared an obituary for the Rev. Malcom MacRae, born in Kyle of Lochalsh. In 1941, he had been sent to the interior of Peru (to replace the Rev. Murdo Nicolson). He had soon married Nurse Annabella MacLeod, of Lewis. For the next 23 years, they were known as the MacRaes of Cajamarca, and had returned to Scotland in 1965. The following February, an obituary appeared for Dr. Kenneth Mackay, born in Alness, and who had gone to Peru in 1926. Two months later, there was an obituary for David Milnes who, with his wife, after ten years at home, had returned to Peru for an additional five years: and later, had returned once more, for one year. (His wife lived on, to die aged 93, in 2010).

In October 1991, an obituary appeared for the teacher Christina Mackay, from Easter Ross, who had gone to Peru in 1923. She had been recruited by none other than John Alexander Mackay, when he was home on furlough in 1922. She had joined the Rev. J. Calvin Mackay in Cajamarca and taught in the school there. After six years in Peru, she had come home to Scotland for three years, and had then returned to Peru. John MacPherson, in his history of the school in Lima, recounts that in 1941 she was returning to Peru when her little convoy of vessels came under German air-attack. Some weeks followed in Casablanca, while her ship was repaired. It then dodged U-boats until docking at length in Buenos Aires in Argentina. A three-day trip by train took her to La Paz, the capital of Bolivia. She then crossed Lake Titicaca by Dumbarton-built steamer and took another train to Arequipa, where some missionaries looked after her until she could get a seat on a plane for Lima. In total, she was to spend nearly four decades in Peru as an educational missionary of the Free Church of Scotland.

In the same decade, obituaries appeared for Nurse Christina Mackay, of Moyobamba. According to From the Frontiers, she had been born in Shawbost, Lewis, had trained as a midwife, and had sailed for Peru in 1932. After Lima, she sailed north on the coast for some days, took the train to the railhead at Chilete, and took three weeks to cross a 20,000-foot mountain range on foot and mule-back. In 1941, she moved to Chachapoyas to replace Marion MacMillan.

She had come home on compassionate leave on the death of her father, but had returned to Peru in 1938. She had come back to Scotland in 1946 because of the state of her mother's health.

In the Free Church missionary bulletin, From the Frontiers, for March 1996, an obituary appeared for the Rev. James Macintosh, born in Glenurquhart, and once legal representative in Peru for the Free Church of Scotland, "in regard to its whole missionary enterprise in that country". He had been, "a noted preacher in English, Gaelic and Spanish".

In the Monthly Record for December 1997, there appeared an obituary for Miss Catherine Mackay, who had died at the age of 103. A sister of J. Calvin Mackay, whom she had accompanied to Peru in the early days, she had been born in Canada. "Her great-grandfather had emigrated from the family croft at Torroble, Lairg, at the time of the Highland Clearances". Her father, Angus, had been Free Church minister in Kingussie, and she had returned home from Peru in 1924 to keep house for him.

A month later, the death of Irene Thomson, wife of the Rev. George Thomson of Moyobamba, was announced. And in the June-July issue of From the Frontiers for 2000, it was announced that Miss Florence Donaldson, from Armagh, had died too. She had been in Peru, in total, for 35 years; and for some of that time had been a Free Church of Scotland Biblewoman in Moyobamba and Chachapoyas.

The passing from this earth of these Andean evangelists, as the second millennium approached its end, brought to an end too what might well be described as the Heroic Age of Free Church evangelism in the Peruvian mountains. Though the centenary of the work of Free Church missionaries in the Andes will be celebrated in 2021, it is not probable that their likes will be seen again. But – who knows, who knows? Yea, saith the Spirit, that they may rest from their labours; and their works do follow them.

– *Iain Fraser Grigor*

1915: John Alexander Mackay goes south

IN ACCORDANCE WITH THE DECISION OF THE FOREIGN MISSIONS'
Committee that I should be sent on a tour of missionary investigation
to South America, I sailed from New York on the Cristobal on 14th
May, a few days after graduation in Princeton Seminary. Through
the kindness of Dr. Robert E. Speer, secretary of the American
Presbyterian Board of Foreign Mission; Mr. Colton, associate general
secretary of the International YMCA; Mr. Inman, executive secretary
of the Panama Conference; and Mr. A. Stuart McNairn, general
secretary of the Evangelical Union of South America, I had in my
possession when I sailed letters of introduction which secured for me
a cordial welcome from evangelical workers wherever I went. These
four gentlemen, not to speak of others, expressed a very deep interest
in my tour, and especially in the prospect of a Free Church Mission in
South America.

On 23rd May the Cristobal reached Colon, on the Isthmus of
Panama. For its size, Colon is one of the most cosmopolitan cities
in the world. Once a notorious death-trap, it is now a comparatively
healthy city, thanks to the careful sanitary supervision of the United
States Government. After three days in the muggy heat of Colon,
during every moment of which I sweated as if in a perpetual Turkish
bath, I passed through the canal. This great waterway, which unites

the Atlantic and the Pacific, is undoubtedly the greatest triumph of engineering which the human brain and head have ever achieved. It is destined within the next few decades to become the highway of the nations. Its motto is, "The land divided; the world united". But how far from being a section of the "Way of Holiness" is the zone around this giant waterway! I can never recall the few evening hours I spent in Panama city – that beautiful romantic city on the Pacific – without thinking of Sodom. Vice in Panama city is more open than in any city which I have ever visited in North or South America. It is to be sincerely hoped that the great Latin American Conference which meets here in February 1916 will be led to initiate some practical policy for dealing with the moral and religious conditions on the Isthmus of Panama, for at present practically nothing is being done for the native population on the Isthmus.

From Panama I sailed on the Palena for Callao, in Peru. On our voyage southwards we touched on Guayaquil in Ecuador, the centre of the Panama hat industry, and at several ports in northern Peru. On this voyage, which lasted a week, we passed from 9 degrees north of the Equator to 9 degrees south of it, and during the whole time had delightfully cool weather. The unexpected coolness of the tropical region of the west coast of South America is due to the presence of a cool current which flows northwards from the Antarctic Ocean.

On 2nd June I reached Callao, where I was welcomed by Mr. John Ritchie, of the Evangelical Union of South America, who came out to the ship to meet me. I spent five happy and profitable days under his hospitable roof in Callao, after which I stayed in Lima. The distance between Callao and Lima is only eight or ten miles, and can be covered by tram in 25 minutes. In Callao I visited the two schools of the American Methodist Episcopal Mission, but my chief interest was in Lima. Lima bears a striking resemblance to Edinburgh. It has landmarks like Arthur's Seat and the Salisbury Crags; and here the traveller may breathe something of the aristocratic, romantic and historic atmosphere of the Scottish capital. For Lima is the traditional centre of Spanish culture in South America. In size, it is a city somewhat smaller than Aberdeen. As to its life, it is quite a modern city. In the colonial period of South American history, Lima was the seat of the Viceroys. Its cathedral, which was built by Pizarro himself, and where his mummified remains now lie in a glass case, is the largest in South America. Its university was founded many years before the founding of Harvard, Yale or Princeton in the United States.

I was particularly interested in visiting the educational institutions in the city. A law student, Mr. Louis Infanta, who had studied for some years in the United States, and who has sympathies with evangelical work, took me through the university. I attended some of the classes in literature and philosophy and was introduced by Mr. Infanta to the rector of the university, Dr. Pardo, who is the president-elect of the Republic of Peru. The head of the Men's Normal School in Lima is an American, Mr. McKnight. I was introduced to this gentleman, who gave me some very valuable information about intellectual and educational conditions in Peru. In addition to taking me through his own institution, he accompanied me on a visit to Guadalupe College – the leading Boys' High School in the Republic. Here we spent two hours together. A more magnificent institution as to buildings and equipment I had never seen, but, alas! It was a sad tale I heard as to the inefficiency of the teaching staff and the miserable educational results which the school produced. Mr. McKnight told me incidentally that young men had frequently come to the Normal School who were supposed to have had four years in a High School in Peru, and who were not able to do the multiplication table!

The churches of Lima claimed a good deal of my attention. They are seventy in number. The outside of the majority of them I found to be plain and unattractive, while the inside of all of them displayed a profusion of gaudy and fantastic images. In every case the image of the Virgin had the place of honour. I saw nothing in painting or sculpture that suggested the truth of the Resurrection. I was present when different types of services were in progress, and was struck with the absence of men. On one occasion I did indeed see a large number of young men at a church service. They were university students, who had clustered around the inner doors laughing and grimacing at the farcical antics of the deluded worshippers and their spiritual fathers. On another occasion, when I was struck with the number of people in a certain church, I discovered posted on the door outside a notice granting a special indulgence from the Pope to whosoever entered the building at any time within a certain period. Other features of the religious life of Lima are the frequency of religious processions, the sight of barefooted friars, and the almost constant ringing of church bells.

The Evangelical Church in Lima is represented by the Evangelical Union of South America and the Methodist Episcopal Church of North America. There are also in the city representatives of the Salvation Army and the Seventh Day Adventists. The last-named sect, in particular, does incalculable harm on the South American mission field. Its missionaries never enter unoccupied territory, but only some places where evangelical work has already begun. They visit those who have been won by the Gospel, and disturb their minds with their doctrinal crudities. Mr. Ritchie is at the head of the Evangelical Union Mission in the city. The activities of this mission consist of a preaching hall, a small elementary school, a printing office and book store, and a monthly magazine in Spanish, El Heraldo, edited by Mr. Ritchie. The staff consists of five workers, including two wives of missionaries. The Methodist Episcopal Church has two preaching stations, and a monthly magazine. While in the city, I spoke on two occasions, once at a weekly meeting of all the Evangelical workers in Callao and Lima, and once at a Sabbath service in Mr. Ritchie's hall. On both occasions, Mr. Ritchie interpreted me in Spanish.

On 11th June I sailed aboard the Ortega for Mollendo, the port of southern Peru, arriving there on the 13th. On the 14th, I took the train for Arequipa. Arequipa, a city of 40,000 inhabitants, is situated at the foot of an extinct volcano, El Misti, 7,000 feet above sea-level, and is popularly known as the most fanatical city in South America. I saw more men at a service in the cathedral of Arequipa than in any other church building in South America. The city has a large number of churches, a university, a famous observatory, and a hospital which is undoubtedly the finest in Peru, but where, nevertheless, an average of fifty per cent of its patients die. The nurses are, without exception, nuns, and are utterly unqualified for their work. Luckless indeed are all those who have to pass under their care; and thrice unhappy are those patients who are known to sympathise with Protestantism.

Leaving out account of the pernicious work of the Adventists, the Evangelical Union has the only mission in Arequipa. It was a great joy to me to meet the staff of this mission, especially the Rev. Mr. Foster. Mr. Foster has a preaching hall where he often has large audiences, and an interesting club for young men. The nursing work of Miss Pritchard, another of the staff, has done more than anything to break down prejudice against the Gospel and the missionaries. Miss Pritchard has access to some of the best homes of the city, and is constantly asked by leading doctors to assist them at operations and other serious cases. I was led to understand that the Arequipan doctors would welcome the establishment of a good hospital; while some of the best families in the city would welcome the opening of a High School by the mission, and would raise no objection to religious instruction being made a compulsory part of the curriculum. Thus is the way being prepared for the Gospel in the most fanatical city in South America.

Leaving Arequipa after a stay of four days, I entrained for Cuzco. This journey of some 400 miles occupied two days. The night was spent on the high Sierra at a place called Juliaca, as no passenger trains pass over Peruvian railways in the night time. It would be far too dangerous in view of the many windings and steep gradients on the line. On the first day we reached a height of 14,666 feet. At this altitude a great many of the passengers were sick with the dreaded "soroche", or mountain sickness, but I did not suffer in the slightest, much though I had dreaded the ascent. It is exceedingly dangerous for any person with a weak heart to attempt the journey across the Andes. On the second day we crossed the watershed of the Andes and one of the sources of the Amazon, and then descended towards Cuzco, which lies at the head of a beautiful valley 11,500 feet above sea-level. The grassy "pampas" or "punos" on the high uplands of

Peru, with their flocks of sheep and herds of llamas and alpacas, reminded me of the mountain pasture lands in my native Scotland. In fact, the physical features of Scotland and Peru have much in common.

Cuzco is the old capital of the Incan Empire, and is still the centre for the great Indian population of Peru. The whole region for hundreds of miles around is hoary with history and romance. Here, also, are found some of the most wonderful archaeological ruins in the world. I stayed in Cuzco for several days as the guest of Dr. and Mrs. Fenn, of the Evangelical Union Mission, which is the only mission in the city. Cuzco has one of the four universities of Peru. Its hospital, though blessed with a better nursing staff than the hospital of Arequipa, is a place of awful squalor. Written above the door of one of its many churches may be read the words, "Come unto Mary all ye who labour and are burdened with your sins, and she will relieve you". I was much interested in the evangelical and medical work of the Evangelical Union Mission, and I owe an unspeakable debt of gratitude to Dr. Fenn and his cultured wife for their kindness. On two occasions I spoke in the hall of the mission.

In the company of Mr. and Mrs. Payne, a newly-married missionary couple, I rode out on the 25th June to the Urco Mission Farm. This large farm, which is in reality a good-sized estate, is the property of the Evangelical Union, and is situated in a beautiful valley about 24 miles from Cuzco. Mr. Payne is in charge of the farm, and is assisted by Mr. Ganton, a Canadian, an American lady, Miss Stockwell, who conducts a school, and a nurse, Miss Found. He has also a native helper who can preach in Spanish and Quechua (the Indian language) and has a "botica" or druggist's shop in the township of Calca, two miles away. When Mr. Payne first appeared in Calca from Cuzco eight years ago, he was stoned out of the place and compelled to flee for his life. Last year he was asked to stand for the Town Council in Calca. He stood, and though he did absolutely no canvassing, he was returned at the top of the poll. The parish priest was also a candidate, but failed to get a seat. Mr. Payne's first motion in council was to have the council meetings held in future on a week day and not on Sabbath – the day on which they had been held for generations. Much to the surprise of the missionary, the motion was carried unanimously. Mr. Payne has already been asked to become Mayor of Calca, and next year he intends to accept the office. Such is the standing which this missionary has in the district that the parish priest dare not now say a word against the evangelical work carried on at the farm. The happiest memories of my whole tour centre in the Urco Valley and in the signs of promise which I saw there for the triumph of the Gospel in that great region of Peru. For the farm is known and its influence felt over a wide surrounding area. I realised this fact during a trip which I took from Urco into the eastern valleys of the Andes.

I had discussed with Mr. Payne the opportunities for a medical mission in the region of the farm. He told me that such a mission was exactly what the region needed. It would attract, he said, thousands of the dwellers in the upland "Punos" and tropical valleys, so, knowing the desire of the committee to find a field for medical mission, I undertook a tour of investigation in order to be able to lay the facts before the committee. I was accompanied by Mr. Ganton and a young Peruvian who acted as our guide. We set out on mule-back; we slept beneath the stars among the trees on the soft sand beside the river – a tributary of the Amazon. Other nights we passed in large "haciendas", or farms in the valleys. At noon on a certain day we crossed the head of a valley among the eternal snows; the same evening we ate our meal of toasted maize and barley far below among tropical undergrowth. Downwards we went through the country of orange and banana groves, through plantations of coffee, rice, and cotton, and through great sugar estates which reach from the snows to tropical heat. I doubt if there is another region in the world outside Peru where it is possible in the morning to drink snow water, to eat the apples and peaches of the Temperate zone before mid-day, and at the evening meal have for dessert orange mangoes, bananas, and all the fruits of the Tropics. On these productive and beautiful valleys on the eastern slope of the Andes we found much misery, sickness, and spiritual destitution.

Often we were hailed in pleading accents from the doors of huts which we rode past asking us to enter if we were able to render medical aid. I arrived back in Urco after an absence of sixteen days with a throbbing heart and my mind made up on the subject of a medical mission.

My mission was chiefly to visit Peru, but the committee kindly gave me permission to visit the other mission fields in South America with a view to gaining all the experience I could. I accordingly left Cuzco on the 25th July by the weekly train for La Paz, Bolivia. That night I spent on one of the steamers that crosses Lake Titicaca. Lake Titicaca is the highest lake in the world, being 12,000 feet above sea level, and the steamers that ply on its waters were built by Denny's, Dumbarton. In La Paz, which I reached on the following day, I was the guest of the Rev. A. Baker, of the Canadian Baptist Mission. Here I spent five most enjoyable and profitable days, visiting, in particular, the university and the "American Institute", a school of the Methodist Episcopal Church, which is subsidised by the Bolivian Government. Taking farewell of friends in this, the highest capital in the world, I took the weekly night train for Areca – a port in the north of Chile – where I went aboard the Limari for Valparaiso. I reached Valparaiso on the 4th August, and found that it would be impossible for me to cross to Buenos Aires by rail, the tunnel being entirely blocked. I had no alternative but to make arrangements for the voyage to Buenos Aires via the Magellan Straits.

In Valparaiso I found the first and only YMCA on the west coast of South America. During the three days of my stay in this city I visited the Union Church, founded by Mr. David Turnbull, of which the present pastor, Mr. Inglis, is a Scotsman; the headquarters of the Bible Society; one of the Presbyterian mission schools; and a State commercial school. The weekend from the 6th to 9th August, I spent in Santiago.

In Santiago, I was the guest of Dr. Browning, head of the "Instituto Inglés", a large mission High School of the Presbyterian Church of America, and undoubtedly the finest school of its kind in South America. Its diploma is accepted in the leading North American universities. From Dr. Browning I received some valuable ideas about the educational work of evangelical missions. On Sabbath morning I spoke to the boys at school, and later in the day preached in the Union Church. Returning to Valparaiso on Monday the 9th, I addressed a special meeting in the YMCA which, it is interesting to note, was the first distinctly religious address given in the institution during its three year history. That night I stayed with Mr. Stark, head of the British and Foreign Bible Society – a Scotsman from Kilmarnock. Embarking on the Orita on the 10th, I arrived at Montevideo on the morning of the 22nd. I spent that day with Mr. Conrad, the YMCA secretary, and gave an informal talk to some of the members in the afternoon. I was particularly interested to meet Professor Monte Verde, a professor in the university, an earnest Christian, and Mr. Conrad's assistant secretary. He opened up to the student problem in South America as it had never been opened up to me before.

In Buenos Aires I was chiefly interested in the work of the YMCA, which had a large students' department, with a graduate of the university of Buenos Aires as one of the secretaries. I learned all I could about the intellectual and religious interests of the students, and visited, in particular, the department of Philosophy and Letters. Mr. Ewing, of the YMCA, and Mr. Hercus, late of the EUSA Mission, were especially helpful to me. On Sabbath morning I conducted a Bible class in the Scotch Church, addressed a widely-advertised meeting in the YMCA in the afternoon, and gave the address in the Methodist Church in the evening. I understand that the afternoon address is being translated into Spanish by the British and Foreign Bible Society for distribution in pamphlet form in South America. During the last two days of my stay in Buenos Aires I was the guest of Dr. Fleming, pastor of St. Andrew's Scotch Church, which is the largest and wealthiest Protestant Church in South America. I also met the Rev. Paul Besson, a favourite pupil of the famous exegete, Godet.

I left Buenos Aires for Montevideo on 1st September, and on 3rd September sailed on the Ruahine for Plymouth, where we arrived on the night of the 23rd. I had hoped to be able to pay a short visit to Brazil on the homeward journey, but exigencies of time did not permit me.

It was with feelings of profound thankfulness to God that I stepped once more on the soil of Old England, having been preserved by His loving care from dangers manifold on mountain, plain and on the sea.

— *Part-one of Mackay's three-part report to the Foreign Missions' Committee; from the Monthly Record, November 1915.*

J. Kennedy Cameron reports to the Mound

THE CONTINENT OF SOUTH AMERICA FORMS A TRIANGLE. THE Equator forms its base. Its vertex is at Cape Horn towards the Antarctic Ocean, and its sides form its Pacific and Atlantic coasts. The vast extent of the continent can be in some measure realised by taking into consideration the length of the Amazon, which rises in Peru only a few miles from the Pacific Coast and falls into the Atlantic. This majestic river is the gateway to one million square miles of the choicest of the world's natural fields of products. Ocean liners from Liverpool can sail up the river to the town of Iquitos, distant from the Atlantic over 2,000 miles, and yet is only 350 feet above sea-level. Steamers of less draught may proceed further upstream for an additional 1,000 miles. To Peruvian territory belong over 10,000 miles of waterway in connection with the Amazon and its tributaries, navigable for steamers of from 4 to 8 feet of draught.

Every country has features which are peculiarly its own. Those to which Peru may lay claim are unique. In no other case can such diverse characteristics be found in combination. The extent of the country is equal to what that of Germany and Austro-Hungary was before the Great War of 1914-1918. Its coast-line is 1,400 miles. A short distance inland, and parallel with the coast, is the vast and magnificent range of the Andes Mountains. Beyond these giant heights the country falls away into the great Montaña – whose forest depths present the largest tract of unexplored territory on earth – the high land itself being termed the Sierra. The Andes, being athwart the Trade Winds, receive on their eastern side more rain than any other part, while on the west, or Pacific side, no rain falls. That region, therefore, between the hills and the Pacific, though its soil is as rich as any in the world, is of itself utterly barren, yet by irrigation it is made to produce rich crops of cotton, sugar, maize, and such-like valuable products.

The mountains are volcanic, and the whole region is still frequently subjected to earthquakes. In 1746 there was an exceptionally severe one. It was accompanied by a great tidal wave which destroyed Callao with its 6,000 inhabitants. The present town stands to the north of where its predecessor did.

The nearest country to Peru across the Pacific is New Zealand, and out in that direction is the deepest part of the ocean. The Challenger Expedition sounded to a depth of six or seven miles, and did not strike the bottom. The highest point of the Andes is 23,000 feet. Away up on these slopes there are deposits of limestone, with innumerable specimens of marine shells. These prove that what is now at so great an altitude on dry land must at one time have been low in the bed of the ocean. Nature at that remote period must have been working in these parts on an immense scale. Indeed in few places on the earth's surface, if any, does Nature produce impressions of greater sublimity than it does on that coast. Along its whole length there is to be seen this endless chain of giant heights rearing their heads far above the ordinary level of the clouds, and appearing in dazzling splendour as the clear sun-rays are reflected from the perpetual snows with which they are clad.

The native name of the mountains is Cordillera, or Copper Mountains. They might as well be called gold or silver mountains, for their mineral resources are varied and of extraordinary value. Large smelting furnaces are at work even in some of the higher altitudes. From these mines Spain drew so much gold that she for a time became the richest country in the world.

Among the hills are great agricultural valleys. They extend for many miles in length and several in breadth. High up also in the bosom of the mountains are large cities and the wonderful lake of Titicaca, which is 3,700 square miles in extent. Its greatest depth is 930 feet. It is at an altitude forty times as high as the top of the dome of St. Paul's Cathedral in London. On its waters one may well be said to sail among the clouds. In Scotland the highest village is Wanlockhead, which is 1,500 feet above sea-level. In Peru there are cities at elevations of nine, ten and eleven thousand feet. Because of the difference of altitudes, the crops cultivated vary from the more tender ones peculiar to the tropics to the hardy oats which are suited to our colder climates.

The Montaña is for rubber and other tropical products the richest field in the world, not even the Congo excepted. Rosewood, mahogany, satinwood, and many such woods, which are valuable for furniture manufacture, are found in abundance. Here grows the cinchona tree which yields the famous Peruvian bark from which our priceless quinine and cinchona are extracted. There is also the coca plant, from whose leaves cocaine is extracted. From Iquitos there is shipped cotton which in some respects has made Peru famous; also sugar of the most luxuriant variety, and coffee of the finest quality, as well as tobacco and many other products. From the Pacific ports are shipped marble, iron, gold, silver, lead, copper, salt, saltpetre, cocoa, rice, sugar, sulphur, cotton, olives, indigo, coffee, and mercury.

The richest fruit-growing part of Peru is the south. There in abundance are such fruits as pine-apples, oranges, lemons, peaches, chirimoyas, paltas, grenadillas, bananas and grapes.

Peru, though south of the Equator, is wholly within the tropics. It has its summer and winter seasons. On the coast, through the winter season, which extends from June to November, a damp mist lies during the night. It is said to result from the cold Humboldt current that flows up from the Antarctic Ocean and strikes the coast of Peru. The contrast between this coolness and the great heat of summer is such as causes the people on the coast to clothe almost as warmly as we do in Scotland, and yet, during the winter, tender plants such as geraniums flourish outside, and many trees and shrubs are gorgeous with flower.

The principal beast of burden in Peru is the mule, which was introduced by the Spaniards after they had conquered the country. Few horses are to be seen. Though motor ploughs are now being introduced, ploughing to a large extent is still done by oxen. The simple form of plough in use, and the goad by which the oxen are driven, recall mental pictures of similar scenes, recorded in Scripture, in Palestine and other lands. On the higher altitudes of the Andes even the mule fails, and there is requisitioned the llama, the largest of the four kinds of sheep that are native to the Andes. The others are alpacas, vicuñas, and huanacos. The load laid on the llama must not exceed a certain weight. Should it do so, the llama will refuse to carry it. Within certain limits, however, it is a useful burden-bearer, and by means of large flocks of them very considerable quantities of goods can be conveyed to the upper reaches of the mountains. Fortunately, however, the use of draught animals can now to a large extent be dispensed with. The motor car is available on the shore level and amidst the valleys of the Sierra. Even the great barrier of the Cordillera has at various places been penetrated by the railways. These provide easy access to the Sierra. Travellers, however, to these parts must be prepared to endure the dreaded soroche, or mountain sickness, and have the strength of nerve to enable them to look down from the mountain heights upon the extraordinary way by which they have ascended. The summit of the railway from Lima to the Interior is about 16,000 feet, and at that altitude men may look up to perpetual snow-clad heights hundreds of feet above. To these frozen heights men by the thousand at one time flocked for gold, because these were the mines by which Spain was enriched. Into the mines the natives were driven and there enslaved in order that the newly found merchants of Peru might be enriched. To the soroche the worst sea-sickness is preferable, and only those people whose hearts are in a healthy condition should expose themselves to the dangers involved in it.

In the heights of the Andes the condor, the largest flying bird, has its home. It is carrion in its habits. It and another vulture of a smaller size are protected as scavengers. Their services are valuable for the health of the community in such a country as Peru, where sanitation has not received much attention.

The dryness of the climate on the coast accounts for the preservation of the valuable deposits of nitrate in the northern part. To the same cause also can be attributed the exceptionally large percentage of nitrogen that is contained in the guano of Peru.

In the Sierra and Montaña, houses have to be roofed as in other countries in a way that will secure protection from the rain. On the shore land it is different. There the roofs are flat, and consist of wood covered with a coating of mud. In the cities they serve as bleaching greens. The walls of the houses are built of sun-dried bricks made from the earth that is in general cultivation. The mortar used is formed from the same source. The outer walls are plastered over and painted. The houses are thus made to assume a clean and pretty appearance, while the internal fittings and furnishing is according to the amount of money which the occupant is prepared to lay out in that direction. The houses do not usually exceed two storeys in height, because of the earth tremors to which the district is subject. The plan on which they are constructed is that of a patio or central court or hall, on to which the rooms open, or around which the houses are grouped, and on to which all of them open, and from which there is egress through the iron gate to the street. The only fire-place is in the kitchen. The want of artificial heating in other parts of the house causes the people to feel the chill of winter greater than otherwise they would do.

Lima, the Capital of Peru, was built after the Spanish Conquest. Its cathedral is probably the oldest and largest in South America. Its altar and candle-sticks are of solid silver. The city is also one of four university seats in the country, and it has interesting zoological and botanical gardens and a museum. Its streets, squares, and patios are rendered attractive with flowers and tropical trees and plants. Its inhabitants are the most cultured and tolerant community in Peru. Talent, beauty, and generosity also abound among them. The city is also a most cosmopolitan one, and is daily becoming more so along with its rapidly increasing commercial importance. Its successful merchants are from many countries, and by them wealth is lavishly displayed. The fields on the shore land are enclosed by walls of large blocks of sun-dried clay, and in the Sierra with hedges of the tall magay oraloe.

Sewage and water supplies in Lima and some of the other principal cities are according to modern requirements, but in other towns they are of a very primitive kind. The sewers indeed are often open surface ones, running along the centre of the streets. In Lima taxi-cabs are numerous, and there is also an excellent up-to-date electric car system. Indeed, no town could be better served in these respects. There are also large shops where things can be bought much as at home.

One thing that a visitor from Britain does miss is the green grass. Outside the irrigated areas there is no vegetation. In every direction there is but the barren parched soil and dust at every step. Where the traffic is heavy the roadways are rough with ruts, and dust on them becomes ankle-deep. Even with the least wind everything gets thickly coated with it, and the germs of disease are readily spread abroad.

* * *

Of the many nations that inhabited America at the time at which it was discovered by Europe, the two most powerful and advanced in civilisation were those of Mexico and Peru. The origin of the latter stretches beyond the domain of history, and is lost in the mists of legend. At the time, however, at which it first came into view it was a great and flourishing monarchy, with its seat of government at the ancient capital of Cuzco. This Inca kingdom embraced Ecuador, Peru, Bolivia, Chili, and parts of Brazil and the Argentine. On the shores of Lake Titicaca, among the Andes of southern Peru, there are monumental remains which seem to give countenance to belief in the existence of at least one civilisation of even an earlier date than that of the Inca.

The Inca civilisation was far in advance of what might be expected on a Continent the very existence of which was so long hidden from the rest of the world. It presents, for instance, a vast contrast to what was to be found in Africa before Christian influence bore upon it for its enlightenment. Though the Inca Indian had evidently no knowledge of iron, yet he could dispense with its use, through his acquaintance with a treatment of copper that secured a hardness that rendered it serviceable for the various purposes to which iron would have been applied had it been available. Hence as a people they were capable of cutting emeralds and other precious stones, as well as of fashioning the most delicate and beautiful articles in silver and gold. From the wool of the vicuña also were manufactured by them articles of dress for the monarch, and carpets and hangings for the royal palaces and temples, as of so fine a texture as to make them coveted by the Spaniards when they invaded the land. In the construction, too, of their palaces, temples, and fortresses stones were used as large as 38 feet long, 18 feet broad, and 6 feet thick. No cement or mortar was used, and yet so exactly adjusted were these huge stones that the blade of a knife cannot pass between them. As in the case of the Temple at Jerusalem, it must remain a matter of wonder how such material could be cut out in the quarries, dressed, and conveyed a distance of several miles over a rough and broken surface, and placed in the walls where they now are. Even with modern appliances the task would not be one easy of accomplishment.

Great wide roads, many of them still traceable, were constructed throughout the kingdom, especially along the Sierra. By means of these a communication, even with the most distant parts of the kingdom, was maintained that was remarkably good for the period. Along these highways were placed at intervals granaries filled with various stores necessary for an army on the march. Barracks also were provided for such troops, and resting places for the ordinary traveller.

Inca religion was the idolatrous worship of the sun. The great temple to Inti, the sun god, was at Cuzco. Its walls were adorned with plates of gold. Its vessels were of gold and silver. Indeed, it is supposed to have been the richest in the world. Gold was so abundant in the country as to have been of little value to the people, and hence the lavish use of it in the adorning of their temple, which became so enriched through the munificence of successive Incas that it came to be known by the name of Coricancha, or place of gold.

When an Inca "was called home", as they say, "to the mansions of his father, the sun", his bowels were removed and buried, and along with them a quantity of his plate and jewels. His body was embalmed – for the secret of embalming was as well known to them as it was to the ancient Egyptians – and placed in the great temple at Cuzco. There the body, clothed in princely attire, was placed in a sitting posture in a chair of gold. On State occasions these bodies and chairs were brought forth and placed even at the festal board. On the other hand, the Inca was not allowed alone into his father's mansions. Some of his immediate attendants and concubines were made to join company with him by being immolated on his tomb.

It was provided by law that every man should marry on his attaining a certain age. To enable him to do so he was provided with a house and sufficient land on which he could maintain himself and his wife. To each child born of the marriage an additional extent of land was assigned. The extent of the holding was again diminished as the strength of the household declined. The people and everything in the country were viewed as pertaining to the Inca, and all was accordingly under government control for the benefit of the community as a whole. Even the very wool of the llama, and of the other sheep, was distributed among the people according to their requirements. The whole population was thus treated as one great family with the Inca at its head. No man could be idle without due cause. No man could be rich, and no man could be poor. Thus the people were deprived of all initiative and were dependent on being led. This was one of the fatal weaknesses in their system that made them an easy prey to the Spaniards.

As the Empire was extended from time to time by the conquest of neighbouring tribes, there was imposed upon these subject races the necessity of acquiring a knowledge of the Quechuan language of the conqueror. He required that throughout the Empire there should be one universal language by means of which communication could be maintained with all parts of his dominions. On the other hand, people of the different provinces had to wear the costume peculiar to their province. Even to this day distinctions among the Inca Indians of the Sierra are observed by differences of costume, especially in colour. By means, therefore, of one universal religion, one universal language, and one universal government, throughout the kingdom, unity was secured, and the Inca was able to exercise a truly patriarchal authority over his subjects.

The Inca people were an industrious race. From the nature of their government they could not be otherwise. To this there remains to the present day abundant testimony in their buildings, roadways, and the cultivation of the soil, and especially in the remarkable system of irrigation that had been introduced by them. This latter work, for its successful execution, required remarkable engineering skills. Even through the solid rock at times the water channels were driven, and that at a time when the use of iron and blasting powder were unknown. By these irrigation works the barren wilderness was made richly productive, and away into the lofty plateau of the Andes, far above the ordinary level of the clouds, were to be found towns and hamlets, whose inhabitants were maintained in a state of plenty through the industrious cultivation, not only of the valleys, but of the hill slopes, which in places were terraced for the purposes of agriculture. The material prosperity of the country would appear to have been far in excess of what it is today. There was a wider agriculture. There was less pauperism, and vice was more in check. The morality of their heathen religion far excelled what prevails today among them under the name of Christianity.

The laws of the kingdom were few in number, but such as existed were rigorously enforced. Crimes of theft, adultery, and murder were capital, as were also blasphemy against the sun god and malediction of the Inca. Rebellion on the part of a city or a province was punished by the extermination of its inhabitants. In the execution of punishment, however, there was not allowed the infliction of unnecessary cruelty, such as is characteristic of barbarous nations, as, for instance, the prolongation of the sufferings of the victim, and the employment of various ingenious methods of torture.

The Inca sceptre descended from the father to the oldest son by the lawful queen, who was usually also a sister to the Inca. In addition to her, a host of concubines shared the Sovereign's affections, and the support of the palace was a first charge upon the provisions of the country.

Each Inca built his own palace, and those of his predecessors were allowed to remain unoccupied. While these royal residences might be placed anywhere throughout the empire, there were centres, such as Cuzco, which had a special claim upon the presence of the Sovereign.

Though tobacco, which is now largely cultivated and exported from the country, was known to the Inca Indian, it was used by him only in the form of snuff. His loved narcotic to-day is the coca leaf. These leaves are from a shrub which grows to the height of about six feet. They are dried in the sun, and with a small quantity of these in his pouch, and a handful of roasted maize, the Indian willingly pursues from day to day long journeys without an undue sense of fatigue. Indeed, he prefers such fare to ordinary food. Its use, however, grows upon him and leads to excess. This is followed with the same baneful effects of habitual intoxication, and a physical enfeebling as result from the excessive use of the drug cocaine which is extracted from the leaf. Alcoholic drinks distilled from maize, and other substances, are also doing very destructive work among these ignorant Indians.

* * *

Of the gold and silver that abounded in Peru rumours had reached afar. These aroused the covetous desire of the Spaniards, into whose hands it afterwards fell, and who were greatly enriched thereby. Francisco Pizarro is the Spanish leader to whom belongs the credit of conquering Peru early in the sixteenth century, and making it part of the foreign possessions of that once great power. His bones are deposited in a side chapel of the great Cathedral of Lima.

The conquest of Peru was rendered easier of accomplishment through the peculiar circumstances that at the time prevailed in the Inca kingdom. The power of the Emperor was absolute. It was so exercised as to leave no room for initiative on the part of the people. They were servilely dependent on the leadership of the Inca. When, therefore, they were, through any cause, deprived of his presence, they were rendered comparatively helpless. It was a fatal weakness in the constitution of the nation, of which the Spanish invader was not slow to take advantage. Further, the last emperor had indicated when he was dying that he desired the kingdom to be divided into two. This was done. Over the northern or Quito one, Atahualpa reigned as Inca, and over the southern one reigned Huascar, with his capital at Cuzco. War soon broke out between the two kingdoms. Atahualpa was victorious. Huascar was taken prisoner by him and placed in confinement. Cuzco also was taken possession of, and Atahualpa extended his sway of both kingdoms. This occurred only a few months before the arrival of the Spaniards. Much unrest prevailed, and the kingdom had been weakened by the war between the rival brothers.

After one or two failures, Pizarro succeeded in landing in Peru with a small force of Spanish soldiers. Great endurance and bravery were manifested by the invaders, not only in overcoming the initial difficulties of getting transported across the Atlantic, and then over the Isthmus of Panama and along the Pacific Coast, but also in facing the many hardships that beset their path in Peru, and the powerful odds that were opposed to them. Few men would face the task. They were, however, urged on by their sordid love for gold. This, with their later treatment of the subjugated races, forms a chapter of Spanish history that forever will reflect discredit upon their undertaking.

By the adoption of a lenient and liberal policy Pizarro made so favourable an impression upon the section of the people with whom he first came in contact as disarmed suspicion and secured for him

easy movement and even kindly hospitality. Everywhere he proclaimed that he had come in the name of the holy vicar of God and
of the great prince of Spain, and that he required obedience from the
people to the church and the sovereign whom he represented. The
inhabitants had no knowledge of what such declarations meant. He
was, however, able through friendly intercourse with them to gather
information which confirmed the rumours that had reached him of
the fabulous wealth of the country, and such reports were a stimulus
to the cupidity of himself and his followers.

After a time he moved towards Cajamarca in the northern Sierra of
Peru, where he understood the Inca then was, for he had determined
to appear in his presence. History records few, if any, instances of a
more daring enterprise. He had to leave the coast on which he was
dependent for retreat should necessity for such arise, and allow
himself to be hemmed in by mighty mountains in the heart of an
unknown country, and with a following of less than 200 men there
face a large army led by a young prince flushed with the pride of
recent victory. On the march he was visited by an envoy from the Inca
with an invitation to the royal camp. Pizarro, however, was of opinion
that the real object of the envoy was to gain information as to the
strength of the white men. This Pizarro gave him, and assured him
that he had been sent by the great sovereign of Spain to congratulate
the Inca on his recent victory, and to aid him in retaining possession of
the position which he had gained.

Having at length overcome the enormous difficulties presented
by the Cordillera, he reached Cajamarca and by finding it deserted of
its inhabitants, he became convinced that Atahualpa was cunningly
laying a trap for him. Instead therefore of proceeding to the royal
camp, which was at a little distance from the city, he invited the Inca
to visit him. This invitation the Inca accepted, and Pizarro prepared to
execute the great feat of daring which he had resolved upon. He had
evidently succeeded in disarming the Inca of suspicion, as he did the
natives on the coast. Atahualpa, richly attired, a collar of emeralds
suspended on his neck, his head adorned with rich ornaments, and
borne by his vassals seated on a throne of gold of immense value,

entered Cajamarca, accompanied by only a small following, and prepared to remain in the city all night. Valverde, Pizarro's chaplain, with a Bible and a crucifix, met and tried to expound to him the true faith, for the propagation of which the Spaniards declared they had come to the country. He besought him to abjure his old faith and accept the Christian one, as that alone by which he could hope to be saved; and also to acknowledge himself vassal to the king of Spain. Such compliance Atahualpa indignantly declined to give. The friar thereupon reported the matter to Pizarro, and urged him on saying: "Do you not see that, while we stand here wasting our breath talking with this dog, full of pride as he is, the fields are filling with Indians? Set on at once; I absolve you!" The signal accordingly was given. All avenues from the city were closed. The Inca was seized and made prisoner. His followers were trampled upon by the Spanish cavalry and his great army completely put to rout. Night fell upon the scene, and Pizarro recalled his troops to their quarters in the city.

An arrangement was afterwards made whereby the young Inca, who was only about 30 years of age, would be set free provided he should within two months, as he promised to do, pay a very large ransom in gold and silver. Couriers were sent, and much gold was collected by them from the royal palaces and temples. Huascar, on learning what was taking place, offered a larger ransom should he be granted freedom from his confinement. Pizarro resolved to have him removed from Cuzco to Cajamarca and have the case of the two brothers there determined. He realised that he had an opportunity of securing one of them as a vassal, and in this way achieve his purpose of attaching the country to Spain. He was frustrated, however, in his design because, when Atahualpa learned what Pizarro's intention was, he gave private orders to have Huascar put to death.

After having his forces augmented, Pizarro distributed among his followers the treasure secured for Atahualpa's release, amounting to over three and a half million pounds sterling in gold and fifty one thousand pounds in silver. He then prepared to march on Cuzco in order to get possession of the great wealth of that city. Valverde, the evil genius of the conquest, realising that the Spaniards could not rule the country in safety so long as the Inca, so much idolised as he was by his people, lived, expressed his readiness to sign the death warrant of the young monarch. But where was the cause to be found that would appear to justify such action? A rumoured rising among the natives, which was afterwards confessed to have no foundation, was laid to the charge of Atahualpa. He was tried and condemned to be forthwith burnt alive in the Square of Cajamarca. The sentence was approved-of by Valverde. There were, however, some who, to their credit, disapproved of the proceedings, and maintained that if the Inca were to be tried it should be before the emperor in Spain. The Inca vainly implored Pizarro to spare his life. At the stake, before the fire was applied, Valverde held up a crucifix and besought Atahualpa to embrace it and be baptised, and promised that, should he do so, he would have the mode of death changed to that of the garrote, or strangulation, the kind of death sentence meted out to criminals in Spain. The unhappy monarch consented, and as a new convert to Romanism he had the name Juan given him in honour of John the Baptist. Thus perished the last of the Incas.

The natives were thereafter wantonly sacrificed to the cupidity and cruelty of the invader. They, their land, and their wealth were appropriated, and unrelatable outrages were perpetrated. It is said that after Spanish occupation was fastened on the land, "in a century nine-tenths of the people had been destroyed by over-work and cruelty". This, however, did not take place without heaven's retribution becoming manifest in the civil wars that broke out among the Spaniards themselves, wherein much blood was shed, and the proud leaders of the Conquest were laid in the dust. Thus ended a chapter of Spanish colonial history as dishonourable as is to be found in the annals of any country. She has paid a great price for securing possession, for a few centuries only, of, "the richest of the colonial jewels that adorned her imperial crown".

Today there remains of the Inca Empire only about 2 million ignorant poncho-clad Sierra Indians, and the monuments of their former greatness in the ruins of palaces, fortresses, temples, roads, irrigation works and baths. The masterly plans of these fortifications and temples, as well as their colossal size, and other works, bear mute testimony to the advanced state to which these children of the sun had attained ere the tragedy of their conquest was enacted in the destruction of one of the most marvellous peoples of which history has record, and a civilization ended which was paralleled with that of Egypt.

* * *

The Spanish Conquest was accompanied with the imposition of the Papal religion. Indeed, it took place in the name of religion, though the love of gold was more apparent as the controlling motive than an interest in the spiritual or moral welfare of the Indian. Spain, however, found it no easy task to exercise control in that distant part of her dominions. Its sea-ports were harried by buccaneers, which kept the country isolated. Lawlessness accompanied the acquisition of wealth ashore. Authority was difficult to establish. So every mode of cruel oppression was exercised on the helpless native, while immorality and other evils ran riot on the part of the conqueror. The professing Christian Church might be expected to have exercised an ameliorating influence, because of its close association with the work of the conqueror.

Valverde was appointed Bishop of Cuzco. He soon by forced native labour had a cathedral erected in the Square in Cuzco. Out of the ruins of the House of the Sun arose a great monastery. A nunnery replaced the House of the Virgins of the Sun. In like manner throughout the country churches, monasteries, and nunneries took the place of the ancient sacred buildings of the children of the sun. Ecclesiastics flowed in from Europe, and great efforts were made to Christianise the Indians by compulsion. Emperor Charles V sent an image of the crucifixion, and it was substituted for Inti, the sun god, and became known as "Our Lord of the Earthquakes". Miraculous powers came to be ascribed to it, but it conveyed no Christian meaning to the Indian, and no effort was made to teach him. He was compelled to give up all symbols of his sun worship, and his conversion to Christianity was completed by the sprinkling of water, for which payment was exacted, whilst to such as clung to their former idolatry no mercy was shown. The very foundations of some of the churches consist of the idols which were thus rendered up under compulsion. It is somewhat remarkable, however, that during the centuries in which Peru remained as part of the colonial possession of Spain, this so-called Christianising work was not proceeded with beyond the limits of the conquered territory. To this day, the Indians of the Montaña remain in their original heathenism. For centuries the Church of Rome has looked on, and has made no attempt to bring light into the darkness of that great forest region. These distant glades did not appear to attract any of the vast army of ecclesiastics with which Peru is burdened. It did not appear to be a land that would be conducive to the ease and prosperity which the early agents sought. The negro Indians of the Montaña remain uncivilised. Some of them wear no clothes. Some wear shirts made from the fibrous bark of a tree. Some wear cotton shirts, and others dye their bodies. Some of them even are cannibals, and the only occupation of all of them is fighting and hunting. Their residences are palm-thatched huts. Their food consists of yucas, bananas, potatoes, and maize. They consist of many tribes, and speak various languages or dialects. By learning new vices they are gradually sinking lower in the scale of humanity. A missionary has written of them: "Rum, Romanism, rapacity, and moral rottenness are conditions which no Indian native can long survive. Unfortunately, that is the only garb in which western civilisation has ever been presented to these children of the forest. Unseen, unknown, another Congo tragedy has been enacted in the dark Montaña, and only a decimated savage population and some degraded traders remain to tell the tale. Alcohol, the bullet and imported smallpox have made such ravages that the complete disappearance of these Indians is a thing of a few years".

In the occupied territory, some useful work was accomplished by the Church of Rome. There is, for instance, cause for gratitude for the lasting benefit that has been conferred upon the Indian natives of the Sierra by their Quechuan language being reduced to writing. Today there are four universities and many schools and colleges. Advantage is taken of these by the white and mixed races, but the Inca Indians of the Sierra are still illiterate.

It is unfortunate that the church which undertook the evangelising of Peru was herself sadly in need of being reformed and purified. Many of her agents in Peru became infected by the spirit of licentiousness that was abroad, and the religious fraternity came to lead a life of ease and indulgence on lands which were worked for them by enslaved Indians. The priesthood accordingly in general came to be characterised with corruption and cruelty. An historian says of them: "The rule of celibacy was generally avoided, religious duties were hurried through, and the instruction of the Indians reduced to an absurdity. Amidst general immorality in the towns, the regulars set the worst example, making their monasteries places of licence and pleasure. The clergy were recruited from two sources; some were the outcasts of Spanish parishes and monasteries; others were mestizos, either idle or dissolute men, driven by disgrace and want to take orders; or else men put into religion by their parents with a view to getting an Indian parish and making a fortune out of these helpless people. The care of souls therefore was sought after only so far as such promised to secure the secular interests on which the hearts of such men were set.

The Inquisition was established in Lima in 1569, and was utilised not for the uprooting of heresy, for there was none to uproot, but to advance the interests of the social order, or what claimed to be such. Any excuse was sufficient to justify a man's being handed over for incarceration in its dark damp vaults, or for trial in its subterranean hall by rack, scourge, wheel, screws or other diabolical invention of cruelty. For two hundred and fifty years suspicion and intrigue were rampant. Freedom of thought ceased to exist, and development of Christian character was rendered almost impossible. While a monopoly of trade was established with Spain, a monopoly of religion was maintained with Rome.

Today sees little improvement. Drunkenness and immorality

prevail. The priests are characteristically ignorant. Their very number forms an almost intolerable burden on the resources of the people. In the country there is one Archbishop, seven Bishops, and a very large number of friars and priests. For instance, in Arequipa there is a priest or friar to every thirty individuals. In the city of Lima, there are said to be six thousand of them; and yet spiritual ignorance of a very gross kind lies like a black pall upon the land. Truly the saying of Scripture finds illustration: "If the light that is thee be darkness, how great is that darkness!" There is no attempt to instruct the people in the teaching of Scripture. Even the subjects of the few sermons preached are the lives of the saints and the blessings which observance of their feast days is fitted to secure. Among the Indians of the Sierra much of their old heathen customs, connected with the worship of the sun, continue to be observed under the name of Christian festivals. Their many feast days, consequently, are days of fanaticism and drunken revelry. Knowledge of the true God and of Jesus Christ is denied them. They are without God in the world. Masses are given and paid for, but of Christ they are left in ignorance, and of the Word of God and its Gospel tidings they have not so much as heard. Mr. Stuart McNairn writes: "Jesus Christ is to these people merely an image they are called upon to worship at intervals; they know nothing of a Saviour from sin. Such is the confusion of ideas among them that in many places their so-called worship is still carried on by means of the old heathen dances, where Christ is worshipped as the sun, and the Virgin Mary as the moon".

The cross is met everywhere throughout the land, but it is a Christless cross. The superstitious worship paid to it is evidenced too in the case of a hill near Lima. On the top of this hill is a heavy cross of wood, and at the base of the hill is a very small chapel. The cross is taken once a year to the chapel to be blessed, and afterwards replaced on the hill. There is a special dispensation for the fifty or sixty men who are needed for the work. Idolatrous reverence for the cross and saint worship abound, and especially Mariolatry, but of Christ and His redemption work there is gross ignorance. The suffering of the Virgin Mary is represented as greater than those of

Christ, and in every respect she is made to usurp the place of Christ. Above the doorway of the Jesuit church in Cuzco are the words; "Come to Mary, all who are burdened and weary with the weight of your sins, and she will rest you". Even a Roman Catholic ecclesiastic has observed that, "there exists superstitious paganism in its most repugnant deformity, and absolute ignorance of the rudiments of the faith".

Till a few months ago civil marriage and divorce were unknown in Peru. The priesthood also exacted such heavy marriage fees that large numbers of the people dispensed with the services of the Church and lived in concubinage. Through this cause, and the general immoral atmosphere in the community, more than half the births are illegitimate. The Peruvian statistician, Fuentes, says that, "a shocking proportion of the people avoid marriage and live in complete libertinage, which increases as one descends the social scale". In Arequipa £12 is the least sum for a Mass, while as large sums as £60 and £80 may have to be paid. At a funeral in Huancayo, which we witnessed, there was no priest present, because the people could not pay his fee, and he would not give his services free. Dr. Mackay offered his services, and they were most gratefully accepted. This instance afforded evidence of how the hearts of the people could be reached, and their sympathy for evangelical religion won, were missionaries available to go among them and show a better way than that of exaction followed by the priest.

The low moral tone of the community is evident from the fact that motherhood is prevalent at the age of fifteen years. Gambling also is freely indulged in by all classes of the people, and that openly in the streets, and wherever men meet and congregate together. Sabbath is not generally observed even as a day of rest from worldly toil. Any cessation there is, is taken advantage of for sports, theatre attendances and political and other gatherings. Among the Indians the day is wholly given to market work.

There are State schools and Church schools. Popish religious instruction is imparted by priests in each, and attendance at such is obligatory, even to the extent of the Confessional and the Mass.

The Jesuits were expelled from the country for a time, but for the past thirty or forty years they are openly exerting their influence among the people, and even conducting schools for the education of the wealthiest of the citizens. The school is one of the means by the use of which the Church of Rome seeks to maintain her influence over the young. Till within the last twenty years religious intolerance prevailed, but now Churches and other Christian agencies enjoy a freedom which the Papacy greatly resents.

A century ago the great world movement that produced the French Revolution made Peru an independent republic. The population, which amounts to over four million, is of a very mixed character: 57% of them being Indians, 23% Cholos, or half-breeds, 20% Blancos, or Whites of Spanish descent. In the coast region this mixture is complicated by the introduction of Negro and Chinese labour. There is, for instance, a large Chinese quarter in Lima, and this presents a missionary problem in itself. These neglected Chinese spend all they earn on opium, and are responsible for the opium dens of the city. The comparative smallness of the population is due to some extent to an abnormally high rate of mortality among the young. It is computed that from 40% to 90% of the young die before they reach 27 years of age. This death rate again is due to the want of proper treatment of childhood, immorality and disease, and the neglect of expectant motherhood.

The country is at present passing through a critical stage of its history. A large foreign element is entering it in connection with an industrial and commercial development that is taking place. The manhood of the country is largely falling away from the Papacy and is being engulfed in materialism. The educated students are agnostics. Religion, such as they know and see around them, in the drunken fanaticism that characterises the festivals of the Church, is to those students a mockery from which they turn away in scorn. They are without the aid of friends and books to direct them to the light of truth and a knowledge of Christ, and so their helpless condition presents a loud Macedonian cry for the sympathy and assistance of the Evangelical Churches. It can, therefore, easily be conceived what a peculiarly difficult field Peru presents to the mission agent. No similar combination of forces – the Papacy, materialism, and paganism – is arrayed in strength in any other country to which the servants of the Cross have been sent by home Churches. Peru, accordingly, calls for specially equipped agents, for not alone with heathenism, but with cultured agnosticism, gross materialism, and prejudiced Romanism, the servants of Christ have to contend. They might well say before such an array of enemies, "Who is sufficient for these things?" Their weapon, however, is the Word of God, and the Lord Jesus, whom they serve, promises to be with them, and His is an arm that is mighty to save.

* * *

Some years ago, in the city of Aberdeen, there was a young lady student who was training for the teaching profession. She found herself influenced to take a special interest in the need of evangelical Christian work in Latin America. Notwithstanding the exacting nature of her studies, she found time to devote attention to this subject of American missions, and the further she proceeded the more fascinating the theme became.

About the same time there proceeded from the Christian home of a respected elder a Highland youth to take a course of study at that famous northern university. He made the acquaintance of Miss Wells, and she found in him an apt pupil for the study of the subject in which she had become personally interested. The result was that he was kept from restricting his outlook to the needs of the homeland to which, like all Highlanders, he was warmly attached. He took the wider and more Christ-like view of the condition and claims of the world as a whole. He and Miss Wells were drawn more affectionately together. Their interest in America developed, and they became so devoted to the interests of Christ's cause in those distant lands that at length they felt constrained to devote themselves for service in them.

Not only, however, were Dr. and Mrs. Mackay thus early led to take an interest in America, but the Lord also prepared them in a special manner for the peculiar work to which they were being called. Mrs. Mackay acquired a place in the teaching profession that assured for her rapid promotion had she continued in the service. Her experience and training were invaluable in the early days of the school in Lima. Dr. Mackay left Aberdeen, after the usual period of study, with a record of brilliant success to which few students attain. He afterwards entered upon the study of theology in connection with the Free Presbyterian Church of Scotland. This course he completed in the Princeton Theological Seminary, where he graduated B.D., and was licensed to preach the Gospel. He further obtained a travelling scholarship, which enabled him to proceed to Madrid, where for a year he studied and acquired a masterly knowledge of the Spanish language. There can be no doubt that had he continued to pursue lines of education, he would have attained to great eminence as a scholar. The spiritual interests of men, however, appealed to him in such a manner that he was constrained to deny himself many tempting avenues along which he could have advanced his own personal interests, and devote his great gifts to the Gospel ministry. During his stay in North America he examined more closely the claims of Latin America. He became fired with a consuming zeal for the manifestation of the divine glory in the deliverance of that vast continent from the forces by which it is presently enslaved.

The Free Church had money allocated to her by the Churches' Commission of 1905 for mission work abroad. She had at the time no agents in the foreign field. She was determined, however, to remain the same missionary church that she was from 1843, and accordingly was looking for fields of operation and agents whom she might employ. The Church had considered the needs of India, and would have gladly entered there, but there were no agents whom she might send, and so she was unable to give effect to her desire to serve that ancient land. Appeals reached her from Africa. To these she was attentive, and agents were found for work in that interesting field. There was also a call for her services from her sons and daughters scattered through the wide colonial fields of Canada and Australia. To their assistance she expressed herself as ready to go notwithstanding the large number of her vacant congregations at home. None of her ministers, however, determined to cross the Atlantic, and all she could do was pay an occasional friendly visit to her children in Canada and Australia. South America had no place in her thoughts. Never had any of the home Churches sent an agent to that continent. It was regarded as already Christian, and only the cry of the heathen had hitherto reached the ears of evangelical Christendom. The fact was overlooked that in South America there are vast regions where heathenism obtains, and also that the heathenism that exists under the veneer of Roman Catholicism is as devoid of Christian life and knowledge as is that of the darkest tribes in India and Africa.

Dr. Mackay at this stage came forward and offered himself for South America. The offer had something so peculiar in it as called for the careful attention of the Church. It was not of her seeking. The field was one in which she had not previously manifested any interest. Indeed, she was largely ignorant of the mission conditions that prevailed in it. She was in search of fields and agents. Here is territory into which there is an open door, and here is an agent eminently qualified for work in such a region. The Lord's hand is surely evident in the matter. While the offer was before her, the General Assembly was addressed by the Rev. A. Stuart McNairn, secretary to the EUSA. The claims and conditions of Peru were so forcibly presented by him, that the Church was relieved of all dubiety as to the path of duty and unanimously resolved to close with what appeared the call of the Lord to her. Thus there were two lines of evidence which converged to determine the path of duty. Dr. Mackay accordingly was admitted as a Probationer, and the usual steps were ordered to be taken for his ordination as a missionary to South America. Shortly thereafter he and his young wife left home for the field of their choice, and there they have since been employed, and have met with remarkable success in the part of the mission agencies that has so far been developed by them.

* * *

The school at Lima forms only a part, though an important and essential one, of our contemplated mission work in Peru. As a field for more direct evangelising work, there has been assigned to us the northern part of the republic, with Cajamarca as a centre. There we shall have the mixed classes of the cities, the Inca Indians of the Sierra, all nominally Roman Catholic, and in addition to these there are the Negro Indians of the Montaña, who lie in absolute heathenism. The commercial language of the cities and of the country generally is Spanish; that of the Sierra Indians, Quechua, in some one of its several dialects, and those of the Montaña Indians are neither Spanish nor Quechua. In this respect Peru resembles Scotland: the commercial language of the country is English, while the language of the Highlander is Gaelic. Agents who are to do mission work among these people must equip themselves by acquiring knowledge of at least one of their languages. The Rev. J. Calvin Mackay has been for a year in such training at Lima, and he is now about to remove to Cajamarca to begin work there. Should his efforts meet with success, as there is every reason to believe that they will, there will arise a demand for other workers. It is impossible at present to anticipate the extent to which work may speedily come to be required. Such developments will entail the employment of native pastors and teachers, as also doctors and nurses, and even industrial workers. In this last direction we may have to do as the old Celtic Church did in Scotland; ie, send out industrial teachers, though it were only to introduce improved methods of husbandry. A tract of land could be secured, and on it demonstration lessons given, as well as other forms of industry taught. In southern Peru such a mission farm is already in operation.

The part of Peru to which our mission efforts are to be directed is as large, it appears to me, as the whole of Great Britain, and it may be enlarged by thousands of miles away into the Montaña, where the Word of God is unknown even by name. So vast is the field, and so great is its need, that we may well tremble at the responsibility which it lays upon our Church. Sister Sarah MacDougall, who is in charge in a very large hospital in Lima, has been having an excellent experience to fit her for work in northern Peru, where she is likely at an early date to join Mr. Calvin Mackay. Yet we may well say, "What are they before so many?" The grain of mustard seed, however, may become a great tree, and undoubtedly we shall reap a rich harvest if we faint not.

For advanced studies many boys are sent from Peru to North America or to England. Such an arrangement entails heavy expenditure. The boys also are thereby removed from parental oversight at a very important age. If, therefore, the same standard and quality of education were provided in Peru, the parents would be disposed to avail themselves of it, and so keep their sons at home. The more efficient, therefore, our school can be made, the wider will be its influence. It is being devolved so as to provide higher as well as elementary education. Boys, accordingly, will be able to take their whole course of preparation there and pass from its benches into the universities and the professions. The peculiar conditions pertaining in Peru have to be kept in view. A large section of the people are educated and highly cultured. A school in which first-class English education can be had opens an avenue along which a valuable influence can be brought to bear on these people. The fact that such valuable secular education goes along with evangelical religious teaching, secures for the latter a place and influence in the upper classes of the community which otherwise could not be had. Successive generations will manifest a growing appreciation of its worth; and before it prejudice, arising from Roman Catholic denunciation, will gradually diminish. Thus, directly and indirectly, an evangelical influence will bear upon the people that will necessarily be beneficial to the cause of Christ among them.

It is from the school also that we must expect to get native pastors and teachers for our work in the Sierra and Montaña. The immense difficulty of reaching the Montaña natives can be overcome only through the employment of native converts, who can live and work among the savage population there and in the tropical conditions of climate that prevail, and which make it a country dangerous to the health of the white man.

But the school, though it has come prominently to notice through its rapid development and success, forms only part of the work of our agents in Lima. Those connected with the mission have been organised into a congregation with a regularly constituted Kirk Session, and public worship is conducted by them every Sabbath Day in the school buildings. Preaching on the streets is not permissible. This avenue of public appeal is, therefore, meantime not open to mission agents. Under divine blessing, however, the little flock at Lima may soon grow into a large congregation, and be a centre of evangelical light and influence in the very capital of that dark country. Such a desirable development will create a field of mission enterprise of incalculable value in addition to that of northern Peru. Such success, however, will call for additional labourers.

At the present time, tract distribution is engaged in as a means of enlightenment. The several mission agencies combine in the work of having such tracts printed and circulated; and there are evidences that this effort is serving a useful purpose. The need for healthy literature in the Spanish language is very great. Valuable service could be rendered were we able to extend this branch of our activities by having a small printing press of our own and men and money for the work. At first it might not pay, but eventually it would do so. It would be a most valuable adjunct to our agencies in the Sierra, for literature can be distributed far beyond the bounds of the direct work of the mission agents, and in Peru much value is set upon printed matter. Friends at home who have money to dispose of for religious purposes could render great aid to the mission by presenting it either with a press or the means wherewith to purchase such.

A wide field for useful service lies open to able men who would be free to deal with the various problems that exercise the student mind. From professional chairs and through literature, much teaching is given that is fitted to poison the minds of the thinking young manhood of the country, especially those of them who pass through the university class rooms, but there is no counter influence of a similar kind. Dr. Mackay is eminently suitable for such a work, and we have reason to believe that it would be work congenial to him. Time necessary for it would require freedom from teaching. The successful discharge of both is not possible for any agent, however accomplished he may be, and however willing. A students' movement conducted on evangelical lines, if successful, would speedily solve many problems with which all departments of the social fabric are presently exercised.

— *Extracted from The Rev. Prof. J. Kennedy Cameron, Peru and its Free Church of Scotland Mission.*

Autumn, 1926: Dr. Kenneth, by mule, proceeds to Celendín...

PLATFORM 2, GLASGOW CENTRAL 11 PM – ARRIVING LIVERPOOL 6AM
– Pacific Steam Navigation Company – arriving Callao 23 days later
– coast-steamer to Pacasmayo, 3 days – train to Chileti twice weekly,
six hours – horses to Cajamarca, 12 hours – change to mules for
Celendín, a day and a half – change again for Chachapoyas, five days
– change again for Moyobamba – (or Bonnybamba – Bonny Scotland
to Bonny Bamba) – six days, and there you are. But it really means
more than that. Even to Callao means more than that.

It means the typical Glasgow Central leave-taking with more
smiles than tears, and the typical pier-head leave-taking with more
tears than smiles, and more noise and confusion than either, and
thankfulness that all one's own folk are in Scotland and not among
the pathetic crowd in the drizzling rain on the pier. Then it means
conceit, tempered with surprise, at not being ill or unashamed
misery if the sea wins, and a glimpse of France at La Rochelle and
several glimpses of Spain at Santander and Coruña and Vigo that
make you wish they were more than just glimpses for the spacious
beauty of the harbours and the quaintness of the folk, the extraordinary variety of brilliant uniforms and the bare-faced swindling
of the loud-voiced boatmen vending their worse fruit at their best
prices.

It means the influx of crowds of poor Spanish emigrants to pack the third-class unbearably, and all day and all night the rattle of the donkey-engines loading thousands of boxes of Spanish onions that ought to have been swinging on a pole over the shoulder of a Spanish youth in a beret tramping the northern villages. It means ten days of all sea and sky and the clock going back half an hour daily and the passengers settling down to fervent likes and dislikes and excess luggage charges from the purser and lightning playing around the horizon and flying-fish playing round the boat and occasional efforts to write Spanish exercises instead of yielding to deck-tennis. Then Bermuda, and Bermuda is worth missing the steamer for. A long launch-run up to Hamilton, a drive in a parasol-covered coach and an impression of an island garden where all is beautiful and luxurious and soft and colourful, so that news of a dreadful hurricane over it shatters a memory of peace.

After Bermuda it means the growing heat, and sleeping out on the boat deck, and the first glimpse of Cuba when the twinkling lights of Havana fade with the fading stars before the sudden splendour of the dawn sweeping up from the edge of the sea into the Heavens, followed by a day of longing for it to sweep back again as the ship lies sweltering in the Cuban harbour where the tall commercial houses rise out of the water on the low piers. It means an afternoon race against a steamer from another country for right of first entry to the Panama Canal the following morning, a night in the strange black-and-white of Colon where Europe and Africa are none the nearer to each other for living in the same town, and then the early rise to miss none of the wonders of the marvellous Canal, and especially the patriotic thrill of saying – "Of course it all depends on these great gates. These gates were made in Glasgow".

The mighty bulk of the steamer is lifted up a step and another step, journeys through a small Loch Lomond with no yellow broom on its islands, travels along a bit ditch and is let down a step without any fuss in the easy fashion in which engineers play with gigantic forces and make the uninitiated marvel at the miracles they work: and the savants explain it casually as, "all the water pressure, you know – nothing in it really – costs the company a thousand pounds per passage through – Scotch gates sure enough".

And then at last it is the Pacific and the line far up to the left is the coast of South America. Night lights twinkling in the distance are the works of northern Peru and the sudden cold that changes the apparel and brings out the overcoats is explained as the Humboldt Current; an explanation which satisfies everyone when it is understood to signify – next stop, Callao.

Callao means sliding past the bleak island of San Lorenzo, ominous for its reputation as the safe residence of suspected political revolutionaries, into all the flurry of getting ready to go ashore, the wait for the port authorities and the fear of not being passed before 6pm, after which no boats are allowed to move in the harbour, the swarm of shore-boats and smart launches, the distant recognition of friendly faces and the hearty greetings at the gangway, then the interminable wait for Customs formalities and eager snatches of conversation with the waiting friends, and at last a rocking tram-car careering madly up to Lima, and the ship already a happy memory.

Lima is a city that leaves a confused set of impressions on one's mind even after a month's stay: a confusion in which the predominating thought is that one is better out of it. The clash of new and old is still obvious, although the victory of the new is so nearly complete, and perhaps it is the rapidity of the change that causes the difficulty. Lima is not at present a reposeful city. Her streets are narrow and her motor-traffic has jumped to a magnitude that needs room and is in the hands of the careless and excitable Latin-Indian bus drivers, whose speed limit is what their machine can reach in the shortest time, and whose faith in their brakes and steering gear is absolute. The Lima motor bus is a test of nerves which custom does not lessen. It is the crash and clatter of the great army of buses, the grinding of suddenly-applied brakes and the scraping of missed gear-changes, that makes the background to memories of Lima, and leaves an unfair impression, for the progress that is being made is steady and determined. There are great stretches of new roads such as the Avenida Leguia to Miraflores, miles of straight smooth-surfaced motor roads lined with trees, there are wide and beautiful plazas, and there are buildings worthy of the historic city. There is a growing grip on the regulation of traffic and on the cleansing of the town that promises to complete, before long, the new order of things, when the whole city will have the order and cleanliness of its fine suburb Miraflores, and such last traces of the old order as remain, such as an occasional open drain, will have disappeared.

But Lima is now, and will be more and more, a city of commercialism and a home of all the nations. The number of races it employs in its public works, in its business houses and in the seaport trade of Callao is extraordinary. That is the second distinct impression it leaves. For us who come from the Free Church of Scotland, the centre of Lima, and a very convenient one too, is the Anglo-Peruvian College, whose so creditable history and varying fortunes and peculiar place in the development and evangelisation of Peru have already been made known at home by those who have the knowledge and ability to do it. To a person whose one idea was to get on to Moyobamba as quickly as possible, Lima consisted mainly of the College and the hospitable home of the Superintendent in Miraflores, and the work in Lima is a matter altogether too big to be entered on by a passer-through. Enough to say that the college is alive with the exuberance of a boys' school and full of the sense of the wise and enthusiastic government of a British missionary staff. It created in this narrow and conservative type of professional man – a medical doctor like me – a decided if temporary regret that he could not throw in his lot with them. The problems and the promises of the Anglo-Peruvian College, and the story of its foundation and development, make a subject worthy of detailed study at home and of strong attraction to the young folk of the Free Church.

But I left Lima to those who know it and got aboard the Huallaga as quickly as possible. Getting aboard was the usual feverish rush, ending up with a couple of hours to spare, looking over the side. The rush consisted in getting boxes out of the Customs House by a government order which arrived late, so that half an hour after sailing time I was still conveying to the sympathetic official my need of immediate release. But in the end, with the greatest of courtesy and assistance, I was dumped, boxes and all, and the precious microscope box preserved unopened, in the motor launch, while a row of policemen, soldiers and civilians all claiming Moyobamba as their birthplace, looked down from the pier. And so at last I found myself aboard the coast-boat, the Huallaga, with a very new riding outfit, a Government contract, and the road to Moyobamba really began at last.

For me it began as, and continued to be, a journey de-luxe, so gracious was the provision made at every turn of the long road, without which provision the inexperienced traveller would have found the journey not only uncomfortable but beset with dangers. I had the great good fortune to be travelling with two gentlemen of Moyobamba itself, who had waited many weeks beyond their time in Lima to take back with them the last item in the list of commissions given them by Miss Soper and Miss Gould.

Señor Manuel Noriega del Aquila, the former sub-Prefect of Moyobamba, the only home-keeping son of a family of lawyers, doctors and engineers, including the member of government for the district of St. Martín and the Lima professor of medicine, is a man of over fifty, stout, florid, placid in most things, but shrewd and more effective than he appears. He is steeped in the political history of Peru and likes to detail his reminiscences of the political upheavals which turned him from a leading citizen of Moyobamba into a fugitive, and brought him again in triumph as a Prefect.

Señor Mariano Valderrama is one of the most interesting and most likeable of characters ever encountered outside fiction. Grave, courteous, correct and at ease in the presence of the highest officials: disreputable, gaunt and steel-muscled in the rigour of the road, driving the muleteers – the arrieros – pitilessly when delay is likely to be dangerous, and yet putting them in high good humour within five minutes of pitching camp, sworn foe (if at times unfair critic) of the priests, and a mine of information on every corner of Peru. Add a horror of ticks and serpents and an absolutely fearless devotion to the doctrines of the Evangelical Church, to his Bible and to his two treasured volumes of Wesley's sermons, and I have given you after all a very feeble description of a man who has led a life of action unequalled in fiction and who has preserved the instincts and the manners of a Spanish gentleman in every sense.

With these two excellent companions, friends from the first moment of meeting, we travelled in company from 19th October to the 5th of December. I found myself at the end of five weeks in the capital waving a somewhat shaky goodbye to the fast receding launch in which were returning to shore the missionaries of the Anglo-Pereuvian College – to me at that moment a boatload of Kintail and Aberdeen and Kingussie, emphasising the stretch of five years that was now between them and me.

* * *

A coast-boat after the lordly ocean liner, and a shuffling out of one port and into another, hugging the line of a bare coast with nothing of beauty or grandeur to compare with the hourly-changing wonder of the ocean, made the trip from Callao to Pacasmayo a somewhat weary three days and nights. Or perhaps not the boat nor the scene was the cause, but the first complete severance from familiar speech and customs, for the Huallaga was a comfortable ship, her deck-space more than ample for the few passengers, and her menus well-meaning. The officers conformed to rule in being Peruvian in all but the three vital posts – a Scots engineer, and an English captain and an English wireless-operator. So speedy and uneventful was the trip that instead of arriving after midday of the Friday, when the only train till Tuesday would have already left, we were rocking quietly in Pacasmayo harbour by six o'clock on Thursday evening, gladly recognising the spruce, elegant and youthful figure in the stern of the approaching shore-boat as that of the Rev. J. Calvin Mackay of Cajamarca.

And so, instead of a weary four days in the deadness of Pacasmayo, there was a quiet and effective word with the Custom's chief, to save from violation the treasured microscope case, a quiet and impressive service in a Protestant home, a quiet and restful night in the hotel, and at nine a.m. I was away on one of the cheekiest railways ever constructed, leaving the sea behind for many a day and by many a mile and range of mountains, while Mr. J. Calvin Mackay embarked on the returning Huallaga to Lima.

Bare and arid enough were the hills, typical thirsty coast hills, up and down which the little train clanked and puffed, and hot and hotter the day despite the open-sided carriages. A welcome interlude was the way-side halt where the cottagers had ready their famous lunch – a great plateful of rice and roast chicken fiercely seasoned, all for threepence, and more desirable oranges and bananas almost for the trouble of eating them. Another hour or two of heat and dust and curves and double-twists like the Kyle railway, and we clattered into Chilete about three o' clock – a depot of goods stores and a few houses.

At once began the (afterwards all-too familiar) din and riot of bargaining for animals, and I thankfully retreated behind speech-lessness and a shady wall, and left the work to my companions who presently announced a departure at three a.m., with the promise of twelve hours in the saddle. So with a sinking heart, I dragged out the khaki and spotless sun-helmet and gleaming brown leather of an Indian cavalry officer and – stipulating only that my mule must be a horse – I sought comfort in the thought that between three a.m. and daylight, the newness might be worked off.

Chilete is a malarial corner and there I first saw to what a fine maturity a well-fed cockroach can reach. But from the moment that a message by telegraph came over the hills from Cajamarca, promising lunch at noon the next day away up on the top, to the pale moonlight confusion of boot and saddle, the time was short and the loveliness of the balmy morning in the soft light and the unexpected comfort of a stocky white horse left me with no complaints. Only as I watched the portly form of Don Manuel and the spare wiriness of Don Mariano, shadows below their broad-brimmed hats, bobbing twenty to the minute to the hopeless bumping jog of a low-bred mule,

I wondered with much inward misgiving if I should not want some spare parts before I either saw Moyobamba or attained to their apparent indifference to the incessant thuds. However, for the moment, my mount was a horse with a tolerable step, the morning mysteriously beautiful, the journey at last really and definitely begun, and good friends climbing up the other side to meet us ahead on the road, so I settled down to enjoy the newness of it all.

The freshness of the early morning was delightful and the daylight was up in time to light us through the ravine where the road is the dry and rocky river-bed, a veritable oven in the heat of the day, and therefore passed-through by most travellers the evening they arrive at Chilete. Our early start served the same purpose and we were through the valley and at the little hotel, La Vina, at the foot of the climb by breakfast time. Breakfast time, as it proved, did not imply breakfast, and the most we could coax out of the halt was a tin of sardines and coffee, with the hope of bananas further on.

As the road began to climb, so did the sun, and it made one feel weak to look up at the great range above, and believe that the road would take us over it by noon. Valderrama had shed the city restraint and enlivened the way with cheery whistling and sudden reminiscences of his first barefoot trek as a young recruit over the same road. As we passed little thatched huts where the good lady squatted in her numerous red petticoats spinning or weaving, he had an apt piece of impudence for each that always left smiles and often changed "haven't any" to the production of a bunch of little sweet bananas. But he sent my heart down into my leggings when he pointed to the highest line of the range far above and remarked that before seeing Cajamarca we would be as high again above it as it at the moment was above us. A deserted group of cottages at a turn of the road produced the sad account of recent bubonic plague which had wiped out the inhabitants.

So in the inevitable single file of the mules, we sat hunched in the saddles, lost in reverie or waking to a point of order or interest or beauty, while the sun rose ever higher and more merciless, and bored in between the shoulder-blades. The road began to take the winding form beloved of teachers of science in explaining laws of force but which to ordinary minds suggests only mild wonder as to how the first horse discovered the advantage of zigzagging up a hill, until at last a single tall telegraph pole over a gap in the skyline announced the top of the ascent. Even patriotic pride in an axiom of home – that there are no Highlands like the Scottish Highlands – could not deny the fact that the view all around from this height dwarfed anything ever seen before. Later,one may argue and compare on points of beauty, but the first impression of the view from height among the Andes is one of overwhelming vastness. The depths and height are tremendous, the colours bold and the very Heavens above made to fit in as a cap fits the head where the topmost peaks merge into the clouds. One could imagine the whole Grampians dropped into one of the ravines and lost.

One thing is missing, whereby Scotland still may claim the prize for soul-satisfying beauty. Here, amid canyon and mountain, green and gold and distant purple, one longs in vain for the low roar of crashing waves breaking on a far shore, or looks in vain for the bright glint of sunlight on the leaping spray of a tumbling burn or the still beauty of the mountain loch. So whereas amid the Ross-shire hills one would have gazed and gazed and (perhaps) forgotten mundane things, here we gave one interested look around and forthwith bethought us of the approaching friends with the promised lunch. An hour or two more of ups and downs among grass-covered hilltops such as the arid coast longs to possess, past the neat white house inviting us to rest and refresh ourselves and our animals, and then there bore down upon us a gallant chestnut mare of great height, whereon rode with practised ease a lady born assuredly under other skies than those of Peru or Spain.

"Well, it's yourself and you will be hungry", said the accent and sentiments of home and, "it is, and we are, and how are you?", said the bruised and empty newcomer. A quarter of an hour served to give a new outlook to life, between rest and a Scotch baking and news of friends, and then on a down-hill road the animals woke up and cantered. Suddenly, over a brow appeared a valley deep down between us and the range that made the horizon in front, a valley sweeping widely round and out of sight to the right. Tucked in at the hill-foot on the left, the sun was lighting up the orderly rows of red-tiled roofs as it had done four centuries ago, when the first hardy reckless band of Spanish adventurers looked down in relieved surprise upon the historic home of the Incas.

Pizarro from this same point on the bare Sierra saw the red roofs and white walls of Cajamarca far below and the white cloud of the Inca tents beyond, and called all his cunning and deceit to the help of his extraordinary daring to satisfy his ambition. His descent shook the old Peru to pieces. Cajamarca is a spot so historic and so nationally important, a very key-city, that the sudden view of it far below, tucked in at one end of its fertile green valley, makes a marked impression on the new-comer. The descent is steep and rocky but the eye is now actively engaged in seeking out detail, as the central Plaza de Armas takes shape, and streets can be distinguished and at last the roof of the Mission House itself. Thereafter, it is but a few minutes till one rides under the arched gateway of the Scottish-Peruvian College and tumbles off the twelve-hour seat with gladness into the atmosphere, inexpressibly welcome, of home, conveyed in a Scottish welcome, a cup of tea and a long hot soak in the mission bath.

The first clear impression of Cajamarca is that this, much more than Lima, is the real Peru. Probably the presence of numerous Indians in their various-coloured ponchos and their conical straw hats is the reason, and truly on a big fiesta day when they crowd in from the villages as they have done for centuries to sell their farm produce, and their home-made hats and harness, the streets are so Indian-crowded as to be almost impassable. In long rows squatting on the ground or behind little tables just off the pavements on both sides of the deep open drain which divides the streets, they are packed close in families offering their wares, a noisy, colourful crowd of people who might all be brothers and sisters, so alike they all are to the eye of the foreigner.

The roads leading to the town carry a constant stream of them, men mounted on mettlesome little horses galloping furiously with flying poncho and waving legs to which the box-stirrups seem to be glued; women piled high on wee donkeys or on foot, all with lively bundle slung on their backs, a pair of wondering bright black eyes peeping out from its shelter, while both hands are busy passing the fluffy white wool from the stick gripped under the left arm in a thread spun by the fingers of the left hand to the winding stick twirled by the fingers of the right.

Cajamarca is a town to linger over. Its setting is its wonderful valley, ringed all round by the mighty rampart of the Andean cordillera so that one feels that getting out of it on anything that cannot fly must be impossible, and the white snaky line of the road that actually accomplishes the impossible but produces the greater incredulity. The real beauty of it is seen from above and one may take a motor-car to see it. Cajamarca has more than twenty cars, and the gymnastics they perform in the narrow cobbled streets, split as they are by the drain, are second only to the achievement of climbing the new road, to the heights that enclose the valley.

Three hours by car from Cajamarca and hidden in a cleft in the mountain range a half-hour's ride from the road, there is an hotel of exquisite cleanliness and comfort, whose raison d'etre and main feature is its hot baths. It has swimming baths filled by a never-ending supply of hot and cold water that gushes from a rich spring high above the house. Yumagual is the name of the place and it makes a delightful resting place. The return to Cajamarca takes one right over the top of the range, and down in a series of alternations between gasps of admiration at the magnificence of Cajamarca's setting, and gasps of horror at the risks of studying it from a Ford car on that mountain road. Yet when one is safe again on the solid pavement and no longer hurtling along a shelf that turns corner on the edge of nothing, the clearest memory is the beauty of the valley when the sudden passing of the summit brings it into view below, while across it tower the equally majestic heights over which must toil the road, as yet unconquered by the Ford, to Celendín, and by yet greater heights to Moyobamba.

It is a fruitful and well-watered valley with its splashes of colour and of cultivation, here and there the road to a tiny village picked out by the line of soldier-like eucalyptus trees. Lower down, one sees the clouds of misty vapour that rises from the hot springs of the Inca baths, and the cactus hedges and eucalyptus that bound the farms and roads, but the town is still invisible, hidden by a shoulder on the left and seen at last as a dark red square almost concealed by harmony with its surroundings.

As to its everyday life, Cajamarca is a busy town. Its commercial importance is considerable, being the geographical as well as the historical centre of northern Peru and the connection with the coast. It is the headquarters of big trading firms, whose goods reach as far as Moyobamba and its villages. It has a hospital growing yearly in provision for the various departments of medical and surgical work. Yet it has kept little of the ancient features. A single wall of the mighty squares of stone which the Indian of old fitted without cement so finely as to leave but a line not to be penetrated by a knife-blade, is left of the room which the unhappy Inca filled with treasure to buy his liberty.

The old Inca baths, in a somewhat discreditable state of neglect, are still in popular use and their natural supply of hot water is as abundant as ever. Beyond that, the visitor sees little of the historic in the city, and it is only the passing glance of the visitor that I give here. As in Lima, Cajamarca for me was the home of the missionary, and that little world of hard work and earnest hope and rich blessing is again outside the scope of my purpose or privilege. As missionary effort, in church and school and dispensary, it is worthy, especially in the Free Church, of a history of its own to be studied with sympathy and pride by those who have an interest in Peru and in missions. But let us go on then, to Moyobamba, still over the hills, and still very faraway.

* * *

There came at last the day, Monday the 8th of November, when the family affairs of my companions and the difficulty of getting animals came to an end together, and we were ready to ride out again, sad for the parting once more with good friends, happy at the prospect of the last lap to Moyobamba and the end of the delays – so thought I in my ignorance, unaware of the fourteen days yet to be passed sitting and waiting. So tiny and ragged were the pathetic wee beasties on which we were to face the Andes that I protested vigorously, but neither my companions nor the arrieros were at all perturbed. "They'll arrive", was all they said about it, and proceeded to make the matter still more improbable by loading-up. First over the saddle went the saddle-bags, leather or cloth, the latter capable of extension almost unlimited, to carry spare clothes and kit and food for the way. This last is always called "fiambre".

Then to each a woolen poncho folded thick to soften the seat, to be at hand in the cold of the heights and the best of blankets at night. Finally, another similarly-cut poncho but of heavily rubbered cloth, a product of Moyobamba, to be slipped over the head as a cape and, when mounted, covering the whole body from the chin down, its long folds reaching below the stirrups. Events have proved it the most genuine waterproof one has ever been inside. As the saddle for such a journey is put on over many thicknesses of saddle-cloth, the end of it is that one climbs into a structure high above the wee mount like the howdah on an elephant, but feeling rather like an elephant getting into a howdah. So with saddlebags packed as tight as kitbag ever was, with spare kit and books and mysterious tins of pancakes and sugar and cocoa and tea and a chicken squashed in on top, our heavy luggage (even to a cabin-trunk) wrapped and sewn in waterproof and sacking, and neatly fixed on the cargo animals, and the old mixed feeling of leaving home to go to a new school, I said a long farewell to the last outpost of the mission, but with the cowardly reservation that maybe I might be making a neighbourly call again within a year.

It was midday when we left, a caravan more purposeful than dignified, and having turned the corner beyond the Inca baths, both Cajamarca and Lima promptly dropped into the region of memory, and loneliness took the upper hand. As soon, however, as the first rough cuesta or climb was over, we were on a wide grassy plain, with a lively breeze to cool the force of the sun, and a far view of the many valleys opening in the line of hills, and companions the more interesting because of the difficulty and necessity of understanding their language.

The cargo mules, lashing out at each other with lively heels, scampered away in front, cooking pots rattling behind the boxes till we sounded like a tinker-tribe on the move or a Ford on the road to Ullapool, the barefoot arrieros trotted philosophically after, and we settled down to the steady trot that sounds so easy till one does it on a mule. Our destination for that night was an hotel at a place called Polloc, in the centre of a great stretch of cultivated land, where herds of cattle are kept, and the hill-slopes are covered with waving barley. After many an up and down, and just as the cold had made me add the poncho to the sweater, we saw it far ahead among its trees and took courage.

But we did not stop there (for the arrieros did not want to pay for pasture) and we carried on into the growing dusk, climbing rapidly out of the plain until the road was no longer visible and then swinging aside to a grassy patch and unloading. There was no possibility of a fire but the boxes were piled-up as a rampart against the cutting wind, we dug out what food was at hand, and made down our beds on the ground. I have never spent such a miserable night, and I mention it to show that the arrieros make the road one of greater hardship than is necessary. They have no idea of looking after their own comfort. As I shivered through the night, I of course took it for granted that I was soft and that the others were hard and accustomed to it. As a matter of fact, I was in far better condition to stand exposure than any of them and felt the cold less. The whole lot lay huddled together miserably cold, and waited for day. It is not that they do not suffer, but they take suffering as a matter of course and do not take any trouble to avoid it, but rather cocaine and alcohol to alleviate it.

They lay down there to wait for the day, they were still shivering and hungry when they loaded and pushed off in the morning, but once the sun rose and turned the frost into glowing heat, they warmed up and cheered up and forgot completely their troubles of the night before. So the arriero goes on from day to day, taking the evil as philosophically as the good, needing only the sun to make him forget the rain, enduring extraordinary hardships from privation and exposure, and a contradiction even in his physique. He can pick up the heaviest box a mule carries, up to 200 pounds in weight, and settle it as a cargo, or he can strap to forehead and chest a load of up to 150 pounds and toddle on with it day by day across the very cordillera, feats of strength and endurance belonging to a strong man, yet he is but a spare wasted figure of a man, and drops off like withering grass in illnesses that need a strong constitution to fight them. Pneumonia, bronchitis, and phthisis wipe-out the arrieros swiftly, and those who escape these are twisted with rheumatism. Poor arriero: it's a hard life and a wretchedly paid one, yet he is like a child in the way he takes life.

He cannot read, although he can trace a painful signature, is easily provoked to laughter and as easily bullied into sullen silence, and his solace and almost his food is the coca leaf. He carries big supplies of it from one point to the other, packed tightly like the green tobacco leaf, and in his belt a little wooden bottle with a broad wire fixed in the cork, to carry powdered chalk. The leaves he chews to get the wonderful stimulant effect of the cocaine, and to counteract its bitterness, he scrapes the chalky wire with his teeth. With his drug, a supply of the crude sugar-cane alcohol, properly named aguardiente (fire-water), and strong coffee with abundance of the treacle-like brown sugar (chancaca), he will carry on more or less indifferent to food, but ready at any moment to put away as big a meal as is offered him. There is little doubt that the cocaine habit, and especially in those more addicted to the poisonous aguardiente, is the real reason for the rapid constitutional collapse of the arriero, as it may be the explanation of his at times incredible powers of endurance alongside men of far better physique and morals.

In the morning, then, we moved off in the grey dawn while Polloc remained shrouded in mist behind, and below, realising with a gasp of thankfulness what would have been our plight had it rained, and with a very bright blue scarf round my ears and a Scottish University sweater peeping through the slit in the bright brown poncho, I felt like a tropical feature for gaudy colour in the bitter cold of the Sierra. An hour later I had shed them all and was listening to the chaff and chatter of the now-thawed and happy arrieros in the warmth of the morning sun.

It is a long day that has to be passed between Polloc and Celendín. The way leads over a halca as the arrieros call the crossing of a height, which is reached by an apparently interminable succession of waves of country, crest succeeding crest hour after hour with no change of view. The summit is known as the "senda mal" (bad road), and not so long ago it was one of the worst parts of all Peru for the sudden attacks of brigands swooping out from the pueblos hidden behind ridges. It is high enough to be cold by day and bitterly so at night, so that very few care to be caught up there at the end of the day.

Here and there one sees the tiny three-feet high hovels of the Indian swineherd or cattle-boy, surely the lowest grade of home-life in all the world. A constant traffic is kept up on the road, for the Celendínos are great business men, and, if well-mounted, make the trip to Cajamarca in one day, while men and animals in a steady procession carry goods between the two towns or to the various villages off the road. Almost without exception the men are muffled in the coloured poncho, and when the inevitable Indian party passes, the women are carrying both baby and a share of the load, while their busy hands are ever spinning the wool for the next poncho.

On this occasion, Valderrama's truly Peruvian forecast that although it was full rainy-season we were to get no rain all the journey, collapsed at the outset, for in early afternoon there came on the most merciless thing in showers that I have ever been out in. The thunder crashed apparently beside us and sheets of lightning lit the leaden gloom that had suddenly overspread the sky. Mournfully, I commented on the early end of his optimistic outlook, to receive the reply – made in all sincerity – that this wasn't really wet, would only last an hour or two, and was rather refreshing than otherwise.

It is a wonderful fact that in all the rest of the journey we suffered nothing from rain, and it was only in a later trip that I realised how exactly right was his attitude.

Rain in the montaña is a title reserved for days on end of the sort of delivery one expects from a hose-pipe, and anything less is just a shower. It is like the way of speaking up Loch Fyne, where there must be a foot of water round the ricks before they will admit that it is anything more than a bit damp. Meantime, we slipped the rubber ponchos on, spread their wide folds over saddle-bags and knees, and to my pleased surprise rode on through three hours of it, to emerge into sunshine as dry and sweet as the kernel of a nut. So passed the first big worry – rain held no more terrors.

Presently, we came to that rare thing on the cordillera, a branching of the ways, one to Celendín, one to Huacapampa, and one to Huauco, mysterious Indian names which sounded attractive to my foreign ear: and shortly afterwards the three places lay spread out before me, far below, as in a picture. Once more a long and narrow valley, and beyond it the ever-repeated line of mighty hills which must be crossed. Valderrama, indicating the highest point, "away up there in the cloud", remarked that from it later on we would get our first sight of the Marañón, the river of ancient Inca history, the river of secrets of gold, which is a great one among the several great origins of the Amazon.

Between us and this rather dismaying prospect lay a beautiful valley with three squares picked-out in dark red; on the left the largest of the three, Celendín, like an architect's plan in its complete regularity, on the right Huauco, and in the centre more hidden by trees, Huacapampa. Señor Noriega for personal reasons desired to make for the last, while I by orders of the mission dared not miss Celendín. However, it was obviously an easy matter to pass from one to the other, once down, and for purposes of the descent I had no intention of separating from the others. Five minutes later, however, I was torn between thankfulness and regret. Looking back now, one can see that there was nothing to worry about, and this descent was by no means the worst on the road, but at the time it struck me as the most foolhardy risk I had ever incurred. The road turned itself into a staircase of rock and mud, its steps of all grades of irregularity, its surface slippery with the rain, but fortunately all between high banks so that the drop at the outside did not obtrude itself. Round and round it went like the inside of a lighthouse, the animals slipping and plunging, and the purpose of the high front and back of the Peruvian box-saddle more evident with every jerk. It was my first experience of what a mule is really good for. Later, I learned just how good they are on bad bits, and how cat-like to keep their feet on the edge of nothing. But it appears to be a point of honour with the mule to trip along on the extreme outside edge of any mountain path, no matter how wide the path nor how deep the drop over which the mule nods its head at the corners. As we continued to slither and bump down, my paralysed brain began to work again, and I thought of the other road to Celendín instead of this to Huacapampa. I asked Valderrama casually, "how does the Celendín road compare with this one?" "Hooh!", he said. "This is a motor road compared with it!" "Oh, direach sin", said I, and resolved to leave the cares of the future to another day.

An hour and a half of the descent and we were in the valley and dismounting at the door of a friend's house, to be warmly welcomed with the rather dampening news that it would be at least three days before animals to continue the journey would be forthcoming. As Celendín has long been a centre much on the mind of J. Calvin Mackay, and had been the scene of several of his most encouraging missionary journeys, it had been his special desire that I should go there to make the acquaintance and enjoy the hospitality of his good friends, and as I – in common with all the other readers of the Monthly Record – had already an interest in the name, I at once sought a horse to take me over. Actually, there is a motor-car, but at the moment the only mechanic was missing, and I accepted the offer of a mount that was, "faster and surer than any motor-car".

He looked good, but behaved so outrageously at first that the owner warned me not to touch the spur to his side on any account. Now, I was certain that the spur had not touched him, and I got more and more puzzled as he snorted and side-stepped along with no sign of settling down. Finally, after many efforts to find out what was irritating him, I gave it up and let him walk quietly along the beautiful, firm, wide road that traverses the whole valley. After the wild bareness of the heights, it was very pleasant to be riding in the evening glow along the tree-lined avenue with the cultivated fields and gardens on either hand, and to enter, in the gathering darkness, the town so often and so affectionately spoken of in the Cajamarca Mission.

My instructions took me to the house of two brothers, shop-keepers, and the warmth of the welcome they gave me was one more of the many proofs of the esteem in which J. Calvin Mackay is held, wherever he has become known. The language was a difficulty, but as soon as they had satisfied their very liberal idea of hospitality, one of the brothers, a stout, pleasant and shrewd man, besought me to visit one or two patients who were seriously ill, there being no doctor in the town. As guide and interpreter, he amazed me with his knowledge of medicine, and his questions showed an almost uncanny gift for relating cause and effect. In answer to my enquiries he told me that in the Lima police he had learned a little, during a long illness in hospital he had learned more and done some dressing of wounds, and since then had read everything medical he could find. Consequently, for the three days of my stay there, he left the shop to his brother and devoted himself to me and medical work, turning the best room in the house into a surgery and himself into a very keen assistant.

The cases presented the usual pathetic majority of chronic illnesses found where there has been no skilled treatment available in time, and made one realise forcibly the benefit that is enjoyed where early treatment is the rule. Cases of blindness from neglect or the attempt to cure by putting impossible things in inflamed eyes were very distressing. Much of the chronic illness occurred in the women, who spend all day and every day at their main occupation of hat making and who, to the sedentary nature of the work and to dietetical errors, add the factor of a harmful posture. They work seated on the ground, cross-legged, and not only bent forward over the hat they are plaiting, but bent forward with a twist of the body to one side. Eight days to make a hat, ten shillings a good price for it, invariably a family of old folks or children to keep, while the men are travelling far afield to sell the products of their labour – it is a constant unremitting grind, that cannot be slackened even for the demands of motherhood.

There were some things, however, that allowed of treatment and relief, and at the end of three full days I was sorry to leave so much unfinished work, and was convinced of the value of a mission nurse – at least – in Celendín. It is a remarkable town in the type of people it produces. They are the most prosperous business men of almost every other town in Peru, and they are found travelling all over South America by inland roads that cross the perpetual snows. In the university of Lima, Celendínos form one of the most numerous and certainly the most noteworthy groups of students, and all alike are marked out by their energy, initiative, intelligence and independence in every sphere of life in Peru. Many of the leaders in Lima circles are Celendínos. A typical product of the district is Aladino Esacalante of Huauco who, as one of the fruits of J. Calvin Mackay's wonderful first visit to Celendín, has developed not only into a fine and earnest Christian but also into a bright and determined student. He is now in his third year at the Anglo-Peruvian College in Lima, having his quarters in a wee room on the very roof, and has a most honourable place in the prize-list each year. He has the fixed ambition to reach Scotland and take the full ministerial course so as to come back to his own people a prepared pastor, and one cannot help feeling that he – along with the two Moyobambinos in Costa Rica – is chosen to do great things yet for Christ in their native land. My hosts also have all the qualities which mark out the Celedíno creditably.

They took a fearless and leading part in the establishment of a public cemetery, and in the long and bitter struggle which followed to prevent the Catholic Church taking possession of its keys; a struggle which has ended in victory for the Town Council, and the removal of the public scandals of the town's life. For a year past they have jointly edited a local newspaper whose purpose is the encouragement of all things pertaining to the town's welfare in public morality and honesty, and the exposure of every act of a contrary nature. Dishonesty and injustice has from the character of its people, always been more difficult in Celendín than in most Peruvian towns, and corrupt officials have generally had a difficult time, but the new paper has made it doubly difficult.

Celendín is full of men of progressive ideas and sound ideals, and to them the missionary visits of J. Calvin Mackay are very welcome. They have long been hoping for the establishment of such a mission among them, and there is no room to doubt that a medical missionary or nurse would have a great and useful work to do and hearty sympathy and cooperation in doing it.

It is a town of about four thousand inhabitants, with the male population fluctuating according to the journeys the men make on business. In some things backward – there is no sanitary service and periodic epidemics of typhoid occur – it has very clear ideas on what it wants, and as a beginning the motor-road throughout the valley and the steady progress of a fine road which will be met from Cajamarca and bring the two towns within a few hours of each other, is a very sound investment. A new and abundant water supply is waiting to be brought, and with it the plans for electric lighting are all ready.

It is an agricultural centre and has a great horse market, for all the region round about is travelled on horse-back, and they pride themselves in keeping good animals. It is here that one sees the peculiar pace of the Peruvian saddle-horse at its best. The rider, instead of having to "post" on a trotting mount, sits as still as in an armchair while the horse moves in a gliding step which is more of a walk than a trot and yet faster than most can trot. It is delightfully easy to pose, centaur-like, hand on hip while speeding through the town on a well-trained mount of the Celendín kind. The whole length of the valley from Huauco to Celendín is cultivated and on the slopes of the sudden hills beyond are patches of barley and maize. They claim a great reputation for their chocolate while yielding to Moyobamba the prize for coffee.

But much as I enjoyed the three days of work and hospitality, I was not sorry when the call came from Huacapampa to go through on Friday night to move out on Saturday. One of the three days was Armistice Day and it was charged with many a memory of the anniversaries of other years, the last of them having been spent in the common-room on the Mound, whence the students who gathered there have scattered themselves already all over Scotland, and to India, South Africa and South America.

Again in the quiet evening I mounted the horse "as fast as a motor" and again he nearly threw me in wild protest and again we sidled and bucked along the road in hopeless fashion. It was some time before I had the gumption to realise what was wrong. Then I whipped off the saddle and found a great, raw sore as big as my hand, which every movement of mine must have tortured cruelly. I walked back and spoke in no measured terms to the owner, who had no difficulty in understanding my meaning, but who in common with my own companions had no small difficulty in understanding why I should make a fuss about a sore on a horse's back. There are no cruelty-to-animals laws in these parts and before I had gone much further I had to get used to the sight of these dreadful sores on many a patient beast of burden.

This night my host, a friend of Don Manuel, was a man who had travelled not only to Bolivia and Brazil, but Paris, of which he had but a poor opinion, and New York, of which he had a poorer. And here at the end of his wanderings he was content with his mud-walled house and some good horses, and as much aji (capsicum) in his food as sent the tears rolling down the cheeks of even my practised friends.

And so on to the Marañón, and next stop Chachapoyas, five days ahead.

— *Extracted from the Memoir of Dr. Kenneth Mackay.*

... *and rides on – at last – to Moyobamba*

ACTUALLY, WE LEFT THE VALLEY FROM HUACAPAMPA, NOT FROM Celendín, and so avoided on this occasion the straight, steep climb by which one leaves the latter and on the top of which climb one ought to gaze reverently down on the Marañón. Instead, we went more over the shoulder and round behind the hill to find ourselves at the mouth of a glen, lost in a very wilderness of mountains, where a white line winding high on the left, and marked out by the shouts of arrieros, showed the descent of the direct road. This was a very short day, for the camping places are more or less fixed by the supply of wood, water and pasture, and early in the sunny afternoon we were lazing on a grassy camping site under the trees at Pauco. A little further on there is an hotel, but my companions, sure of a dry night, preferred the open, and indeed it had every attraction. The fire was speedily got going and the first pot of road-fare swinging over it.

As it was the same pot morning and night for the rest of the journey, it deserves mention once and for all. Two things that are easily carried and that keep indefinitely form the staple diet of the road: rice and dried meat. The rice is boiled up and salted, a lump of meat per man hacked off with the arriero's ever-ready knife, the twelve inch long machete, and thrown in, and when the rice is soft it is supper time or breakfast time, as the case may be. At times it is preceded in the cold parts by a cup of upe – a steaming hot gruel of toasted ground maize that passes the lips as if cold, and then scalds all the way down your oesophagus and heats you right to the toes. Almost always it is followed by the very Peruvian coffee, made in the same pot by boiling up in the water a tremendous lump of chancaca, the brown unrefined sugar from the cane, and adding coffee grounds. It is fearfully strong with a bitter flavour and in the absence of milk it feels worse than medicine at first. In time, one gets a taste for it, that refuses to be put off with imitations. As to the chancaca in it, one may safely say that the arriero would sooner have this beverage than food, but he would rather have it minus coffee than without the full measure of his treacly sugar.

At this early stage of the journey we were amply provided with more perishable luxuries, but the broth as it came steaming from the pot was sufficient assurance that we should not have much to complain of, unless it were the monotony. As day succeeded day, I found that at breakfast we were too busy getting ready to worry about the latter fault and at the evening meal, invariably made on arriving at camp whether at three or eight, hunger and the comfort of stretching the weary legs made a daily new sauce.

To finish at once with the food question, the arrieros took what we gave them and carried on with their bag of beans and biting hot aji, while we were able from time to time to add eggs and fruit to the menu. In short, food never once presented itself as a problem, because of the experience of my fellow-travellers in providing the unadorned essentials and leaving the luxuries to the fortune of the day. On the other hand, there is constant suffering on the road among those who start overloaded for the first three days and find themselves with nothing durable thereafter.

To return to Pauco, I left them to their coffee and made myself thoroughly pleased with the life of the road over a cup of tea, before getting the beds down under the trees. It was altogether beautiful there in the silence of the hills, studying the changing chart of the heavens above, as the full light of the moon began to pick out the waving line of the mountain tops and to throw the whole valley below the line into deep darkness. It had the effect of familiar music, moving to a sense of reverence and soothing with a sense of rich peace. Then, from the valley below came a cheery whistling and the driving shout of a late traveller urging on his beast, and presently a lad was deep in excited conversation with my friend.

All the way from Moyobamba, driving his mule with its load of one thing and another to sell in Cajamarca, all alone, making use of the moon to reach Celandín that night; yes, the Inglesas were well; there was talk of a gringo doctor coming but they had heard that tale before; he had left his mother sick but he hoped she would not have to wait the coming of the aforesaid mythical doctor to get better. And when he was introduced to me, he silently struck a match, saw the undeniable "pacuchu" (this is a word in Quechua) and forthwith in great delight entered on the symptoms of his mother's illness till Valderrama tactfully told him I could not understand, but that he himself would make it all clear to me before we reached Moyobamba.

They fell to talk of the roads ahead, of the state of things in their home town, and in fact had a good old gossip while my sleepy thoughts tried to follow the lad's course from the promised land of Moyobamba to under the trees at Pauco. A little later his voice came ringing down from the climbing path above us as he made his rapid ascent in the bright moonlight singing, with the Indian catch in the wail of his voice, the runs and lilts of some old Inca song. Higher and higher and fainter and fainter came the sound of it and, listening and wondering, I drifted into sleep that lasted undisturbed till the stamping of the mules and the odour of the breakfast broth brought me to my feet in the warm glow of sunrise.

A full hour and a half of hard breathing and hoisting and adjusting and tightening of ropes and blinding of vicious mules by tying a poncho over their heads, and the bare-footed arrieros with their whole kit slung in the knot of a poncho over their shoulders drove the cargo with shouts and blows down the glen road and we leisurely saddled up and followed to cross the famous Marañón and taste the tropical heat of Balsas on its bank. This was a ten-hour day in the saddle, and perhaps the hardest of the whole journey. For an hour or two we rode through a shrubbery of scented hedges promising abundant flower and fruit a month or two later, but as the sun rose and began to search us out, the road began to descend steadily until everything was dry and stunted, and burning sand or rock took the place of cool grass and undergrowth. The loops of the Marañón enclosing fresh patches of green in their brown, turbid curves shone far below, and following the crest of a shoulder of the mountain, the road took on the steep zig-zag down into the blasting heat at just the hottest part of the day.

Yet this was the wisdom of experience, for Balsas is the victim of a very resistant form of malaria and few who sleep there by night escape it, and so although thinking with warm sympathy of those who endure such heat in India, I was well content to endure three hours of it to escape the malarial infection. Balsas at midday was like an oven, grilling in the heat of the tropical sun straight overhead and with a breath of wind that added to the heat, so drying and burning did it pass over the face. Thankfully, we tumbled off in the shade of the little post-office and sucked orange after orange while the telegraphist and his wife hastened to bring cooling drinks of the fruits of the place. A pathetic little place is Balsas, its raison d'etre being almost entirely the needs of the postal service and the arranging of a depot and relays of mules. Men, women and children appeared dried-up by the sun, anaemic and yellow with constant malaria, and utterly lethargic, although possibly in the cool hours of the evening the place might change its aspect very considerably.

It lies on the river level in a curve of its swift, silent, dark-brown flood, the first village of the department of the Amazons and separated from that of Cajamarca by the famous bridge of the Marañón which we had crossed five minutes before entering. The bridge is no mean feat of engineering, constructed nineteen years ago by an Italian engineer, who on the final day and in the last tests, impatient with the hesitation of some of his workmen, himself proceeded to test a stay, which collapsed and dropped him in the river. He was drowned but his bridge stands as the only crossing of this early source of the mighty Amazon. In the rock face high above it, one sees to this day remnants of the line of an ancient Inca road, hewed as was their custom in the solid rock and at a level half-way up the cliff. Tradition says that there was once a bridge of stone as well; a greater marvel of engineering than the present suspension bridge of chain and wire and planks.

As we mounted again in the glare of the dry, hard sand and rode by the river and under the loaded lemon trees, transferring not a little of their load, Valderrama flung his hand out in a typical and expressive gesture towards the piled masses of mountain which fronted us in a tumbled heap disappearing in the clouds, and told me that we were at the very foot of the climb which on the day after next would place us on the summit of the great cordillera for the first time (for one crosses it twice in the great detour between Cajamarca and Moyobamba). This particular summit is known as Callo-Callo, with the simple tale attached of an old-time Indian woman hushing her greeting bairn all the way across it in bad weather with the injunction conveyed in these words equivalent to "wheesht then, will ye".

Nowadays a different route to the top is open which cuts out the weary climb on which we were at the moment entering, and in fact they pointed it out to me at the time as an old road that ought to be reopened. However, up we had to go, winding round and round on the cliff edge, the mules following each other with their family perversity on the extreme outside edge, and ever farther and farther below the little bee-hive huts of Balsas and the two patches of green ringed by the brown band of the loops of the Marañón. By the end of that afternoon, I personally was heartily sick of that particular view. The breathless hot air was loud with the unceasing chatter of a chirping creature which ought to have been at least as big as a house to be in conformity with its vocal powers, but which when distinguished with difficulty against the bark of the stunted leafless trees proved to be a tiny insect of about half an inch with a kind of concertina in his chest.

Slow as the progress necessarily was, it was sure, and little by little the oppression of the heat gave way to freshness, dark clouds began to loom ominously above us, and we came out on a plateau on the crest just as the rain began to fall. Two minutes more and we were in our shelter for the night, while the storm burst into fury outside. A hopeless shelter it appeared to be, this tambo of Carrisal. Tambos are huts provided by the government at convenient points for the shelter of travellers, and consist of four or more posts supporting a roof of thatch. Some, more luxurious, have side-walls of stone. The difficulty is that, in the places where they are most needed, the wet and cold have caused the shivering arrieros to pull a bed and fire out of the thatch of the roof until there is nothing left of it.

Apparently that had happened in Carrisal and – the work of renovation falling half on each of two villages, Balsas and Leimebamba – the latter had fulfilled its part by doing one slope of the roof, but Balsas claimed that side as geographically its part, and refused to do the other. Result for us, half a roof, which nevertheless proved very much better than none. In fact, with the raging of wind and rain, with the crash of thunder and the flashing of lightning all around, more than a dozen of us enjoyed a hot supper, a dry, warm bed and a sound sleep. It sounds very ordinary but to me, tired-out and prepared at first sight of the place for all the horrors of a soaked kit at that altitude, it came as the greatest mercy of a day that had been a sort of breathless thanks for the preserving care of the Most High to find, at the right moment and in face of such improbability, not only shelter but comfort.

Something similar were the feelings of a young man whom we found waiting in the tambo. He had left Celendín for his home in Chachapoyas five days before, returning from seven years of study in Lima, and here on the heights his animals had wandered, and for three days nothing had been seen of them. His food was finished when we blew in. The company was completed by the arrieros and a number of old men and women, Indians of the very poorest sort, drummed-out of their tiny colony near Cajamarca to make the best of their way to where they had originally come from, near Chachapoyas. Two of them, old women over seventy, were confident of surviving the rigours of the route. Much talk of people and places, drawn out by Valderrama with his knowledge of most corners of the montaña and of the Quechua tongue, went on in the firelight, as is the custom of the tambos of the cordillera road where people pass as ships in the night, and if the exiled old folks accepted grateful bite and sup from our steaming pot, they insisted with equal dignity on our tasting their beans and aji. At break of day they were toddling wearily on their way while the whole squad of arrieros scoured the thick bush for the missing mules. How the old Indians survived the frost of Callo-Callo, I do not know.

We camped that night in a site known as Old Tambo, which proved the newest and best of the lot, reaching it by a four-hour's march which brought us once more high above the shoulder of yesterday's climb to look down again over the valley of Pauco. From my vantage point the view all around, save for the drop into the Marañón, was a vast area of mountain tops, reaching into the infinite distance like a tossing sea frozen into immobility and capped with the white clouds for foam.

Once more, we were just into shelter when the rain came down with a right good will, and presently there whirled in on us a party from the other side of the mountain, led by a fat and streaming Indian lad bearing an ancient umbrella. Then there appeared, when the wraps were removed, a delicate young woman carrying an infant, and from a wooden cage-seat strapped on a cargo mule she pulled a lusty couple of bairns loudly demanding food. She was a capable body, and in no time had them all fed and bedded, had investigated our business and admitted her own, and obviously thought little either of the difficulties of the journey or the dangers of the weather.

The early morning was bitterly cold and we lay watching the dense wreath of mist that shrouded the summit of Callo-Callo creep slowly down until its clammy fingers were all about us and the arrieros bringing in the mules had to be guided home by constant shouting. Under such conditions no-one attempts to pass the summit – "the halca is bad", says the arriero and brews himself another cup of coffee philosophically, and then it is no use being in a hurry. On this particular morning loading-up went on in the mist and, sure enough, by the time breakfast was over, the white was melting into sunshine and a glorious day for the crossing was unfolding.

The road was not so heavy, for the last of the ascent is the least steep and difficult, and by noon, muffled in scarf and ponchos again, we were drinking cold upe on the top, where even at this altitude, probably 12,000 feet, the cattle were grazing on the grassy slopes around. Of course, the Moyobamba road is by no means the highest nor the most rigorous on the Peruvian Sierra and here there is no snow, only cold winds and rain. The descent on the other side was more gradual but rapid, and followed the cleft of a tiny spring issuing from the hillside at the top which rapidly grew, as we followed it down through a narrow and fertile glen, into a rushing mountain burn, and then into a fairly wide and deep river, the Udcubamba, whose sweeping course ends in the Atlantic more than 3,000 miles away. All the streams beyond Callo-Callo find their way to the Atlantic thus, and as our Moyobamba Mayo joining the Huallaga also empties itself in the same Marañón, the rivers may be said to make light of the enormous distances and heights that lie between Celendín and the Amazon ports.

* * *

By the late afternoon the character of our surroundings had completely altered and the road ran by the riverside among the green pastures of a glen called Pomacochas, a truly Indian-sounding name. Here the arrieros insisted on camping and had we had a tent I should have been delighted to stay with them. They make themselves snug by stretching a sheet from a rampart of cargo to the ground, but we were without shelter and so, leaving them, we pushed on for another couple of hours to the pretty pueblo of Leimebamba, Señor Noriega especially sighing plaintively for the eggs and new milk to be had there.

Poor man, he had had a sore shake-up in the morning, and even now he pales at the thought of it. At an innocent-looking rise and turn of the road, over three of four rough stone steps, his fine white mule had slipped and, making a lunge forward to recover, came up to the sharp bend at the top with such impetus that it reached the edge of a drop of several hundred feet. The rider's weight was too much for it, and for an awful moment they balanced there. Then he threw himself clear on the inside, and the mule recovered, while Don Manuel picked himself up, somewhat bruised with the fall and his cheery red face for once a sickly white.

And now his desire for eggs and milk was disappointed, for some soldiers had passed some weeks before, and had committed such depredations among the poultry that the villagers had removed all their livestock to the hills behind the pueblo. To complete an unfortunate day, he was bringing two boxes of fine rabbits through to rear in Moyobamba, and on this night one of them went into the pot. One had died in Balsas, and six now remained. The difficulty of getting anything out of the Leimebambinos as a result of the conduct of the soldiers is evidenced by the tale of the present judge of Moyobamba who, coming with his delicate wife, had so misarranged his fiambre as to reach here with nothing, thinking to replenish in the village. He did so in the end only by using his revolver with accuracy on one or two hens in the woods behind. Yet, on a later journey, when I encountered the same "haven't any" reply to every appeal, as soon as I had prescribed for a sick baby they trooped along with aprons full of hens and eggs.

The telegraphist in this place turned out to be a cousin of our hosts in Celendín, and a keen reader of the literature supplied by the mission, and was consequently both interested and helpful. We put up at the Royal Hotel. That was the name traced in purple letters across the whitewashed front of the newest building round the village square, but as an hotel all it offered was a space to make your bed down. Talk of the escape of Señor Noriega brought out several tales of tragedy at that same point on the road, where it is running as a shelf along the steep side of a basin whose bottom is a rich farm belonging to a masterful old lady who lives in Moyobamba. Three men in the smoke of a bush-fire went over the edge on one occasion, and recently a radio engineer has told us of the loss of a mule and its cargo of instruments at the same point They got it two hundred feet down, the cargo pulverised, the mule dead with not a bruise to be seen on it.

The following morning, we had to wait for the arrieros from Pomacochas and so the start for us was late and the day short. Señor Noriega as sub-Prefect was carrying heavy military cargo and the animals were tiring, so that our progress was a little slower than it might have been, but all the more pleasant. The way for three days now led us through a completely different type of country. From precipitous rocky staircases up and down, and a path on the edge of abysses, we had a garden walk by the riverside. Instead of the piled masses of mountain peaks, like a stormy sea all around and capped by the clouds, we found ourselves in a cleft with steep rocky sides so covered by trees and ferns and grasses as to be a very Perthshire glen. In the bends of the stream were narrow strips and wider spaces of rich green pasture and round and among it all the luxuriant under-growth, for this is a stretch of montaña in the dip of the Sierra. The road wound leisurely up and down the right bank, sometimes close by the river, now rushing deep and silent as it gathered volume, sometimes altogether shut in by the trees, sometimes climbing over a cliff of rock rising sheer out of the water, till from high above we looked straight down into the river again, and always a fresh view tempting one to linger in its peace and rich beauty.

On the second day, we entered an avenue of wild fruit trees and all the air was full of their faint, sweet perfume, while here a covey of birds all dressed in green, and there a single little splash of red like a poppy blossom with wings, butterflies of countless sizes and colours, and the cry from the cool depths of the wood of a bird called the quien-quien. Orange, lemon, pineapple, and the buds of the much-prized chirimoya, its scent a delicious sweetness like the taste of pineapple, all full of promise but not yet of fruit. Here, the people might have stepped west from Egypt or Arabia, for they dislike the national hat of straw and wear a turban-like cloth wound round the head which, with the copper tint of their skin, gives them a very eastern appearance. Lots of cattle are here and all the males kept as bulls so that at times their appearance was far from reassuring, but as a matter of fact they are exceedingly tame and gentle.

Again, we passed the nights in tambos but as a result of the milder climate of the glen, the roofs had been left whole and one was very comfortable in the camp-bed. Out of the camp-bed, however, it was insufferable, for in the dust of the floor and the million crevices of the walls, lurk the waiting garrapattas, the female of the species feeding long and full in the quiet of the night upon the blood of the unwary traveller. These ticks lie, apparently for centuries, in the dust until warm blood comes near and then with one accord they rise and sharpen their lancets and proceed to operate. So in the morning we counted our spots, and for the rest of the day scratched them.

The evening scene at this tambo remains a picture in my memory. From the vantage-point upon which the hut was built, the river in its close-woven hedge of trees separated us from the steep straight line of cliff running as a rampart three-days long, beyond which lie the pueblos of the gold-mines. Away down the river, the cliff ends in a shoulder and the sky opens out in the promise of the end of the narrow glen by tomorrow night. It is a poetic sky at the moment, a wonder of delicate colour. Below are the mules rolling and kicking in grateful abandon, now that the burdens and all the friction of tight-drawn ropes are cleared from their weary backs.

The arrieros, with a running fire of argument and friendly abuse, are divided among their nightly duties, raising the rampart of boxes, and covering them against the possibility of rain, fetching food and water to where the two boys are bent over the fire preparing the inevitable caldo (broth) of rice; my two companions superintending the cold-shoeing of Don Manual's white mule, for up to this point the animals have all gone bare-foot, but must now be shod or go lame; and myself on my camp-bed watching it all and waiting for the nightly chorus of "cuidado, cuidado" (carefully, carefully) when it came to moving the case containing the Milton microscope. As the night drew in, and the music of the running water made the background to the rustling of the trees and the low voices of the arrieros, the whole became a miracle of restfulness, so that for once the ceilidh round the fire faded into contented silence and all was peace.

The following night we left the cargo at the bend of the Udcubamba where it sweeps round the cliff-foot to seek the Marañón, and began to climb out of our Perthshire glen to Sierra country again. The darkness found us warmly welcomed to a fine little farm-house whose owner keeps a room specially for travellers who care to accept his hospitality. Here at last we had milk in pails and eggs cooked a dozen at a time. There was one interesting touch, at the sound of shouting and rattling of tins outside. Our host snatched up an ancient musket and fired forlornly out of the bedroom window while remarking "tiger". As far as I could make out, the tiger is a species of wild-cat or even puma, which occasionally harasses the cattle. One particularly beautiful creature we saw on this farm was a Royal peacock in all his pride and glory.

Now we were back again among the ups and stony downs of the Sierra, a long day on the tired animals that put us in the evening within sight of Chachapoyas at last, two hours away on the slope of a hill that faced us across another of these deep sudden cracks in the face of the Sierra, that make the road ten times as long for the mule as for the crow. So there we stopped, finding a room in a kindly little house where we got our beds down, and where the three lads of sixteen downwards and their eighteen-year old sister who were keeping going the farm of their dead parents, might have spoken the purest Ross-shire Gaelic, so exactly similar were they in manner to any family in a western croft. Mitupampa they called it in Quechua, which means mud-plain, and for that reason we dropped the idea of making ourselves clean and pretty for arrival in Chachapoyas, and rode into it the next forenoon as weather-beaten a band of gypsies as was ever expelled as vagrants from the avenues of Bearsden.

The night before, the discussion had been long and eager over the day of our arrival in Moyobamba. A week that night, I was told, I would be cleaning-up for an early entry into the town. With the never-ending journey brought into proportion, I lay awake wondering and hoping. But I might have postponed these exercises, for a week that night I was still in Chachapoyas, and the calculations were still being as optimistically made anew each day of delay.

* * *

Its name for me will always be Chancho-poyas, for chancho means pig, and here for the first time I saw pig-rearing in all its crude disregard for the welfare of anything but the pig. They lie at the doorsteps in their wallows, root and dig all through the streets, and have right of entry into the kitchen and assume it in the living rooms of the poorer houses. They are not there in dozens but in hundreds, all black, with the myriads of wee black coolans grunting and squealing and burrowing under their placidly sleeping mothers, while the mules step round them and the wee boys walk over them. From this Sierra town down into the montaña this is the rule, and a terrible state of matters it is from the point of view of public health and epidemics, for the worse the dirt and crowding, the more do the pigs flourish and increase at the expense of the children.

Chachapoyas, then, is a town set on the slope of a hill above the bend of the Udcubamba where it turns away round the corner of the long range to seek the Amazon, and the whole department of which it is the seat of government is the department of Amazons (always in the plural). Its three provinces in their forty thousand square miles have a population of 100,000 souls, of whom 6,000 live in the capital and the rest are in the numerous pueblos and pueblocitos of the provinces. It gives some idea of the enormous responsibility involved in a missionary effort for northern Peru – the realisation that in simply passing from Cajamarca to Moyobamba one leaves unprovided-for 16,000 in the province of Celendín and 100,000 in the department of Chachapoyas, and that that journey is merely a line that does not come within many miles of other centres and areas of a similar needy nature, without referring to the vast stretch of Indian Loreto.

The population of the department of the Amazons is almost entirely agricultural, ploughing with a light wooden scraper which rather tickles than turns the earth, and which is drawn by two oxen pitilessly held together by the crossbar on the horns, and supporting a plough-beam of great length and weight. Maize and beans are the staple products, with barley and potatoes near the town, and down in the valley bananas, oranges and grapes. Wine-making and the sale of whole-meal flour to Moyobamba form a big part of the local trade, while almost continually from the Indian villages beyond the cordillera come in small quantities of gold. There are good-enough shops, but the town is not a thriving one. On the contrary, it is more given over to laziness and the vices of drink and gambling than most of the Sierra towns, deriving its means of support in small part from the efforts of some hard-working farmers and, in much larger part, from the exploitation of the Indians of the surrounding villages. The hire of animals and of bearers for cargo is one of the mainstays in the latter sense, and it was only by a ten-days' wait and at a stiff price that we were on this occasion able to secure the animals for the remainder of the journey.

These ten days were quiet and lonely, but there was rich compensation in the peacefulness of the walks with a book, out above the town to moorland that might have been the uplands of Lanark, but for the blue mass of tumbled peaks that bounded it and that looked down on the other side to the plains of the montaña. Sub-Prefect Noriega was the subject of much polite attention and held an afternoon levee each day, which served me very well as a period of Spanish instruction, and which led to my appearing at the lunch table of the Dean of Chachapoyas, a church dignitary of some importance but a very genial and hospitable host, and so very like a minister of the Free Church at home in his person and his manner that it seemed very extraordinary to hear him pouring out torrents of Spanish. My two friends spent much spare time and money buying hampers and filling them with rolls of the local bread and small cheeses, for if they should have arrived in Moyobamba after their long absence without these delicacies of Chachapoyas, their friends and relations would have felt like the bairns in Alness if Auntie had come home from the wonderland from which the south train brought her without the box of butterscotch.

Over and over again, citizens of the town related the story of the coming of J. Calvin Mackay from Cajamarca three years before on his way to Moyobamba, when in his room he was waited upon by a resolute company of the most fanatical Romanist women to warn him out of the town with the utmost despatch. I think anyone else would have fled forthwith, but so great was the courtesy of their reception by him and so very different his appearance from the roaring lion of a heretic that they had been worked into a fever against, that their warning is still unspoken and instead they asked for and got an exposition of his faith in the form of pure Gospel truth, and retired in good order and shown out with the most calm and friendly politeness.

A thing which has not yet been forgotten and is continually being retold is the last of the incident. Someone raised an insulting shout as the ladies took their departure, and got for his share a rebuke that took immediate effect and that has placed the seal on Mr. Mackay's standing in Chachapoyas, quite unknown to him, as "muy caballero" (most gentlemanly) and "de mucha cultura" (weel brocht up). The importance of it is that these people now assume that all Protestants are of the same character, and the ridiculous and once generally-accepted calumnies of the character and life of the missionaries have been dealt a knock-out blow. It makes one realise how far-reaching can be the effect of one's everyday thoughts and actions in establishing contact with new people, and how very close must be the missionary's watch on himself and his dependence on Divine grace in his daily "walk and conversation".

* * *

It was Monday, the 29th of November, three long weeks from the day we left Cajamarca, when at last the noise and bustle of loading up, the heaving of boxes, and straining at ropes and kicking of mules, betokened the start of the last lap – really, the last. The Chachapoyas hiring is done from the pueblos nearby, and to save the better animals, any old mules are sent in to take the travellers out on the first day to the pueblos where the hirer lives: our destination this first night was a village called Daguas at six hours distance and we left at noon. It is true of many occupations that it is easier to keep going when tired than to start again after stopping for a bit. This is especially true of riding on these mountain roads, and from the simple stiffness and soreness in the saddle, and the irritation of sun and flies, this first day remains in memory as a bad one, in spite of the satisfaction of having passed the last "junction" and having no further changing of mules to do, or delay to expect. Yet thinking things over as the hours went slowly past and the animals jogged patiently and mechanically up and down the braes, I was compelled to take stock of the whole three and a half months since I had received my commission in Inverness. I was drawing near to Moyobamba in a frame of mind considerably altered from that in which I had left Scotland.

Our road took us by steep and rocky ascents and descents through a deep ravine on whose sides, far above, cattle seemed to be clinging like flies, so little foothold could be seen. It reminded me of the sheep on the sides of the Quirang on Skye, feeding quietly in spots that showed no way either of access or of descent. Swinging over the ravine from a tree at the head to another at a bend 300 yards away ran the telegraph wire made visible by the simple plan of tying a coloured rag to it at intervals. Out of this canyon the road made a steep and sudden climb, leaving for the present the river and the "high road" to take us to Duguas, which now appeared as a sort of battlement to an isolated hill of such steepness that it had to be climbed much like a lighthouse. The only reason, on the face of it, for having a village perched thus on a peak must be the historical one of a safe refuge and look-out in hostile territory, and Daguas may well have been a brigands' stronghold in days not very far back. But once our bargain for the mules was struck, the house and hospitality of the hirer were liberally at our disposal. The hill-top proved to be surprisingly wide, in a cup-shaped depression holding a small village with its little school and several crofts whose lanes were overgrown with perfectly genuine brambles.

Next morning, early, appeared the mounts for the five days ahead, and they were good. The patio of the house presented a scene reminiscent of horse-sale day, with some twenty-five saddle and cargo mules and as many men, women and boys tied-up in apparently inextricable confusion with harness and ropes and boxes. Conspicuous among them all was the old grandfather of the tribe, a veteran of ninety years with a beard still black and hands still strong enough to chastise a troublesome boy or mule. Both he and all the family knew that we could not be sent-off in ship-shape fashion if he did not supervise, and it was pleasant to see how the rough arrieros did just as he told them and accepted his rebukes. This old man, who had never been out of sight of his mountain home, had all the appearance of a typical veteran of a west-coast fishing village in Scotland, and even in Spanish his speech, and indeed that of all the country folk, had the same trait, had the softness and lilt of the old folks' speech in the Highlands. The owner of the house, his son, looked an older man than his father, and investigation of his condition showed that the mystery of disease is universal. I had not looked for diabetes in such a place as this.

In twos and threes, the arrieros who were to accompany us got their mules loaded and away, and at length the patio was sufficiently cleared to show that there were three cargoes without mules. Then it turned out that three mules were to come with an Indian from some little distance, and that he had been at a fiesta the preceding evening, so that he would probably not remember his contract for a day or two. We did not take things quite as philosophically as that, and immediate messages were sent to "bring him in the alive or dead" style that is needed in these cases. However, about noon the perspiring young Indian appeared with his animals without having received our message. The poor fellow had left home at four a.m. to join us, but two of the mules had broken away from him. How he had recovered them I cannot imagine, but on the journey he several times showed a degree of strength and endurance amazing in a lad of his size.

Thus starting several hours after the others, we made slow progress down the steep hill-side, along a river-valley and up a rocky climb to a bare wilderness of rock which seemed to last for hours, until we came suddenly upon as green and lovely a plain, enclosed in the loop of a broad river, as ever a farmer could wish to see. At one end of it clustered the huts with the telegraph office, but the whole populace was at work together, exactly like a turnip-hoeing at home, digging and deepening the furrows with wooden spades instead of the plough, and carrying down among them some half-dozen drills at a time. They were certainly carrying out more thoroughly than I had seen in all the Sierra the maxim of going deep and turning well over, and the finished work was a series of straight, well-turned furrows of black rich soil to cheer a ploughman's eye. Molinopampa or "plain of the mill" it is called, and there is not a more fertile or more green and pleasant stretch of land – well-wooded, well-watered and rich in pasture and in grazing herds – till one comes again to the shores of the Cromarty Firth and the good fields of Easter Ross.

Cheery greetings passed between the workers in the fields and my companions and – ascertaining the camping-place of our arrieros – we began to push-on in fear of darkness. Leaving the open plain, the road entered the silence of dense woods, broken only by the beautifully tuneful note of a bird called by the arrieros the sorsal. With the last of the daylight we forded the slow quiet water of the Ventilla with feet crossed on the mule's neck, and startled a flock of wild duck on a great pool nearby, and then, leaving the river, took to a rocky climb again in the darkness. A faint white gleam was all I could see ahead, but the animals plodded on quietly and surely, an eerie feeling for the rider in unknown country, until after two hours the sound of rushing water was heard and we were back again at the Ventilla.

A few moments more and we were dumping our kit and sipping hot coffee while Valderrama arranged that we should have "dinner in the morning", since sleep is as good as food and easier to get in the dark. We were settled in what appeared to be a tambo, but was in fact simply the wooden bridge over the river roofed over with thatch, and it was a new and very pleasant sensation to drift to sleep in the shadow of the mountains to the music of the running water ten feet below the bed.

Puente Sicse it is named, and for a camping site it is delightful. To be wakened there in the dim early light and watch the stars go out, and the mist rise from the wooded slopes around, hear the music of birds, feel the cosiness of the camp-bed in the frost and drenching dew of early morning, enjoy the fragments of the breakfast broth that should have been last night's supper, and then as the sun comes up in genial warmth, feel a sense of well-being and comfort that readily turns to deeper thankfulness and worship as one looks ahead to the day's task – the crossing of the highest and steepest part of all the cordillera on the way to Moyobamba. For morning and evening worship on this journey one continually returns to the same two sweet and familiar psalms, in the morning looking around and ahead, the travellers' song, "I to the hills will lift mine eyes, from whence doth come mine aid", and in the evening, in thankful rest and comfort, "The Lord is my Shepherd, I'll not want".

This is the big day. By eight a.m. the cargo was all ahead and we had started, but it was half past ten before we reached the foot of the mountain at the tambo of Ventilla. This part of the road simply climbed a hill to come down again to the river which had made a great detour, and should have been done the day before but for the delay. However, even half past ten at the foot gave us time with good animals to get over the top, and the day was beautifully clear, a matter of vital importance. The summit is called in Quechua Pischcuhuañunan, which means "the place where the birds die", and while the crossing can be done in about four hours, if the day be threatening and there comes on the fierce wind dreaded by the Indians, accompanied by the driving small rain or drizzle, the cold is intense and the difficulty of breathing an agony. No sensible person attempts to cross on such a day, but at times a poor fellow in a weak and sickly condition, in the anxiety to get on, or from inability to hurry, gets caught, and lying down to rest, drifts into unconsciousness, and dies. There was a matter of ten rough crosses in all at various stages of the crossing, each with its story in almost the same terms: "the halca was bad and the man was sick".

Our day was as good as could be desired, and we went up in good spirits. The ascent is very steep, much steeper than Callo-Callo, and literally consists of a series of staircases of rock with periodic landings, two to three hours of steady climbing. Over and over again, looking up, one marks the distant telegraph pole on the farthest ridge, only to find on reaching it that there is another ridge with another pole as far up again. However, the scramble and struggle ends at last on the wide bare crossing of the shoulder just below the peak, and here at the spring of coldest water we made our upe of maize meal and rested the animals.

Not a living creature was to be seen, only the bare rock of the hill, until turning the shoulder we began the descent, and saw the first approach to a loch which I had seen in the Sierra, where between the point of Pischcuhuañunan and another known as Cochaconga lies a silent dark stretch of water where wild birds make their home. Here for us the sky suddenly darkened and in a moment down came the thunderstorm of rain and hail. The road in its descent clung to the side of the mountain and speedily became a rushing mountain burn with miniature waterfalls, through which the mules plodded doggedly, while we sat hunched in the saddles, effectively covered in rubber capes, and were thankful to be over the top in good time.

Along the left ran a deep valley and there the storm seemed to concentrate until the lightning sheets appeared to be bursting up from below us and the thunder to be at our very feet. While it lasted, it was an awe-inspiring experience, but in an hour the capes were drying in the sunshine and we came to the end of the crossing and prepared for the abrupt descent. As on Callo-Callo this began in the cleft of a spring, gradually swelling into a river, and with it began the undergrowth and trees which indicated the transition from Sierra to montaña, and which stretches to the Atlantic. At last I was looking down into the montaña, and no Andes now separated me from Moyobamba, some four days distance down below in steady descent.

* * *

Certainly, that part of the descent immediately before us was anything but steady, for it terminated in an hour of winding between high walls of rock down a dripping and slippery staircase of rock, in a series of slithering plunges that made me recall with a grin of deep sarcasm my feelings of dismay in the descent to Huacapampa. Of course the simple process of dismounting and going down on foot would have made the thing perfectly simple, but it was soon over without mishap as we came out of the staircase at the river Bagazan. At the moment the storm of the afternoon had transformed it into a raging torrent and it took all the skill and force of the arrieros to force the animals safely over. This is one of the points of sudden rise and fall of the rivers that sometimes holds up the mails for many days. Once across, we were finished for that day, camping for the night at a tambo by the river.

This being the coldest and wettest point of the whole journey, the tambo is continually being destroyed by the shivering arrieros to make fire and bed, and we found it with only a corner of the roof left. However, the night looked like being dry and it gave us shelter enough. A few hundred yards away there is a cave of rock which is used when the tambo falls in. The surroundings on this particular night were such a sea of mud that bare feet came off best. The evening was spent steaming wet clothes and hearing tales of the road exchanged between the arrieros and the cattle drivers who were taking their bulls down from Chachapoyas and Molinopampa to sell as butcher-meat in Moyobamba and Rioja.

All the trials and troubles of the road, which for me had not been one tenth of what I had heard prophesied, and which given good health and careful preparation need never be very serious, were now over, according to the repeated assurances of my companions, and the rest would be a pleasure-ride through scenes of beauty. Personally, I came to consider the next three days as the worst and most trying of all. Certainly, there was no more climbing of heights or walking on the edge of nothing, but instead the road lay through an interminable wood, with the promise of coming out into daylight always a little way ahead, and the branches and creepers dripping wet overhead and compelling the constant protection of the face with the arm.

The footing of this part of the road is very uneven and rocky, but it is more the sense of being so closely shut in by the forest and the impossibility of seeing ahead or around that becomes very wearying. After some three hours of great contentment with our woodland path, the wonderful variety of its gorgeous flowers, and the towering height of its trees hidden for their first ten feet in impenetrable thicknesses of undergrowth which frequently transformed our road into a tunnel, I asked Valderrama when we would be out into the open again. He said, "this goes on to the Atlantic ocean", and I found he was not exaggerating very much, for except for the open clearings by the rivers, such as that in which Moyobamba is, the whole of the montaña to the borders of Peru and into Brazil is this incredible mass of forest and tangled vegetation, teeming with wildlife and penetrable by man only with an axe.

So we passed hour after hour plodding on without change of scene, but with a distinctly warmer temperature than hitherto, until in the late afternoon we came to the lip of a deep, deep cup with forest-clad sides, into which tumbled a noisy stream. Far away below us in a clearing at the bottom of the cup was a tambo, our hotel for the night. This place is called in Quechua "Ushcu", the hole, and a very good name too, as I thought while we repeated a descent like that of the previous evening and came out half an hour later at a very respectable and water-tight tambo, close by the river.

There was quite a storm during the night but we remained once more snug and dry, and I began to gather from the change of temperature in the night that the Andes were really behind us for good. So slow, so tormentingly slow, is the progress of each hour on this journey that it comes almost as a shock to realise the enormous heights and distances that get left behind as the days go past. The journey becomes almost the end in itself and one forgets that life consists in anything more than the bustle or rest, morning and evening, and the patient sitting in the middle all day. This monotony was to me the only hardship of the journey, and especially those last two hours of the daily nine or ten, when false hopes of the arrival within ten minutes are continually being raised. "Just a wee bit further", says the arriero, or "an hour or so"; when there are still three good hours to go.

The heavy loads of official goods carried by the sub-Prefect had caused the animals to tire considerably and they did not reach Ushcu that night. Consequently we made a two hour move in the morning to the house of a telegraphist at a point called Pucatambu, the second office out of Moyobamba, there to wait the cargo, but by the time it arrived the day was so far advanced and the weather so bad that in view of a particularly bad descent ahead and the absence of shelter, we spent the day there. The telegraphist proved to be a remarkable man. Beginning with his lonely little hut there by the roadside, seven years ago he set to work to make a clearing and to plant it. It grew, he employed and housed some Indian workers, and cleared more, brought a sugar-mill from Iquitos, built all kinds of labour-saving appliances for drawing water up to the peak of the hill on which his house stands, and now presents for the admiration of the forest-weary traveller a great stretch of what was dense forest on the steep slopes above the river, now flourishing with sugar cane, bananas, yuca, maize and pasture, fenced in with barbed wire. He has a little colony of Indians who regard him as a kind of father and whom he feeds and clothes. He produces the whitest sugar in the district and dispenses in the cleanest house on the road the most liberal hospitality.

To my mind, the one tremendous pity is that most of his mechanical ingenuity has gone to the production of alcohol from the sugar cane, for though he himself is temperate and has a great contempt for drunkards, he makes no small profit from the sale of drink. Yet the industry, application and intelligence which have wrested the land from the forest and surrounded his house with glorious roses, when his colleagues along the wire in better situations have been content to rest on their wages, are so unusual that he cannot be considered as less than a most remarkable as well as hard-working man. He has worked out his religious position to what he considers the same fixed basis as his sugar mill. He will have none of Romanism because he has long watched it at work in its priests, and his religion, as he puts it, is to love and help his neighbour, his neighbour being every man who passes his way until such a man abuses his kindness.

Thereafter it is equally part of his religion to see that the man who does him an ill turn pays for it. His practice in regard to the first part of it is worthy of all praise, for he is known far and near for hospitality without grudging. I fear he is likely to be pretty grim in the accomplishment of the second part too. He had many questions to ask that day about the Protestants and what they professed, and the tangible fruits of that religion, in the well-known work of the English nurses in Moyobamba, appeared to him as a very real religion. Anything more vital than good works he did not want to hear about, but he willingly accepted and set about reading copies of the Gospels which I was able to give him. A remarkable man for his environment and opportunities! I have since helped him by telegraph through a dysentery outbreak among his family of Indians.

Leaving at eight a.m. on Saturday morning the house of our hospitable friend, we found the road in the most slippery condition which the combination of red clay and constant rain can produce, but there was bright sunshine overhead and a host of beautiful objects, gorgeous butterflies, and birds and flowers now taking on a tropical appearance, to shorten the way. A little more than two hours, the road sometimes through woods, sometimes through a deep cut between high banks of moss-covered rock, so that feet had to be smartly moved from the stirrups to escape bruising, brought us to the top of the great brae down to the plain of Moyobamba. It is called the Ventana, or window, because of the sudden opening of the scene at one point where, far below, a great plain unfolds itself as far as the eye can reach. Valderrama was waiting for it and with a flourish introduced me to Moyobamba, represented in the expanse of plain by the single conical peak of the Moro. Though I call the scene a plain, it is to be thought of not as a stretch of prairie, but as the same dense mass of forest as that through which we had just come, now spread out below like a carpet of the densest texture and the darkest green. Of the towns of Rioja and Moyobamba and the many villages, we could see, however, nothing from this window.

The brae itself is the worst piece in the whole road. Being very steep, it is continually being worn by the rushing rain-waters and – as it has systematically been neglected by successive authorities who pocketed money meant for repairs – it has for long been impossible to come down it on horseback. Consequently we strapped everything on the saddle and began a perspiring plunge down for two hours. Some bad jumps there are for the animals and it is small wonder if goods get damaged on the way to Moyobamba.

Once down, the whole character of the going changed. No longer was there rough and broken rock for footing, but firm earth and level going, and at a house called Dry River at the foot, we fared richly on bananas and papayas and fruit drinks. As Valderrama said, "now we're at home, we'll want for nothing". All the afternoon we rode at a trot again, almost for the first time since Chileti, through avenues of trees and wide stretches of fern and bracken to the orange trees of Rioja, and in the late evening of Saturday I was seeing my first patients in my own official "parish", and experiencing the relief of my doubts as to whether the climate would be a sore trial or not.

I rather spoilt things for my good companions by preferring not to arrive on Sabbath in Moyobamba, but when they were a little on their way there came a summons from the nurses to a case in the hospital, and in company with a young member of the congregation who had come out to meet me, I followed them. Twice between Rioja and Moyobamba, the mules have to be stripped to swim the rivers, first Tonchima and later Indoche, the traveller and his goods crossing in a canoe made of a hollowed tree. Between the two, in the little village of Calzada, famous for the richest and juiciest oranges in the world, we overtook the others, or rather I did, for my companion had stayed behind at a small bridge in the depths of the wood, where the mule would be neither coaxed not compelled to cross. Eventually, with the help of the arrieros, they practically carried it over.

At the second river a number of citizens were waiting to welcome Señor Noriega and they extended to me a very warm welcome with appreciative reference to the nurses Miss Soper and Miss Gould. Half an hour later, those ladies themselves and members of the congregation met us on the road, and we entered Moyobamba in force. A short meeting of thanksgiving in the little church and I was enjoying once again the hospitality and the atmosphere of home, and marvelling to find myself actually in Moyobamba in the mission field opened up by Misses Soper and Gould – who had preceded me, over that long, long road from the coast, more than four years before.

– *Extracted from the Memoir of Dr. Kenneth Mackay.*

The 1930s: Alexander Renwick
heads for the Amazon

AFTER A FEW DAYS WE STARTED TO CLIMB THE MOUNTAINS TO CROSS over from Cajabamba to Cajamarca. At dusk we came to a large hacienda, where the manager received us most courteously. He provided for ourselves and our horses, but, that night, I had my first experience in Peru of wrapping myself in a poncho and sleeping on the floor. It is not half so hard, or so disagreeable, as might appear.

In the morning we were early on our way. Even those elevations were teeming with life – cultivators on the hillsides, shepherds caring for their flocks, men and women constantly on the move. In a few hours, however, we were out on the uninhabited uplands, called hereabouts the chalka: the cold and exposed regions too inhospitable for cultivation.

In the afternoon the mists came down on these Andean heights. My friends were not nervous, but, for a time, we lost the way. Finally, we emerged from the mists and saw below us the primitive community of Laymina with its Indian huts and straw-covered roofs. It was at a height of about 13,000 feet. There might be nearly forty of these dwellings. We were heartily welcomed into one of them for the night. A prominent item on the menu, I remember, was toasted Indian corn. It was not particularly palatable to the uninitiated, but these humble folk gave us of their best and we were truly appreciative. There they live on this cold, wind-swept mountain-side, frequently enwrapped in the Andean mists; and, at other times, buffeted by the merciless rains. They were a sturdy race. Many of them disdained shoes and stockings, and their clothes were nearly all of home-spun materials. Tonight, again, we slept on the floor on skins – this latter a luxury. I question if there was a bed to be found in the entire village, for we occupied the most pretentious dwelling in the community. Placing our saddles as pillows, and wrapping ourselves in our ponchos, we composed ourselves to sleep. Truly, "a man's life consisteth not in the abundance of the things which he possesseth". In the morning I felt as fresh as if I had slept on a bed of down, and I had learned not a little of how other folks live.

The path leading down from this mountain height was exceedingly steep – so much so that, at times, it appeared more prudent to walk than to ride, but I was to find, in a few days, that in comparison with some others, this path was first class. In three hours we had reached the valley below, and under a clear sky we travelled cheerily via Hualqui and Jesús to the far extending campiña of Cajamarca, a place which must ever be associated with the tragic story of Atahualpa, the last of the Inca rulers.

On a sunny afternoon in November, 1532, Francisco Pizarro and his small force of 106 infantrymen and 62 horsemen came across the bleak Cordilleras and got their first glimpse of the beautiful plain of Cajamarca. They had had a rough journey, of about a week's duration, from Motope, near the present Lambayeque. Their experiences were exactly the same as those of the modern traveller in the parts of the Andes where roads have not been built. Says Prescott: "It was so steep in many places, that the cavalry was obliged to dismount and, scrambling up as best they could, to lead their horses by the bridle. In many places, too, where some huge crag or eminence overhung the road, this was driven to the very edge of the precipice; and the traveller was compelled to wind along the narrow ledge of rock, scarcely wide enough for his single steed, where a mis-step would precipitate him hundreds, nay, thousands of feet into the dreadful abyss!" The more I learn of Peru, ancient and modern, the more respect I have for the marvellous accuracy of Prescott, and there is certainly not a word of exaggeration in this description.

Great was the astonishment of the Spaniards when, from the heights above, they saw, in the distance, the valley of Cajamarca, "enamelled with all the beauties of cultivation unrolled like a rich and variegated carpet of verdure in strong contrast with the dark forms of the Andes that rose up everywhere around it". They were to prove the truth of what they had been told so often, that the glory of the Inca Empire lay in the mountains and not on the coast. They were surprised at the fine, solid buildings of stone they now met with, and the aqueducts and irrigation channels which enabled the diligent husbandman to make this region a picture of prosperity such as they were to find later in innumerable places throughout the land.

The traveller who today comes up from Pacasmayo to Chilete by a very slow train in which he is rendered grimy by the dust which blows in from the deserts, takes a car at Chilete and, if he is fortunate enough not to meet with landslides, arrives in about three hours at Cajamarca – the total time from the coast being only some nine hours. Nevertheless, even under such conditions he cannot but be impressed with the majesty of the Andes as he climbs up above San Juan and sweeps round sharp curves along the very edge of terrible precipices. It may be that the sun will be shining pleasantly, as it was on 15th November, 1532, when Pizarro arrived, but it is just as likely that he may be enshrouded in a thick mist which will make him very cold and miserable. When, however, he comes over the crest of El Gavilán ("The Hawk"), he will see a sight not at all unlike what those rugged Spaniards saw more than four hundred years ago when they crossed the mountains somewhere further to the north. There is the lovely valley with its fields showing up in varied tints of green and yellow, stretching along for some fifteen miles with a breadth of from six to nine miles. In some ways, it reminds me of the valley of the Spey at Kingussie, Scotland, but the former is ten times as wide. Nevertheless, there is a resemblance, and it is all the more remarkable that my colleague Mr. John Calvin Mackay, head of the

Scottish Mission at Cajamarca, should have come, precisely, from that charming little town in the Grampians.

One of the first things one notices on coming in sight of the Cajamarca valley is the hot vapour rising in clouds from the thermal baths some miles away across the plain at the ancient Kónoj where the Inca Atahualpa had a pleasant residence. "The bearded thieves come up from the sea", (as the natives called the Spaniards in 1532) saw this same sight, but no longer do we see the white tents spread along the hillside behind, where Atahualpa had tens of thousands of his warriors encamped, on beholding whom, a feeling of dread struck at the heart of the small band of Spanish adventurers – men of iron though they were.

Alas! that the Cajamarca of those days, according to the accounts of the chroniclers, seems to have been infinitely superior to the city of today. It had then about 10,000 inhabitants. Today it has some 13,000 but in those days, the Spaniards were impressed by the architectural science of the people, and their fine, strong buildings of hewn stone – "the best they had yet seen in the country". Excluding the churches, there is not a building in the place today which would attract one's attention.

Pizarro's secretary, Francisco de Xerez, in his Conquista del Perú, records that the people of this city were superior to any that they had seen on the other side of the mountains, as was shown by, "the superior style of their attire and the greater cleanliness and comfort visible both in their persons and their dwellings". I have often visited Cajamarca, and no man would think of writing about it in this strain nowadays. If we leave out the landowning, professional and merchant classes – who are delightfully cultured – the people, as a whole, present a picture exactly the opposite of that described by Xerez in 1532. Indeed, it would be hard to find a more untidy or more miserable-looking set of Indians than those of this community. The open sewers in the middle of the street attract one's attention as they do all over the Sierra, but fortunately there is a plentiful supply of water flowing swiftly through them down the hill, and the air is the healthiest one could wish for; thus the evil effects are counteracted.

Anyone coming here naturally looks for the plaza where Atahualpa, the last Emperor of Tahuantinsuyo, was treacherously taken prisoner and where he was later executed by the Spaniards – a plaza which they declared was greater than any they had seen in Spain. But Cajamarca, today, is poor in Inca remains, though there is still pointed out, in what is now the hospital of Bethlehem, under the care of Roman Catholic nuns, a room which is alleged to have been Atahualpa's prison. Here, it is said, the captured monarch made the astounding offer to the Spaniards that he would fill the room with gold to a point which he marked with his finger on the wall, nine feet from the floor.

The baths of the Inca at Kónoj (called also Cuñu) are well worth a visit. According to Xerez, there was one bath, "to which there came through a pipe, water so hot that one could not put his hand in it. The water rises boiling in a nearby hill". He also says there was a smaller bath here. Garcilaso de la Vega tells how, at each of his residences, the Inca had magnificent baths, adorned with gold and silver, and that the water flowed in pipes of that metal. Today, there are six of these baths under the control of the municipality. There is no doubt that one of these is the same as was used by the Inca, who, Xerez says, "went into it by steps". The size of the bath is as large as an average bedroom, and one can swim about in it to his heart's content. Gone, however, are all the ornaments of gold and silver and the pipes of these precious metals. Neither are there now any royal apartments standing nearby, and few recall that it was here that the Inca received in haughty majesty, with six hundred gorgeously clad attendants, Hernando Pizarro and De Soto, the emissaries sent by the Spanish chief with his ill-omened invitation to dinner. You can purchase there from Peruvian maidens of the present day lemonade or soda water, but gone for ever are "the dark-eyed beauties" of the court, who, in the Inca's day, served in this same place, "sparkling chicha from golden vases of extraordinary size", as Francisco Xerez and other eye-witness tell us. The water for these great baths comes from immense springs of hot and cold water which rise almost side by side only sixty yards away. These waters are strongly impregnated with sulphur, and are highly valued by the inhabitants.

I had tarried longer at Cajamarca than I had intended, and it was time to get away on the long trail across the Cordilleras to the Amazon. The description of the journey would almost need a volume for itself, but a very brief summary must suffice.

The first day's ride to Huauco in the valley of Celendín was about forty-eight miles. We were able to do it on horseback. Henceforth, we must use the faithful mule, for horses would perish in such a trip as we were now commencing. Our way lay along breezy uplands and great open spaces, past shepherds and shepherdesses pasturing their flocks in the lonely places – irresistibly reminding one of biblical descriptions of pastoral life. My faithful companion for the first week was to be Sr. Alejandro Huaman, an ex-cavalryman – as genial a representative of his country as one could find. We set out laden with provisions sufficient to carry us on for seven days until we could replenish our store for the next stage at Chachapoyas. An important element of food on such a journey is dried meat – and we were well supplied. On this first day we had experience of how easily our horses could fall on the slippery hillside after rain. We had contracted mules to be ready at Huauco. On arriving there we found they were still roaming on the hillside miles away. This meant delay next morning, and alas! even when they were brought, they were found to be badly shod. The muleteer, however, assured us he would get this rectified at Celendín. Thus we had, perforce, to spend the night there – only a few miles from our starting-point. We found, when too late, that the muleteer was a deceiver, and that he got his mules only partly shod. This was to cause much inconvenience.

Early next morning we were in the saddle. We started out from an elevation of well over 8,000 feet in this delightful valley. In about three hours we attained the summit of the ridge and sat down to lunch. The sight in front of us then must be one of the grandest on the earth's surface. There, right beneath us, was the immense gorge of the Marañón, a tributary of the Amazon. This river, even here, is as big as any in the British Isles, and yet it appeared no more than a thread almost straight beneath us, so tremendously deep was this canyon.

On the other side of the valley rose ridge after ridge of the mightiest mountains one could imagine. I was astounded when Don Alejandro told me that our way lay, precisely, over those mountains. He pointed out a path which could be discerned here and there in the far distance running along the very summit of a narrow ridge where it seemed as if the traveller might topple into the abyss by a wrong step to the one side or the other. At first I thought my friend was joking when he told me we had to pass that way. Had I not known for a fact that men and women have been crossing these mountains for generations, I would have said it would be utterly impossible for anyone to do it. "Tomorrow evening", he said, "we shall sleep at the tambo just beyond where you see the path on that distant height".

It was long past dusk when we arrived at the Hacienda Chuqumayo on the banks of the Marañón. We had descended from the biting cold of the high Andes into this malaria-infested gorge of sweltering heat. Our path had been so steep and rocky that in many places it seemed to be inviting disaster to ride. It looked, often, as if some mighty giant of mythology had scattered the towering crags and immense boulders on every side in sheer caprice. On some of the shoulders of these rocky heights we saw considerable numbers of deer – apparently enjoying perfect peace with the calm assurance that even the most foolhardy huntsman could not approach them.

There were many travellers, men and women, encamped in the farm yard of Chuqumayo. The blazing fires in the open air made a cheerful sight in the dark; and man and beast were glad of the sight of food. The mules were the most demonstrative, whinnying continuously as we came to our camping-ground. Good cheer prevailed around these camp fires, but all were tired, and soon most of the travellers sought sleeping-places in the shelter of a wall or boulder, with the sky for a roof. I remember, especially, an army captain from Chachapoyas who looked the very picture of content while he lay in the open air with his saddle under his head. Long before dawn cooking operations had begun and my friend Don Alejandro proved his capacity. Soon we were across the river and were facing the great ascent towards Huilka – sometimes able to advance only along the bottom of a stream, sometimes climbing zig-zag up the steep mountainside. In certain places the path consisted of steps cut out of the rock, rising up like stairs on the hillside; and, not infrequently, the gigantic cliff shut out the light of the sun. Up we toiled for some hours, and then on that lofty height occured an incident which I shall not easily forget. One of the cargo-bearing mules had gone on in advance along the path. It had lain down to rest. When rising again it came too near the edge of the precipice and went crashing down, bounding from rock to rock, and was dead long before it reached the bottom of the ravine about 1,000 feet below. The necessity of retrieving the valuable cargo delayed us, and that night we had to sleep at Huilka, far up the face of the mountain. When our muleteer lost his animal he exclaimed almost in tears: "There's 145 Soles gone!". Up on the mountain he met an acquaintance who comforted him with the words: "Well, if he is dead, he is dead. We must all die". This fatalistic philosophy had an astonishingly soothing effect on our arriero and not one word of complaint escaped his lips thereafter.

Early in the morning we were again on our way, hoping to make up for lost time. The path moved up in zig-zags, and as we got ever higher the view became more and more impressive – the endless series of peaks and the glimpses of immense valleys producing an indescribable feeling. Travelling along the very edge of the abyss, I found it decidedly disconcerting to notice how my mule always got as near as possible to the verge of the precipice, no matter what I could do. This is an outstanding characteristic of these animals. It was explained to me that most of them had been used as pack animals. They had learned that if they kept to the inside of the narrow path, their load scraped against the rocks, which was disagreeable. Hence they keep as near as the outside as they can. I must say, however, I found it decidedly uncomfortable to be balanced in this way over the very edge of chasms sometimes more that 1,000 feet in depth.

It now began to rain – such a rain as I have never seen. The wind, too, arose, and a gale on an exposed peak in the Andes is certainly not a matter to be trifled with. I had on an overcoat, and above it a woolen poncho; and over all that a first-rate rubber poncho. In spite of this, the rain passed through it all as if it had been a cotton sheet. On we went, however, for hours, but no sooner did we manage to wind round one elevation than we always saw another awaiting us. It seemed interminable. At Tambo Viejo we found two men looking with scared faces at the lowering mountains and afraid to proceed. Up above us the wind made a most peculiar, eerie sound, swirling round the conical peaks. We resolved to face the pass of Callo-Callo, and when the two men at the tambo (a shelter with a roof but no walls) saw that we were proceeding, they resolved to follow suit. As we reached the summit, the cold and rain became almost unbearable. The gale was so strong that we could hardly force our mules to face it. Again and again they tried to turn back. They had good reason. There, by the wayside, were innumerable skeletons of their kind – faithful beasts which after many a journey across these terrific mountains had become weakened and could not stand the exposure of this cold region, and perished. Down we went on the other side – along a path which was rocky in parts, muddy in others; and, in some places, took the form of stone steps down the hillsides. At last we came to the extensive green meadows of Yulli – which reminded me more of English meadows than anything I had hitherto seen in Peru. We had travelled thirty six miles from the Marañón river. In good weather we would have enjoyed the journey, but we could not feel much enthusiasm on arrival at Yulli, for our clothes were all drenched – even those we had in our bags. We were taken in by a kindly old Indian couple. There was no bed, and we had to lie on the floor for rest. I had a fevered sleep and during the night became unwell on account of the cold and the wet. In the morning, however, we pushed on to Leimebamba, which was about twelve miles away. I was cheered by the knowledge that there was a hotel there – the Royal Hotel. I had visions of a hot bath, hot drinks, and some comfort for a sick man. My expectations were doomed to sore disappointment. The place was hopelessly untidy. The owner could give us a room, but nothing more – not even a bed. I had to depend on my travelling companion, Don Alexandro, for every kind of attention – and the people of the village would sell nothing. They bore a grudge to travellers – for they seem to have suffered at their hands in past times.

In the late afternoon, the muleteer came in to say he must return home – his beasts could go no further, he said, for they had no shoes. The fault for this was entirely his, but I gave him a pound and asked him to have them shod right away. He blessed me fervently and assured us we would now get on rapidly. He said we would start at 6.30 a.m. We were ready before then, but he did not turn up till 8 – and when he did come, he was obviously under the influence of drink. He had spent my money on liquor. Soon afterwards Don Alejandro found him stealing out of the village with the mules. It was only with difficulty he saved him from taking a saddle we had got for the journey.

Here, then, we were, stranded in this inhospitable place. To find fresh mules was a real problem, and we were held up for twenty-four hours until Don Julio Jauregui, a farmer some miles away, came to our help.

The weather now became delightful and the thirty nine miles to Chachapoyas were covered without any incident. This town stands in a wide, open valley, at the relatively low level of some 7,500 feet. It is the capital of the department of Amazonas and has a population of only about 4,000. It had suffered a great deal from a recent earthquake, and the inhabitants had much to say of their experiences. I had a feeling that their stories lost nothing in the telling. It was good to find ourselves in the comfortable and hospitable home of Don Pedro Quiroz. It was luxury to sleep in a bed once more, especially as I knew I would not see one again for six or seven days.

I have found in Peru a decided love for the mystic and the mysterious. Don Pedro told us of a remarkable incident which had occurred at a distance of some three days journey from Chachapoyas only a few years previously. A man and his daughter coming from Guayabamba stopped at a certain point after dark to camp for the night. He descended a few yards below the path when suddenly his daughter heard agonising shrieks, and soon these were repeated, now at a distance. Next day her father was found by a search party six miles away. There lay between a jungle so thick that they could only get through it by cutting paths with machetes at certain points. They declared that it was impossible that he should have been carried there even by a body of men. He bore no marks except where he had been strangled, and a few pricks from thorns on his face. What had happened to him? I cannot find an explanation. Don Pedro, however, and most of the community did not hesitate to attribute the tragedy to the work of malignant spirits.

At Chachapoyas I bade good-bye to my excellent friend Don Alexandro Huaman. He had been my companion for over 160 miles. I was now to be accompanied, for almost as great a distance, to Moyobamba, by Don Hilario Vasquez. We came to Daguas, a delightful place with its green hills, and thatched houses scattered here and there across the landscape. A gentleman from Habana, near Moyobamba, asked if he might ride with us. He was Sr. Lopez Lozano, an amiable gentleman whose knowledge of local conditions was valuable. On this particular day I found that my new mule had a habit of taking long leaps, and this was somewhat disconcerting. Descending these steep hills, it was nothing to come to a break in the path where the mule had to leap down about three feet, from one level to another. The effect was the shaking of one's bones which, at the end of the day, left me completely exhausted. Night after night I laid me down with a feeling of almost helpless weariness. One evening we came to a bridge over a small river near Ventilla. It was an uninhabited place; but on this evening, no less than forty slept there, some on the bridge and some under it. We lit our camp-fires and cooked our supper, chatting sociably for a time. The simple life made us all feel a sense of human kinship.

The next day was a memorable one. Leaving the green pastures, we climbed into the wild rocky country above Tambo Noriega. The path was very steep and for a long distance consisted of veritable stairs cut into the rocky face of the mountain. Our poor bestias – our beasts – got quite puffed out and took a long time to ascend. So steep was the climb that in many places we had to hang on to the mane of our mules to keep on our saddles. We were now crossing the far-famed cordillera of Pischcu-huanuna, "the place where the birds die". This Quechua description is true to fact. There is neither bird nor animal of any kind to be seen for several leagues. Yet the pastures were wonderfully good and would easily support great flocks; but in spite of this, every living creature seemed to have forsaken these elevations. The only explanation I can think of is the sudden changes of temperature which occur here, and which are destructive to life. It is a common experience for travellers to die on Pischcu-huanuna, especially those who leave the hot forest region with insufficient clothing to face the terrible cold of the heights. Several mounds were pointed out to me where the dead had been left by their friends. When one of those terrible storms breaks out, and a traveller weakened with fatigue and soroche (mountain sickness) dies, it is considered dangerous for his friends to wait to bury him. To avoid the same fate, they must hurry down to the lower altitude without delay. Hence they cover the body with stones and pass on. It seems callous, but what can they do? In that high region there was a lake to the right. I was warned to keep dead silence for, if not, the demons of the storm might sally forth from its cold waters! I spoke, and lo!, the thunder began at once to roll along the heavens. I suppose it nearly always does so at this spot.

Nothing could be more absolutely lonely than the path across this elevated plateau, which became a sort of rolling country although it must have been about 14,000 feet in height. We overtook a small group of men carrying three lepers, each of whom sat in a sort of chair – half box, half chair – strapped on the back of a carrier. This is a common method of crossing the mountains, and there are certain Indian communities which have earned their livelihood, for generations, as burden carriers. These poor lepers had already been carried for nearly a fortnight, and they had still to go 186 miles to reach the Huallaga river, where they would descend on a raft to Yurimaguas, finally, to reach the Leper Settlement below Iquitos, hundreds of miles away. Truly, the one half of the world does not know how the other half lives.

That night our royal residence was the large cave at Bagasan. Some fifteen persons slept there, and I must say that being a cave-dweller was to me not at all unpleasant, even if Bagasan has the reputation of being frightfully cold.

We now entered the forest which I was to have constantly before my eyes for well nigh 3,000 miles. The farther in we penetrated, the thicker it became, and the more gigantic the trees. Not seldom we found our path barred by some enormous trunk which had fallen across it. On such occasions the only remedy was to circumvent the obstacle by cutting a new passage through the jungle with our machetes. In not a few places the traveller runs the risk of being strangled by the tough trailing plants and stems which hang across his path from tree to tree. One morning, when riding along at a good pace, I suddenly found my neck in one of these natural halters. It needed herculean efforts to make my mule stop, for it was not accustomed at any time to rendering swift obedience, and if it did not stop, disaster was almost certain. For a few moments it appeared as if I were to come to the same miserable and untimely end of Absalom, in the wood of Ephraim.

One fine, fresh morning we arrived at the Ventana, the remarkable descent which travellers have to negotiate on their way to the Moyobamba area. There was joy in the air. Thousands of birds sang in the sunshine and my companions also broke into song. I found, to my surprise, that these natives of the woods could whistle a tune as melodiously as the birds themselves. As far as I can remember, the descent of the Ventana took the better part of two hours. It was at once obvious that we could not ride down this mountain. Enormous rocks and boulders were scattered about on every side. The trail wound in and out among these, and across terrible declivities. We drove our mules in front of us, and down they went making a terrific clatter over the rocky path, while the natives kept ever after them with hoop and halloo to make them face the abrupt descents where it seemed a miracle they did not break their legs. We found it hard enough to clamber down on foot. I could not imagine anyone riding down the Ventana; and yet I was told that a placid and unobtrusive English missionary nurse did it on her first journey to Moyobamba, quite unconscious that she was doing anything heroic. At the bottom of the Ventana we were on the level, with the mighty forest all around, with clearings at intervals, where some small homesteads peeped out from among the trees. We spent the night at Rioja, a town of a few thousand inhabitants, with a hospitable people who carry on an active industry in the manufacture of Panama hats, the materials for which are abundant in the locality. This industry is a common one throughout the department. Some of these hats are remarkably fine and the best varieties need some three weeks of hard work to make.

A ride of twenty-four miles more across flat, wooded country brought us to Moyobamba. The most interesting feature was the crossing of the rivers on the way. In each case we were ferried across by a boatman, while our mules had to swim across.

Over four weeks had passed since I left Lima. I was now both weary and grimy after that long journey through the wilds, and it was with no ordinary feeling of content that I rode, accompanied by a regular cavalcade, into the patio adjoining the house of Dr. Kenneth Mackay, where a real Scottish welcome awaited me right in the interior of South America.

This town has about 7,000 people and is the capital of the beautiful and fertile department of San Martin with its population of 75,000 – less than one human soul to the square kilometre. To me, Moyobamba was highly attractive with its wooded hills in the distance, and the morro – a massive rock – rising in solitary majesty from the centre of the plain.

Nature is prodigal in this locality and every kind of tropical fruit can be grown with ease. A hostess there may place a salad on the table containing over a dozen different kinds of delicious fruits – not for love of display but because there is nothing else so easily obtained. The coffee, oranges, and grapes of Moyobamba are specially delightful. There is no garden of Eden, however, without its serpent, and this lovely region has its own ills – chiefly in the form of tropical ailments. Dr. Kenneth Mackay, of the Scottish Mission, was by far the most popular man in the province, and well he might be, for he was the only doctor within a week's journey. Each year he had about 14,000 consultations, and with very few facilities performed many major operations (with the help of two nurses) which would have been worthy of a city hospital. In one district he had completely cured thousands of persons from a loathsome skin disease, the Yaws, akin to leprosy, and so saved them from life-long misery.

The people of Moyobamba are particularly attractive. The Spaniards arrived here in 1539, seven years after coming to Cajamarca. The fact that they should have penetrated so far, in spite of all their preoccupations, shows their remarkable spirit. The leading families of today are their descendants. Here, in this isolated field, they have preserved the gracious manner and the human kindness which were characteristic of quieter ages than our own. Some of the leading professional men in the country are natives of this department. The people, as a whole, are clean and intelligent. Even some of the poorer folks, who use neither shoes nor stockings, have a native grace and charm of manner which many a West End society lady might envy.

On 5th February I set out again for the Amazon, accompanied by the genial Don Eduardo Cifuentes as guide and friend. Our route was to lead us through Pintu Yaco, Roque, Tabalosos, Lamas, Tarapoto and Shapaja. It took us four and a half days to arrive at the last-named place, on the River Huallaga.

We arrived at Roque – a large village with thatched houses – after a miserable day of torrential rain. We were soaked to the skin; the mules had kept falling on the slippery path, or sinking into the marshes, and we were truly glad to reach an abode for the night. We put up at the house of a man who, not long before, had been chief of the gendarmerie at the capital of one of the departments. He had been unpopular, and when the revolution occurred in August, 1930, he was attacked by a mob which took his possessions. He had to flee in dire poverty, and he and his wife were now living here. They treated us very kindly and it was a pleasure to be with them. He was a man with a fine face and military bearing, and as I conversed with him I could not help marvelling at the strange chances which make some men popular and others unpopular. He secured from a neighbour a large ox skin on which I slept comfortably, on the floor, all night.

In the darkness I listened for some time to what I thought was the sound of heavy rain. I was amazed to find in the morning that it had been, in reality, a horde of red ants – a particularly fierce variety – devouring a rubber overcoat in a corner of the room. This led to a talk on the fauna of the locality, and I was interested to hear of a jaguar which in six months had killed no less than 200 pigs before it was finally shot. The region abounds in jaguars and black bears. The previous day we had seen a splendid specimen of the wild pig which a peasant had just shot. It was dark in colour, with bristly hair – and was smaller than the domestic variety.

Time was pressing, and the steamer for England left Iquitos on an early date. We had thus to push on with all speed – on one occasion travelling all night. We found that here, as elsewhere, nature had her charms by night as well as by day, but the natives strongly dissuade one from journeying in the dark, for fear of serpents and wild beasts which prowl in the forest.

I remember coming to the large village community of Tabalosos before dawn. The moon was in her last phase and giving a gentle light. The scene was beautiful and tranquil as we passed the small clearing in the forest. A few fire-flies were fluttering about here and there and, now and again, we heard the notes of a night bird. We had reached the village when scarcely anyone was astir, for it was barely 5 a.m., but a man marched from house to house loudly beating a drum to summon the people to some joint public task. Whatever those folk may be, they are certainly early risers. Soon after leaving the community we saw a ruddy glow in the east signalling dawn. Then, all together, at the same instant, as if in obedience to a command, the countless thousands of birds and chicharras (a kind of cricket) in the woods struck up a veritable chorus of welcome to the sun. I have seldom seen anything more remarkable, and it seemed, for all the world, like a mighty Hymn of Praise to the Creator.

Crossing a very turbulent river by canoe, managed with an expertness worthy of all praise, whilst the mules were nearly exhausted swimming the fierce current, we proceeded up hill and down dale through the forest till we came to Lamas, a remarkable Indian community of 12,000 people – of a different race from those in the high Andes – where Sisters Soper and Gould, far away from their well-loved England, were sacrificing themselves in their humanitarian and spiritual work for that simple people.

At Shapaja, on the river Huallaga, we had to wait for a raft to carry us down to Yurimaguas. Launches cannot ply on this part of the river because of rapids, and so passengers have to journey downstream on rafts for, roughly, 160 miles. After two days we succeeded in securing a passage from a farmer who had come downstream with a cargo of cotton. He had two rafts, each about fourteen feet by ten, made from the light wood of the topa tree. In the centre was a raised platform, to make things easier for us should the raft sink under the water at the rapids. The worst of these were directly below Shapaja, where the river had cut a path through the mountain. The bogas (the nearly-naked natives who managed the raft) were strapped to their posts to avoid their being carried away by the turbulent waters when the whole concern temporarily disappears in the flood, on descending the cataract. They insist on being fortified for this trying experience by a good draught of aguardiente every time they make the voyage. Much depends on the height of the water in the river. Sometimes the raft can scarcely be saved from being dashed to destruction on the rocks and, at other times, it may be detained, revolving for an entire day in a whirlpool. We were peculiarly fortunate when we passed, and got through that terrific gorge without a hitch. After that, we floated down in peaceful water with a brilliant sun overhead, and the illimitable woods on either side.

The owner of the raft was a cheerful, good-natured agriculturalist of about fifty-five years of age – with side-whiskers turned grey. He had with him two daughters aged about seventeen and eighteen, whom he treated with devoted care and affection. He was taking them to an institution at Yurimaguas to be trained in domestic economy. In the course of our leisurely journey down the noble river he became friendly, and asked me how I would feel if I had to rear a family of eighteen, "in these hard times". I said it certainly seemed a big handful. Some days later, on the launch from Yurimaguas to Iquitos, he told me he had proposed to a very young lady at the former place. I was surprised and said with sympathy: "Oh! You're widower then". He replied, almost indignantly: "A widower! No! I'm a bachelor". My astonishment knew no bounds. To this really kind-hearted man, it never seems to have occurred, for a moment, that there was anything improper in rearing a family outside the bonds of matrimony. There are not many like him in English-speaking lands, but let the Anglo-Saxon be careful how he casts stones, in these days, when there is so much to blush for in the matter of sound morality, in other places as well as in Latin America.

We had got well away from the mountains and were floating quietly downstream at about four miles an hour. In a few days I would travel by launch and then by steamer down the river, but this flat, wooded country would continue, almost without variation, to the mouth of the Amazon, over 2,400 miles from where I then was. It was now the 12th of February and, travelling in the fastest possible way, I could not reach London until 8th April. Before me lay that wonderful journey along the greatest inland waterway on earth, almost under the Equator and, after that, the Atlantic Ocean and … Home! It was good to think of the homeland, and yet back yonder in the far distance was the mighty wall of the Andes fading away under the sunset sky.

The call of blood and kindred was strong, and I longed to see again the cliffs of Albion, but voices from the mighty Cordilleras, where I had journeyed so many days, were already calling me back.

– *Extracted from: Dr. A. M. Renwick, Wanderings in the Peruvian Andes.*

The Rev. John Calvin Mackay, Kingussie.

Highland Wedding, Cajamarca, Peru, 1927. Front row, from left: Christina Mackay, Easter Tore; Annabella MacLeod, Lewis; Margaret Fraser, Achiltibuie; Dr. Kenneth Mackay, Alness; behind him, the Rev. John Calvin Mackay, Kingussie; and seated, far right, almost certainly Calvin's wife Rachel.

From top-left, clockwise: Rev. James Turnbull, Rev. Murdo Nicolson, uncertain; Mrs. Turnbull; Annabella MacLeod.

National Assembly, Iglesia Evangélica Presbiteriana del Perú,
Lima Seminary, 1977.

Back row. *Unidentified; Luis Torrejón, ex-Moyobamba; Kees Lam, Holland;*
Heraclito Aguilar, Suyubamba; Andy Fraser (just visible at the back), Sierra;
James Macintosh, Lima; Santiago Castañeda, Tambería; Willie Mackay,
Lima; Heráclito Guerrera, Moyobamba; Señor Lamas, Lima; Manuel Moraes,
Moyobamba; Pedro Arama, Lima.

Front row. *John MacPherson, Lima. Gerrit Plaisier, Holland; Pedro Merino,*
ex-Cajamarca area; Archie Boyd, the Mound; Juan Silva, ex-Cajamarca;
Nicolás Lopez, Cajamarca; Aquiles Más, Rioja; (in the back),
Teofilo Chikibala, Suyubamba; Alexandro Montenegro, Rioja;
Hermogenes Correa, Celendín.

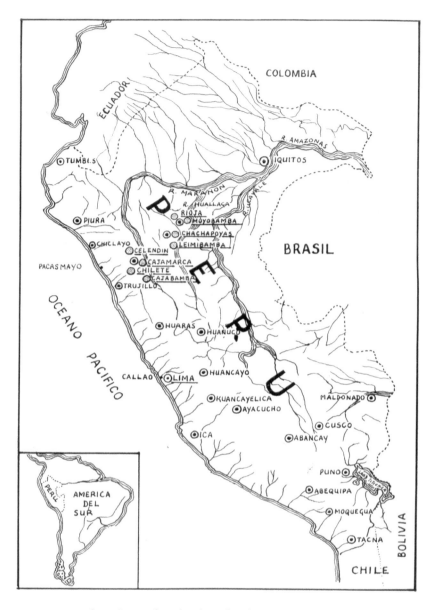

Map from "Free Church Of Scotland Missionary Enterprise: South Africa, India, Peru, 1900-1949". Mission stations underlined.

Missionary Enterprise: a mid-century appraisal

HAVING ESTABLISHED A MISSIONARY BRIDGEHEAD ON THE COASTLINE of Peru in the Colegio Anglo-Peruano [later Colegio San Andrés] at Lima, it was not long until the Free Church began to push the frontier of her spiritual influence towards the interior. After all, her aim in entering the country was not education, however desirable as a handmaid of the Gospel, but evangelisation, and upon this she definitely embarked in 1921.

The pioneer of this advance was the Rev. John Calvin Mackay, a son of the Kingussie manse who, after a brief ministry at Nairn, realised his life ambition when, in the summer of 1919 he, with Mrs. Mackay and their infant daughter, set sail for the land of the ancient Inca. A preparatory period was spent in Lima acquiring proficiency in the language, assisting in the rapidly developing school, and proclaiming the evangel as opportunity offered. After some two years gaining experience of the country and its ways, the time seemed opportune for launching out.

In May 1921, Mr. Mackay made what might be termed a reconnaissance visit to Cajamarca, the mountain capital of northern Peru, as a likely centre for evangelical witness in the interior. On the journey he struck-up a companionship with an entire stranger who turned out to be an American educationist on his way to open an office in Cajamarca. At first somewhat reserved, it was not long until the American discovered that his travelling companion was indeed el caballero protestante – the Protestant gentleman – as he afterwards came to be known in the northern uplands of Peru. The result was a lasting friendship, which proved of practical value in later years.

Arriving in Cajamarca, Mr. Mackay lost no time in making contact with friends and likely sympathisers to whom he had letters of introduction. A visit was made to the nearby village of Jesús (pronounced Khay-soos, with emphasis on the last syllable) where lived Don Alejandro Llanos, a colporteur who afterwards became a devoted servant of the Mission. After securing accommodation in an upstairs flat on the main street of Cajamarca, Mr. Mackay returned to Lima, sold off, and with Mrs. Mackay and their two children hit the trail for the interior.

Cajamarca, the key to the evangelisation of northern Peru, lies on the main highway from the coast to the Montaña or forest region of the interior. On this highway, which lies entirely within the territory allocated to the Free Church by mutual agreement amongst the main missionary agencies at work in the country, are situated such towns of importance as Celendín, Chachapoyas and Moyobamba, on the direct route, with Cajabamba somewhat off the beaten track to the south.

To reach Cajamarca one has to cross the lofty ranges of the Western Cordillera, where the road rises to a height of 12,000 feet above sea-level. Nowadays the journey may be made from Lima in comparative comfort by bus, or more speedily by plane; but in the days when the Sierra Mission of the Free Church was started, no such facilities were available. Then it was a wearisome adventure by boat from Callao (the port of Lima) to Pacasmayo in the north, thence by train to Chilete at the foot of the Andes, with the last lap somewhat dangerously on horse or mule-back along the perilous paths which climb the shaggy steeps, descend the dark ravines, and skirt the dizzy precipices which characterise the western range of the Andes.

A town of some 12,000 inhabitants, Cajamarca nestles beautifully in a green valley about four miles broad by twelve long, watered by two rivers. In this favoured valley, on farms of varying size, grow all the crops of the temperate zone; the main industry being farming, agricultural and pastoral, with the concomitants of tanning and leather-work.

The town itself is both ancient and historic. A seat of the ancient Inca, it was here that the fatal blow was struck at the Inca empire and civilisation by Pizarro, the Spanish conqueror. The house where the ill-fated Atahualpa, the last of the Inca emperors, was kept prisoner, with the room which he filled with gold as ransom for his life, is still an object of interest to the curious traveller. It was to this ancient city and strategic centre that the Rev. J. Calvin Mackay took the evangelical witness in July, 1921.

The opening chapter of our mission in the Sierra is as romantic as any chapter of pioneer missionary enterprise; but a full account of those early days can come only from the missionaries who were there. Here, only a token is offered.

The upstairs flat rented on the main street of Cajamarca, consisted of two or three bedrooms, a dining room, and a large sitting room where friends were invited for worship on the Lord's Day. Thus in Cajamarca, as in the early days of Christianity, the Church began, "in the house". One of the apartments was set-out as a reading-room, where Bibles and good literature were available. This reading-room was freely patronised by the young people from the local Colegio, and from this there gradually grew Bible-study groups. To begin with, little more could be done than win the confidence of the people and make known the purpose of the missionaries' coming. It was the waiting time – by no means the easiest period in missionary experience. Meanwhile, a Christian home was being set up in the community, an evangelical witness was being lit, and little by little, in shops and by the wayside, contacts were being made whilst, in the neighbouring village of Jesús, the humble cottage of Senor Llanos provided a welcome opening for Gospel meetings.

In December of the same year (1921) the limelight was focused on the Mission when Mr. David C. Brackenridge of the British and Foreign Bible Society, together with Señor Pedro Ayabacha, an ex-soldier and experienced colporteur, visited Cajamarca. They set up their stall in the market-place and there displayed their wares for sale. The Scripture portions were rapidly disposed of, as were also the other portions. Before the Society's representatives had completed their stay the Mission had a visit from the Superintendent at Lima, Dr. John A. Mackay. On the recommendation of a friend of his, a professor at Lima university, now visiting his native Cajamarca, the local theatre was engaged for a public meeting. The meeting was duly held and widely advertised. A local newspaper had the temerity to publish an account of the proceedings including a report of Dr. Mackay's address, or rather what the editor – a rabid anti-clerical – thought Dr. Mackay should have said! This gave publicity to the Mission and threw the glove right at the priests' feet. The challenge was not ignored.

When the visiting evangelicals left the town the Rev. Calvin Mackay and his little daughter had occasion to accompany them, thus leaving behind Mrs. Mackay and their infant son. Returning one evening from a visit to a friendly "Cajamarquina", Mrs. Mackay had slipped into her hand a note containing a warning that an attack was determined on the mission-house that very night. The report having been confirmed, contact was quickly made, through the home just visited, with civic and other authorities. Several of these were known to be friendly, thanks very largely to the good offices of the American educationist already referred to. The husband of the lady above referred to was local fiscal (later fiscal of the nation, a post comparable to the English Attorney-General) and largely through his influence a civic order was issued forbidding more than two people to congregate in the streets, while two soldiers were posted at the entrance to the Mission premises, a precaution continued for some time. The church bells, which were to have given the signal for the attack, were never rung: the project of the priests had been thwarted.

Alarmed and riled by this official frustration of their malign purpose, the priests embarked upon another scheme. Every Sunday, leaflets were distributed among their flock containing instructions on how to counteract the poison of the "heretics". But their ill designs God overruled to the advantage of the Mission by making them the occasion for advertising the evangelical cause.

Nothing more violent than an explosion of dynamite underneath the windows of the Mission-house was experienced until January of the following year, when the feast of San Sebastian became due. Such occasions, with their mass processions and religious excitement, always provided an opportunity for the malicious designs of the priests, and on this occasion they determined to take advantage of it. The procession, led by Indian musicians, and carrying the inevitable image, stopped in front of the Mission premises, when the image was made to face the balcony. Then a semi-illiterate member of the procession climbed onto the balcony of the house opposite and proceeded to stumble through a document inciting the crowd to attack the Protestants. Before he had finished, the interested spectators in the Mission-house were fascinated to see a smartly-dressed young man mount the balcony, displace the loud-mouthed speaker, and himself begin to address the crowd. He directed his appeal to the young men in the procession and, reminding all that the Constitution of Peru guaranteed freedom of worship, like the town-clerk of Ephesus he warned the assembly of the possible consequences of that day's proceeding. Adroitly appealing to the amour propre of the citizens, paying tribute to the culture of the town and reminding them that the strangers in their midst belonged to a great nation, he completely won over the better element of the crowd.

The apprehensions of the missionaries and their friends that another attempt would be made about Easter were only too well founded. On this occasion the procession approached from the opposite direction, but with the same destination in view and with the same wicked design in mind. Like others in similar cases, the defenceless missionaries resorted in prayer to their Heavenly Father. Then, as the excited procession drew near, Mr. Mackay posted himself behind the street door so that, in the event of a break-in, the ladies might escape unmolested. But prayer was heard and fears were falsified. For some reason, unknown and quite mysterious at the time, the procession did not halt before the Mission-house. Not until two years later did the missionaries receive the explanation of the mystery. The human instrument of deliverance was again the young lawyer who had provided such an effective master of assemblies on San Sebastian's Day. This time his mother and sister were determined he should not intervene in favour of the Protestants, and were prepared to restrain him, by force if necessary. Feigning weariness and disinterest, he lay languidly in a chair, while his friends watched the procession. He contrived, however, to keep himself informed of its progress. When he had ascertained that it was now near to the Mission-house he suddenly leapt to his feet, darted into the street, and taking up a position alongside the "mayordomo" or manager, tactfully escorted the procession past the Mission premises. On being asked by the suspicious mayordomo what had brought him out he ironically replied, "Oh, I am feeling very religious today". When he had reckoned that the procession had reached a safe distance beyond the Mission-house he suddenly took leave of the marching throng, saying, "I've paid my respects now, I think I'll get back home". By Divine intervention and human instrumentality another anxious situation had been surmounted. But the battle for the expulsion of the "heretics" was not yet over, as the following episode shows.

On returning home one day Mr. Mackay remarked to his wife, "I am tired raising my hat to people on the street this morning; everyone is greeting me with lifted hat and 'Good day, Mr. Mackay'." The explanation came later. It was the friendly-disposed reaction of the enraged citizens to another attempt by the priests to ostracise and boycott the Protestants and thus drive them from the town. The priests had printed and circulated a leaflet entitled, "Neither Bread, Water nor Greetings", amounting virtually to an expulsion order. But this crude and callous attack on the Protestant missionaries not only miserably failed to achieve its purpose, but aroused such resentment in many of the citizens as to elicit this outward demonstration of sympathy and goodwill. The Mission had weathered the initial storm; the missionaries had come to stay, and not without a measure of goodwill on the part of the more enlightened members of the community.

As the fierce blasts of winter cause the tree roots to take firmer grip of the earth, so the storm of persecution served to establish the roots of the Free Church Mission in the respect and goodwill of the people of Cajamarca. The work continued to grow and prosper until it became apparent that a more adequate meeting-place than the homes of the Christian believers was required for Christian worship. Upon the Rev. Calvin Mackay devolved the task of planning and preparing for the erection of a church. The actual building of the church, largely financed by the contributions of the young people of the Free Church (through the "Penny Brick Fund" opened in the pages of their monthly magazine, The Instructor) became the responsibility of another master hand.

The Rev. James Turnbull, a graduate of Glasgow University and a qualified teacher, who took the Divinity Course of the Baptist Church, responded to the appeal of the Free Church Foreign Missions' Committee for a teacher to take charge of the Mission School at Cajamarca. Under the practical supervision of Mr. Turnbull the plans for a new church initiated by Mr. Mackay gradually took concrete shape and were eventually completed and attractively materialised. The church was opened for public worship on 11th January 1936, amid profound local interest. Guests included Dr. Renwick, the Superintendent of the Peruvian Mission, Dr. and Mrs. Money, Señor Aldama, and Nurse Annabella Macleod (now Mrs. MacRae). Local personalities present included the Mayor, the sub-Prefect, and Judges, together with several of the leading professional and business men of the town. The congregation of over six hundred included Indians from the mountain villages in their native ponchos. The inaugural service had a good press and impartial observers were not slow to pay their tribute. By faith and fidelity, by practical love and Christian witness, the missionaries had won the day and the evangelical mission had come to stay.

For about a year before leaving the field – which he had to do for family reasons – Mr. Turnbull had the able assistance of the Rev. Murdo Nicolson, a young Free Church minister of promise who had offered for service on the foreign field. During this year of partnership, determined effort was made to evangelise the numerous villages around Cajamarca, such as Asunción, Jesús, Laymina, Hualqui, San Marcos, and Ichochan. On Mr. Turnbull's departure, Mr. Nicolson, now saddled with full responsibility, threw himself with evangelising zeal and youthful ardour into the work of extending the Kingdom of Christ in the mountain region of Peru. The method followed was to begin with a general visitation of the village announcing the preacher's arrival and the time of the service in the evening. At the time announced, or thereabout, the congregation drifts in one by one, some boldly, the majority with diffidence. The singing proves an attraction and serves to publish the fact that a Gospel service is being held. In this way, the seed of the Kingdom is sown from village to village, watered by prayer, and the results left with God. It is only thus that the cords can be lengthened and the evangelisation of the Sierra effected.

When Mr. Nicolson found it necessary to relinquish the work in the hill country of Peru, a worthy successor was provided in the Rev. Malcolm R. MacRae. In some respects of different stamp from his predecessor, Mr. MacRae is not a whit behind in evangelical zeal. In the absence of much-needed help from home, but with the assistance of Peruvian evangelists and the aid of an American jeep, recently acquired and remodelled very largely by his own hands, he has set himself the task of continuing and developing the village work of his predecessors. A virile and as far as possible a self-supporting Christian congregation in every village of the territory is his bold ideal, and towards its realisation he had laboured with ceaseless and self-sacrificing endeavour. Towards this end land and property suitable for the erection of churches are being acquired wherever possible. But to prosecute this work effectively ministerial help from home is urgently required. There is need for not less than two other ordained missionaries to man this field.

The organisation of the Church has not escaped Mr. MacRae's attention: proposals for this have been laid before the Foreign Missions' Committee. At the moment of writing the time is not ripe for constituting a Presbytery, but a scheme has been devised that will give higher status to the Peruvian pastors, and more responsibility to the Peruvian Church, with a view to the ultimate development of a complete Presbyterian system of Church government.

In the pages of the New Testament, the Apostles frequently acknowledge a debt of gratitude to co-workers in the Lord, many of whom remain unnamed. Similarly, the Free Church missionaries in the Sierra, and the Mission from its inception, owe much to the warm friendship and manifold labours of devoted Peruvian workers, many of whom in this case also must remain nameless. This record would not be complete, however, without a brief reference to one or two of these fellow-labourers for the Master.

Alejandro Llanos, already a believer, had returned to his native village of Jesús when the Free Church Mission entered the Sierra. Contact was early made with him and he was engaged as Mission colporteur. In this capacity he prepared the way for more systematic village work of the missionaries in later years. Llanos was a welcome visitor in many homes and thus the missionaries found a ready welcome in districts where his unobtrusive ministry had preceded him.

When it was found necessary to open a school in Cajamarca, Medardo Diaz, a young man from Celendín, already connected with the congregation, agreed to teach some classes, and conducted services during Mr. Mackay's absence. He married Señora Julia Velasquez, a young believer from his native town who, after taking a course at the Bible Training Institute at Lima, rendered valuable service to the Mission.

Among the eager souls in Celendín who had sent to Cajamarca the interesting telegram which was the means of starting work at Celendín was Daniel Cabrera, a shoemaker, whose anxious questionings, prompted by previous reading of the Scriptures, were satisfactorily answered for him during the early days of the Mission.

Moving to Cajamarca, he identified himself with the Protestant congregation and sent his children to the Mission School.

After definitely casting in his lot with the Protestants he never looked back, but became diligent in spreading the Good News of the Kingdom. As a carpenter he proved a willing and efficient trades-man in the construction of the Cajamarca Church. His son-in-law, Alejandro Huaman, who was in the joint service of the Mission and the British and Foreign Bible Society, and David Cabrero, were the first elders of the church. They took their ordination seriously and delighted to help with the work of the congregation and to accom-pany a pastor or a missionary nurse on their respective itineraries.

These are but a few. There are many others whose sincere friend-ship and earnest endeavours were invaluable to the missionaries, but the limits of space forbid their mention here.

The work of evangelisation employs every legitimate agency for the achievement of its purpose. Chief of these is the Gospel preached in season and out of season for, "faith cometh by hearing, and hearing by the Word of God". To this end regular church services are conducted, cottage meetings are held and individual contacts made; advantage is taken of markets and religious fiestas where people congregate in large numbers; while the printed page touches a wide constituency, seen and unseen, often unreached by the human voice. Other agencies, too, ancillary to the great work of soul-saving, are employed to good effect, among them nursing and education.

To begin with, Mrs. Calvin Mackay, a trained teacher, gave lessons to a number of children, one of whom was Esperanza Rojas, now a teacher on the primary staff of the Lima College. When, in 1924, the Rev. J. Calvin Mackay and Mrs. Mackay went on furlough, Miss Christina Mackay, a member of the Lima staff, took charge of the school in Cajamarca, where she remained for a number of years, doing excellent work with some Peruvian assistance. A public request that the Protestant School should provide secondary education for girls led to the formation of a secondary department under the direction of Mr. Mackay. In the first year, about a dozen girls enrolled, and one of these later passed to Lima, where she took her teaching certificate and returned to Cajamarca to open a girls' school on her own. At the opening ceremony she paid eloquent tribute to the training she had received at the Mission school. The school had many encouraging results, spiritual as well as educational; several of the girls attending having been brought to a personal interest in the Gospel through the instruction received there; one proceeded to the University of Lima, took her teacher's training and is now a valued member on the staff of Colegio San Andrés.

In 1928, Mr. Turnbull, to whom reference has already been made, took charge of the school, where for some time he had the assistance of Miss Norah M. Ridgeway. The elevation of the Sierra, however, proved injurious to Miss Ridgeway's health and she was forced to retire from the Mission. By 1933, circumstances had so altered that a reconsideration of policy became necessary. After mature deliberation it was decided to close the school as the need which had called it into being had been met, and the money and man-power thus released could be utilised in much needed evangelisation of the surrounding area.

This aspect of the Mission's enterprise cannot be too highly evaluated. Of primary importance from the humanitarian viewpoint, and in bringing a Christian witness of love and skill which even the most obtuse and bigoted can understand, the nursing mission has proved a valuable handmaid to the Gospel. In the early days of the Mission, it opened doors which would have been completely closed to any other form of approach and by deeds of loving skill broke down many a prejudice against the evangelicals. Children were sent to the Sabbath School out of gratitude for attention received from the nurses. The need for this indirect approach is not now so pressing, since prejudice has to a large extent been lived down by the work and witness of the missionaries; but the need for the missionary nurse is as great as ever.

The inception of this work in Cajamarca is inseparably connected with the name of Sister Sarah MacDougall, a household name in the area where she initiated the work following a spell as matron of a hospital in Lima. A member of a Highland family with evangelical traditions, a skilled nurse and a capable administrator, possessing a commanding personality and a high sense of duty, Miss MacDougall is the beau-ideal of the pioneer missionary nurse. Her devoted service to the Cajamarca community has won for her civic recognition and a place in the life of the town seldom accorded a foreigner. The success of the work she inaugurated is amply vouched for by the approach made to her by the "Voice of the Andes" Mission to organise a similar work in Ecuador.

In 1927 the nursing mission received a welcome recruit in Nurse Christina Mackay, from the island of Lewis. To her fell the honour of inaugurating the work in Celendín. Nurse Annabella MacLeod, from the same island, gave skilled and devoted service at Moyobamba and Cajamarca, and even after her marriage to the Rev. M. Macrae, her domestic responsibilities have not prevented her relieving the missionary nurse when occasion demands.

The first patient to attend the clinic at Cajamarca was a member of the evangelical congregation. Others came after dark. The sister of a director of one of the schools came by night, and the treatment proving successful, the work was advertised. There is no longer such reticence or secrecy. Bearing its own credentials the nursing work has gone steadily on and developed almost beyond recognition.

While zealously devoting themselves to their professional duties, the nurses never lose sight of their missionary calling. By a word spoken in season, a tract given out, a Bible or Gospel offered, they seek to interest their patients in the soul-cure every sinner needs. Their efforts often seem as bread cast upon the waters. Not all who consult the nurse for bodily health are willing to acknowledge their soul's sickness or submit to the specific for salvation prescribed by a Protestant. One such case brought to the Mission-house refused Bible and literature. No coercion was used. The sick-room, however, was situated next to the dining-room, where family worship was conducted. The patient heard, and left the hospital a converted woman. Ten years later, her husband testified to the blessing received by the whole family through his wife's change of heart.

The "Lady with the Lamp", not only of physical healing but also of spiritual life, is still a necessary adjunct to the work in Cajamarca. But for the effective carrying out of this enterprise, a minimum of three nurses is required, two for the Cajamarca district and one for Celendín.

The Cajamarca Mission celebrates its semi-jubilee in August, 1946; and it was surely a felicitous providence which enabled the Rev. J. Calvin Mackay and Mrs. Mackay, the inaugurators of the work, after a prolonged absence the homeland, Mrs. Mackay for family reasons, and Mr. Mackay invalided by a serious accident sustained on the field, to be present and to join with their colleagues in thanksgiving to God for the, "great things He hath done". An official of Lima university once remarked to Dr. Renwick that it is nothing short of a miracle that there should be an evangelical mission in Cajamarca. If so, then a miracle has happened. A quarter of a century of missionary endeavour in manifold service and varied experience has not been in vain; seals are not wanting to the faith of the Church and the zeal of the missionaries.

The mission in Moyobamba will always be associated with the names of two pioneer nurses, Miss Soper and Miss Gould. In the early 1920s they had a vision of the need of this particular area and set out with the purpose of starting work there. These were the days before the excellent plane service, at present in operation, linked the Capital with the remote areas of the interior of Peru. To reach Moyobamba involved a hazardous journey on mule-back over a range of giant mountains that reach in places a height of over 20,000 feet. But these two brave ladies were not daunted and they set out entirely dependent on God for they received no official support from any missionary society. The extent to which the work had prospered under the manifest blessing of God can be gauged from the number of buildings taken over in 1928 when these two missionaries joined the staff of the Free Church Mission in Peru. The mission then possessed a church building capable of seating 200 people, a living house, a small hospital with two wards of ten beds and two small private wards. The mission also possessed its own small cemetery, rendered necessary because of the opposition of the Roman Catholic priests to the burial of Protestants in their burying ground. The two enterprising missionaries who started this work, Sisters Soper and Gould, remained with our mission in Moyobamba for some years. After a time they felt the call to go deeper into the forest region and founded the present Lamas mission in the Huallaga Valley. The Huallaga (pronounced Wa-yaga) is a tributary of the Amazon and waters a prosperous and populated area. The two missions and their staffs are on very friendly terms and help each other from time to time in a practical way.

Readers will want to know something of the conditions prevailing in our Montaña Mission territory. The position of the Montaña makes it practically self-supporting. The far distance from the coast, and the high altitudes of the Andes, make imports costly and almost prohibitive. Many of the inevitable hardships of life in such a region are compensated for by the prodigality of nature. In this tropical climate grapes, oranges, figs and bananas grow quickly and luxuriantly and these form a large part of the native diet. The town of Moyobamba is the capital of the province of San Martín. Here are centred police and military headquarters and a court of justice to deal with provincial causes. Moyobamba is also becoming a place of growing importance for air traffic with as many as three different companies landing planes at the local air station. The town has a population of about 7,000 inhabitants and is an ideal centre for an evangelising mission.

The story of the Free Church Mission in Moyobamba will be always linked with the names of two doctors, Dr. Kenneth A. Mackay and Dr. Harold C. Lindsay, who ministered there in succession. The doctors were ably supported in all their evangelical and medical efforts by a noble band of devoted nurses. Prominent among those are the names of Miss Marion MacMillan, Nurse Annabella MacLeod (Mrs. N. MacRae), Nurse C. Macdonald, Nurse Rebecca Fraser (now Mrs. Milnes) and Nurse Wilkinson. The flourishing Sabbath School, more than 200 strong, is largely due to the work of Miss Flora Matheson (Mrs. Harold C. Lindsay) who went out as a Bible-woman and did invaluable work in visiting the homes of the people.

When Dr. Mackay took over the Mission in 1928, his influence and opportunities were largely increased by an official appointment as medical officer of health for the whole Moyobamba region. In his official capacity the doctor took over the supervision of the town's hospital as well as responsibility for the mission hospital. In this large province, with a population of 25,000 inhabitants, he was the only medical man within a week's journey and many and exacting were the claims upon his time and energy. The period of his administration saw the development of the mission hospital and the addition of a fine out-patient department; the growth of the congregation and the initiation of evangelistic activities in the neighbouring villages under native pastors. He also encouraged young girls from the congregation to go to him to train as nurses, a policy which greatly assisted the development of the mission work both on the medical and evangelical side. When Dr. Mackay, for family reasons, returned home in 1938 and handed over to his successor Dr. Harold C. Lindsay, he left behind him a name respected and loved as a man, physician and pastor and a work of God well established and developed.

With the advent of Dr. Lindsay there begins the intimate and cordial relation with our friends of the Irish Evangelical Church, a church which has contributed so generously both in man-power and money to our missions in Peru. Dr. Lindsay's first period of service coincided with the war years and was in consequence unduly lengthened. When recently he was home on furlough, he was able to give a detailed account of the work going on in this most interesting part of the field.

To get a more intimate picture of the actual work of the Moyobamba Mission, we may conveniently consider it under three sections.

The importance of a mission hospital in a strategic centre such as Moyobamba cannot be overstated. It is indeed the only efficient surgical unit in this area. Many abdominal operations are undertaken successfully by the mission doctor. During the past twenty years the incidence of appendicitis has risen sharply and it is not uncommon to have to treat as many as fifteen cases in one year. Excellent work has been done in the war against tropical skin diseases, some forms of which, such as yaws, the mission has practically succeeded in stamping out. Malaria and hook-worm are widely prevalent, with disastrous effects on the natives, especially tragic in the case of children. Against all these ills our medical mission continues to wage an unceasing war.

The hospital day begins early at 6 a.m. when the nurse or Bible-woman assembles the staff for morning prayers. At 6.30 a.m. a short service is conducted in the out-patient department before consulting begins. The demand for the doctor is so great that each patient receives, at the start of the day, a ticket with a number which lets him know when to appear for consultation. A room full of patients awaiting their turn, gives the Bible-woman her opportunity. A Bible portion is read and the Bible or a New Testament is offered for sale. Those who do not wish to buy are not allowed to go away empty-handed; they are offered free portions of the Scriptures and tracts. They are supplied through the kindness of the Scripture Gift Mission, to whose helpfulness we record with pleasure our indebtedness. This has been going on for 25 years now, and so there is scarcely a home in Moyobamba where the word of God has not entered. It has been the means of leading many into our ranks and it is interesting to find that many cases have come to light in which the written Word by the Spirit's power has been sufficient to bring conviction and conversion. The out-patients' department also provides an excellent opportunity for the Bible-woman securing effective contacts with the people and a faithful follow-up has added to the congregation and brought children to the Sabbath School.

The best opportunity, however, is provided within the walls of the hospital among the in-patients. An unexpected visit there in the morning will find most of the patients reading God's Word. The time of evening prayers in the wards has a particularly softening effect upon the patients. It touches them to learn that they are mentioned by name at the Throne of Grace and to find that their needs, physical and spiritual, are being committed to the care of the Good Physician of body and soul. So the doctors and nurses commend the Gospel of the Grace of God and not without saving results. Nursing work, particularly maternity work, is carried out in the town and many a door otherwise closed to the Gospel has been opened by reason of the Nurse's visit. It may not be generally recognised that the Hospital is not only self-supporting financially but also aid-giving. The considerable earnings of the doctor and nurses are put into the mission funds and have been used to extend the hospital and to acquire property necessary for the life of the mission.

And so El Hospital Evangélico, as it is known, fulfils a varied and useful function. It touches a wide section of the community. In one year, Dr. Lindsay reports, the hospital served as varied a clientele as "a sister-in-law of the Prefect, a member of the Supreme Court, and an Adventist pastor from Lamas".

Our mission hospital has created for itself a very warm place in the affections of the people of Moyobamba. A lot is still required in the way of new items of equipment and the hospital and its works deserve a large place in our prayers and interests.

The real test of a solid missionary work is the establishment of a strong congregation with a healthy congregational life. In this great aim the mission has not been unsuccessful. In Moyobamba there has now been established a church with a communicant membership of about sixty and a fellowship of adherents numbering about 350. The standard of church membership in full communion is maintained at a Scripturally high level so that, as far as humanly possible, the foundation of the work is soundly laid in accordance with Apostolic precept and practice. Peruvian social usage and local customs are of such a character that great care requires to be exercised in the case of all applicants for admission to full communion.

The growth of the congregation soon rendered the old church building (seating capacity 200) wholly inadequate and a new building was urgently required. This has now happily been secured, with the generous cooperation of the home churches, at a cost of 15,000 soles (roughly £750 in British money). Seated to accommodate 600, the church was formally opened on 31st July, 1941, with great enthusiasm. Representatives from the other Peruvian stations of our mission were present, among them, most appropriately, Miss Soper from Lamas. The presence also of the Prefect of Moyobamba, members of the judiciary, the chief of police, and local army commandant indicates the position accorded to our mission by the community. It was Dr. Lindsay's determination that the congregation itself should contribute to the building of their sanctuary, which they, although poor, did with great goodwill, contributing one tenth of the total cost. The most of the remainder came from the good friends in the North of Ireland, who gave most liberally.

The walls of the new church are composed of mud blocks. This may give the impression that it is shoddy and poorly constructed. That is not the case, for the blocks are so made that when hard they have the durability of concrete. Altogether, it is a solid, compact building with a pleasing appearance, and, occupying a more central position than the old church, it had already attracted increasing numbers to its services.

One of the most encouraging features of the congregational life in Moyobamba is the Sabbath School. There are over 250 on the roll, with a good average attendance. Children come whose parents are not connected with the Mission, but who may have benefited through the nursing and medical work, or have been visited by the Bible-woman. The children are sent out of a sense of gratitude and respect. There in the Sabbath School the ground-work of an intelligent Christian confession is laid. For although many may drift away from the Mission in the "difficult teenage", the instruction given cannot be wholly lost, and when in later life these are arrested by the power of the Gospel, their Christian profession will be more intelligent with a background of Biblical doctrine. The Westminster Shorter Catechism is the doctrinal manual used, and the children find no difficulty in memorising its contents. Indeed, the memory faculty is highly developed in the children of the forest region. The difficulty lies in getting them to understand what they repeat. But is not this the teachers' trouble all over the world?

Credit for the development of the Sabbath School goes to Mrs. Lindsay. Her work of visitation, when, as Miss Flora Matheson, she was Bible-woman in Moyobamba, brought many a new recruit to the Sabbath School. The coming of the children to evangelical teaching involves for them no small persecution at the hands of the R.C. authorities, and they are subject to a "war of nerves" by the nuns in the day school. The nuns, who run the main kindergarten work, "make it a rule of entrance to their institution that the child must not attend the Protestant Sabbath School". But in spite of this the children come and the work prospers.

The success of the work owes a great deal to the native pastors, who have ably supported the missionary from the beginning. While the ultimate aim of our Mission, as of every mission worked on the Apostolic model, is the setting up of an indigenous Church, self-supporting and self-controlling, it will be recognised that too rash development of the indigenous Church system may well lead to the complete subversion of the young Church. A step in the right direction, however, is the training of native pastors. This has been done in Peru through the good offices of the Theological Institute in Lima. Moyobamba, and the neighbouring villages, especially Rioja and Calsada, and the Sierra Mission at Chachapoyas, owe no small debt to the Peruvian evangelists trained in the Institute in Lima. At present there are four pastors attached to our Moyobamba (and Chachapoyas) Mission. These are Señor Manuel Morais, Señor Alejandro Tuesta, Señor Luis Torrejón, and Señor David Landa.

These, all with varying capabilities, form a very fine team of workers, Señor Morais, the senior pastor, is temperamentally of a somewhat impulsive nature, but he preaches, "right valiantly the Gospel of Grace", and exercises an acceptable ministry. Señor Tuesta has been with the Mission since childhood. He is a gifted young man, with a good record in the Institute in Lima. Possessing a Cambridge Diploma in English, he teaches in that subject in the College in Moyobamba. Señor Torrejón was mentioned in the Assembly Reports on one occasion for his stand against Romish superstitions; this took place during his period of conscription in the Peruvian Army. One day, when all were ordered to attend an annual parade to Mass, he refused. He justified his conduct to the priest and commanding officer, but was told he must submit for disciplinary reasons. On being referred to a higher officer, his case was upheld. Señor Landa, the last recruit, was a carpenter, and he gave two days a week to the evangelisation of the villages. When, for health reasons, he had to give up heavy work, he took a course in the Institute in Lima and gave his full time to the ministry in the Sierra, especially in Leimibamba, the outpost of the Moyobamba Mission district.

These Peruvian workers could better themselves in other walks of life. The problem of the rising cost of living is felt as acutely on the Mission field as in other parts of the world. It is the Church's responsibility to see that they are given an adequate remuneration which will relieve them of anxiety and secure their much-needed service to the development and extension of the Mission. Prayer is needed for those men, exposed as they are to temptations unknown to the Church at home.

The evangelistic activities are not confined within the four walls of the Church, nor within the boundaries of Moyobamba. Along with the regular church services, there are "cottage" meetings in houses lent for this purpose by members of the congregation. Those who are shy of coming to the church do not have the same reluctance to attend a house service. Thus a wider field is touched, and visits to the homes of the people bring them into personal contact with the Gospel.

Evangelisation of the villages is not neglected. The two larger towns in the Mission area, Rioja and Calsada, have the nucleus of Protestant churches. They are now anxious to have a place of their own to worship in. The Huallaga region has been taken over by the Lamas Mission. Our attention has now turned more towards the foothills of the Andes, and Chachapoyas, where Nurse MacMillan has done heroic pioneer work, an important centre midway between Cajamarca and Moyobamba, has been occupied. To take full advantage of the opportunities which are open to us here, the presence of another missionary from home is urgently needed.

Our Mission is on very friendly relations with the other evangelical body with whom we share the field, the Lamas Mission (which is the only other evangelical mission in the department of San Martín).

The Seventh Day Adventists are also at work in this part of Peru. As their name indicates, they observe the seventh and not the first day of the week as their Sabbath. Their peculiar views on fundamental doctrines of the faith, and their subversive emphasis on work-righteousness, place them in a category by themselves. Their method of approach in some districts is to encroach on the labours of other Protestant missionaries and by a process of proselytizing win over support to their own cause. Their methods have not met with any particular success in our area, but their presence is one more reason why we should be diligent to occupy the whole field as quickly as possible.

— *Extracted from: Free Church of Scotland: Missionary Enterprise.*

The Rycroft Commission:
Indians of the High Andes

THE TERM "INDIAN" WAS USED BY THE SPANIARDS IN THE SIXTEENTH century when referring to the inhabitants of the New World, because they thought they had reached India by a westward route from Europe. Of the many peoples in the New World at that time, the Peruvians and Mexicans were the most outstanding as regards accomplishments, cultural advancement and power. We are concerned in this study with the Indians of Ecuador, Peru and Bolivia who are the descendants of the subjects of the Incas, and their predecessors.

The source of the Inca civilisation which the Spaniards found in 1531 is lost in the mists of fables and legends, as is the case with any prehistoric peoples. Archaeological evidence and certain traditions point to a prehistoric culture dating back anywhere from 200 to 600 B.C., though there is no general agreement as to where it developed.

Three theories are held by different archaeologists and historians: one, that this early culture developed on the coast of what is now Ecuador and Peru; another that it began in the Andean mountain region; and a third, that there was a parallel development on the coast and in the mountains. Philip Ainsworth Means held this last theory, maintaining that the Proto-Chimu and the Proto-Nazca civilisations developed on the coast while that of Tiahuanaco flourished in the Sierra from about 100 B.C. until 600 A.D. The second Tiahua-naco Empire, he claims, dates from 600 A.D. to 900 A.D. after which time the Inca Empire appeared. Some maintain that the Tiahuanaco civilisation dates back as far as four or five thousand years.

Whatever the exact origin of these early civilisations, one fact stands out clearly, and that is that a great cultural empire known as Tiahuanaco was formed previous to the Incas of the Andes. The extensive ruins on the shores of Lake Titicaca testify to this. No one knows why Tiahuanaco as an empire disappeared but it is generally believed that it was in some way the inspirer, or creator, of the Inca civilisation which followed it.

The most persistent legend tells how Manco Capac and his sister-wife Mama Ocllo, the children of the sun, came from the island in Lake Titicaca, bearing with them a golden wedge, and were directed by Viracocha, the creator, to take residence and build a city where this should sink easily into the ground. The prince and princess journeyed northward from Lake Titicaca and founded the imperial city of Cuzco, the people worshipping them as children of the sun and sovereign chiefs. They civilised them and taught them arts such as agriculture, spinning, weaving and metal work.

Historians agree in affirming that the appearance of Manco Capac marks the beginning of the most remarkable empire ever seen in the Americas. When the Spaniards arrived in 1531, this empire extended as far north as Ecuador and as far south as Chile and Argentina, with a population estimated by some at fifteen million. This empire, called by the Incas Tahuantinsuyo, gave unity and organisation to many scattered primitive tribes. The conquest of the tribes which formed the nucleus of the empire was mostly, though not always, pacific. The Incas used cunning and method though, naturally, they were trained warriors. They seem to have had a golden rule, "do not destroy". Even when force was required to subdue a people, they did not touch the villages or the crops; nor did they believe in pillaging or taking booty. Immediately after subduing a tribe they set up their sun worship and took the local gods to Cuzco, the capital. The curacas or chieftains were also taken there to learn Quechua and to be instructed in the Inca manner of civilisation. They also transplanted peoples from one region to another.

The Inca government was absolute, theocratic and despotic. The ruling Inca was not only the centre of political authority, he was also of divine origin, being a child of the sun. Every subject entered his presence without shoes and without raising his eyes. Socially, the population was divided into the aristocracy or nobility, the priestly class and the common people. Families were grouped in communities called ayllus and these formed the basis of the social structure which we find today. They were agricultural communities, pastoral communities and those of mixed type.

The social system of the Incas was not communistic as we understand communism today, but rather collectivist. Land was considered the property of the state and was divided into three parts, one for the Inca, one for the sun (or the priests), and one for the people.

By means of irrigation and terracing of mountain-sides all available land was under cultivation. The Indians were skillful farmers, and raised corn, manioc, potatoes and cotton, while in the south of Peru and on the Bolivian altiplano they tended flocks of sheep, llamas and alpacas. All who could work were obliged to do so and the aged and infirm were cared for. But the individual was robbed of freedom and initiative for he was part of a meticulous paternalistic system which arranged for the amount of land he was to work, the supplies of food he was to have, where he was to live and whom he was to marry. The empire was given cohesion by an amazing system of highways running north and south along the coast and through the Andean mountain ranges for over two thousand miles. Flocks of llamas, as beasts of burden, and fleet-footed messengers used these highways, while stores of grain and other foods were kept at intervals along the road to be used for moving armies or in case of famine.

These people were remarkable for their massive stone buildings, the genius for which they seem to have inherited from former civilisations, and the archaeological remains of which can be seen at Tiahuanaco and Chavin. Fortresses, temples, palaces, bridges, aqueducts and other impressive stone constructions were built at a time when the use of iron and steel, cement and mortar and traction animals such as horses and mules were not known among the people of the Andes. Modern engineers are baffled as to how stones, weighing as much as 260 tons, could be quarried, carried many miles and cut with such precision in angles and curves that one stone fitted perfectly with the adjoining one so that a knife cannot be inserted between them. There are, of course, many theories concerning the methods used by these Inca and pre-Inca peoples. For example, one theory maintains that they used the juice of a herb to soften the granite and make it workable.

The Commission visited the amazing ruins of the Fortress of Sacsahuaman where some of these huge stones can be seen. This fortress is built on an eminence 700 feet above the city of Cuzco in the south of Peru, and consists of three stupendous stone walls built in tiers with the stones placed in zigzag fashion, for some four hundred metres. Immense blocks of stone are fitted together as skillfully as the inlays of a cabinet maker. Twentieth century military engineers marvel at the ingenious design and defensive qualities of this well-known fortress.

Equally remarkable is the Lost City of the Incas, Machu Picchu, discovered by two British missionaries in 1905 and publicized in the United States by Hiram Bingham in 1911. The ruins of this white granite city built on a pinnacle about 2,000 feet above a river gorge, and surrounded by a galaxy of towering peaks, twelve, fifteen and twenty thousand feet high, provide one of the most awe-inspiring spectacles in the western hemisphere. Standing amid these impressive ruins one could not fail to hold the designers and builders in high regard.

The story of how Francisco Pizarro with his handful of Spanish soldiers conquered this vast empire by stratagem and treachery is too well-known to need repeating here. He followed the example of Hernán Cortés in Mexico, capturing and executing the ruler, who in this case was Atahualpa, and soon found that there was no organised resistance to the conquest of the whole area.

Some writers point out that centuries of oppression had made the Indian submissive and meek, submerging his personality, already indolent and fatalistic. They also believe that the excessive drinking of the native liquor, chicha, in fiestas and public ceremonies lasting several days, as well as the chewing of the coca leaf, tended to atrophy the mental faculties of the Indian, reducing him to an automaton obedient to the voice and will of the Inca, who regulated the life of his subjects individually and collectively. The Inca Empire was closely knit together but there was no concept of nationality in it.

The Spaniards were amazed to encounter such weak resistance, as well as the lack of leadership and adequate defence. The Indian had very little to defend, however, and perhaps that is why he had no incentive to resistance. He had no spiritual possessions such as liberty, dignity and honour; the only material goods he possessed were a few household utensils. As for the land, he only had the use of it, and even the house or hut he lived in was not his.

The coming of the Spaniards did not improve the lot of the Indian; it greatly aggravated it. Whereas the Inca had reduced the Indian tribes to servitude for the common good and supplied his needs at the same time, the Spaniards enslaved the Indians for their own selfish ends and deprived them of an adequate means of livelihood.

History has recorded what is probably the almost unparalleled barbarity and inhumanity ever practised by a conqueror toward the conquered. The king of Spain was moved by the evils perpetrated against millions of defenceless human beings, but even the enactment of regulations and laws by the mother country could not stop the acts of abuse, greed, and cruel oppression.

The most valuable lands were divided among the conquerors who were supposed to civilize and Christianise the Indians. In exchange for a small plot of land on which to build a hut and grow his food, or the right to pasture his animals, the Indian worked for his master on the land or with his animals and also performed personal services.

Many Indians were forced to work in the mines where conditions were such that the majority never returned to their native villages. From the paternal tyranny of the Incas the Indians passed to that of virtual slavery under the Spaniards without receiving any social or individual benefits.

The lack of social and political status, together with the abuses and cruelties practised by the Spanish conquerors stunted the growth of all the domains under their control. In Peru the population which was said to be more than eight million when the Spaniards arrived, was about two million at the time of Independence.

Clodoveo Jaramillo Alvarado, an Ecuadorian writer, says, "Neither the state nor the church contributed anything to the education and regeneration of the Indian and his incorporation into the juridical life of the nation. The state, which inherited from the theocratic regime a disdain for the Indian, continued to consider him an outcast. Conservatism which imposed class inequality as well as government by the aristocracy and the clergy, denied the Indian instruction or any rights, putting him in the humiliating position of a servant. For this reason, since the destruction of the Inca Empire, the Indian has lived on the fringe of justice and law, on a plane of inferiority, denied the essential attributes of human personality".

Deprived of his land in the valleys the Indian retreated up the mountain sides or into the bleak cold plateaux, beyond the reach of his rapacious exploiters.

But one thing stands out: whether he gave tribute and service to the Spaniards or withdrew to his mountains, the Indian retired into the inner recesses of his being and became what he is today – almost inaccessible to the civilised world. To his conservatism he added sullenness, despair, and an undying hatred of the white man.

What about the Roman Catholic faith which the conquerors sought to impose? Here also the Spaniards achieved practically no success. The one thing they tried most to destroy – the pagan religion of the Indian – survived. Catholicism accommodated itself to ancestral superstition and pagan practices. The Spanish clergy brought the Indian neither a religion of love nor a Christian morality which could have given them a rational conception of life.

* * *

The hacienda peon – and many generations of his ancestors before him – is born upon the land of his patrón and supplies the labour needed for the varied tasks of the hacienda. An estate of from 500 to 1,000 acres requires the work of from fifteen to forty families, depending upon the nature of cultivation and working arrangements between patrón and peons. A large hacienda of from 50,000 to 100,000 acres may have a resident population of five hundred or more peon families scattered over it.

While differing in minor details, the general pattern of relationship between patrón and peon is similar throughout the Andean republics. The peon is granted the use of two or three acres of land upon which he may live, raise subsistence crops for his family, and pasture his animals. As a rule, he builds and owns the hut in which he lives though he has not even a squatter's claim to the ground on which it is built nor to the land which he is allowed to cultivate for himself. In the highlands of southern Peru and on the Bolivian altiplano, where the pastoral industry partly takes the place of agriculture in the Indian economy, considerable areas are allotted to the peons for the grazing of their sheep and llamas. In the case of one large property near Ayaviri, Peru, ten percent of the grazing land of the hacienda is marked off for the sole use of the huasipungueros (part-time peons). The manager said this was for two reasons: to segregate their poor strains of Peruvian sheep from his own highly-bred stock, and to keep the peons from stealing the hacienda sheep. Some of these peon families grazed as many as two to three hundred of their own animals.

The land assigned by the patrón to his peon varies widely in productivity – from steep and stony hill slopes to fertile bottom lands. In the same farming district between Otavalo and Ibarra, northern Ecuador, the Commission inspected haciendas on which the peons were struggling with difficult terrain and unproductive soils, and other estates where they had grown on their squares of bottom land as fine stands of wheat and barley as those produced by the fields of their patrón.

The plots assigned to the peons are usually located at a distance from the "big house" and this necessitates a long walk to and from the cultivated fields of the hacienda. Upon a large hacienda in central Peru, comprising 6,000 acres (nine square miles), a group of thirty-five peon families lives at a distance of four miles from the central grange upon an elevated section of the estate where only wheat and oats are grown. They form a community by themselves and seldom visit the intensively cultivated bottom lands of the estate. These are worked by a small group of full-time, trained labourers who operate on more modern lines of cultivation under the immediate supervision of the English patrón. The upland families each cultivate two acres of land for themselves, raise their own grain and vegetables, and pasture twelve to fifteen sheep, two or three cows, a pig or two, and a few goats. Of the six-day working week, the peon usually gives three days to the patrón and the other three days he devotes to his own interests. Throughout the Andean highlands, Sunday is a holiday on which no regular work is done.

Such intermittent and haphazard labour, as would be expected, is very poorly paid. On haciendas visited in Ecuador, peons earned from forty to eighty centavos a working day, or five to ten cents U. S. (The average wage was from forty to fifty centavos).

Of the twenty-two peon families of the Ayala hacienda, near Ibarra, northern Ecuador, each has a "square" (eighty-four metres square) of land for its own use. They work this land and sell some of the produce, but do not hire out for labour. The men are the only wage-earners and receive sixty centavos per day.

At Colta, near Riobamba, central Ecuador, a huasipunguero is paid fifty centavos per day in cash but is also given his food which, with the use of land, is estimated to be the equivalent of the wage of town labourers who get from two to four sucres per day. In southern Peru, the English manager of a 10,000 acre hacienda pays full-time workmen from fifty centavos to one sol and his huasipungueros twenty centavos (three and a fifth cents U. S.) per working day, plus the use of the land and grazing rights. This latter right is paid for at a comparatively high price in the open market.

The regular workmen on this hacienda are given, in addition to their cash wage, a pound of maize and five ounces of coca every morning. The manager had formerly followed the Peruvian custom of supplying a daily meat ration to his workers: that is, killing a sheep a day for each ten men. With the mounting value of his blooded stock, he could not afford to kill a 200-sol sheep daily for ten men so he began to pay his workers more and required them to feed and cook for themselves. The intermittent workers are given one ounce of coca per day.

At the government experimental sheep hacienda near Ayaviri, the skilled full-time workers are paid from one to two soles per day (fifteen to thirty cents U.S.), while the huasipungueros get forty centavos, plus food, one ounce of coca and the right to pasture their cattle, sheep, and llamas. The sixty families of peons living on the 55,000 acre estate of the Yucara hacienda near Juliaca, southern Peru, upon which 29,000 sheep are grazed, receive fifteen centavos a day (two and a half cents U.S.) cash wage. In addition, however, each family is given the use of five acres of land to cultivate for itself and grazing rights for from sixty to four hundred sheep and a few cows. These people work three days a week for the hacienda.

Under the traditional Bolivian hacienda system, upon the eastern shores of Lake Titicaca, the huasipunguero is paid no cash wage whatever. He is given from one to three acres of land and grazing rights for his sheep, and in return he works on an average of four days a week for his master. The pongo custom is generally in force whereby the patrón may requisition, without payment, a measure of the peon's grain, chickens, a goat or a sheep for use on his own table. He may also call out a boy or a girl from the peon's family for service in the "big house" or for work in his city residence – again, without payment of cash wages. The peon families are rotated, taking turn and turn about in providing this impressed service. The patrón also takes all the manure from his peon's stock as fertiliser for his own fields. The peon cannot leave his patrón's employ without his permission. He is usually in debt to his employer and is also held to his environment by traditional bonds and a fatalistic inertia. The landlord considers that everything which lives off his land or is raised upon it is his.

In striking contrast to this sombre picture of serfdom, the manager of the Canadian Baptist hacienda at Guatajata, Lake Titicaca, after many years of training his peons and preparing them for land ownership, now pays his unskilled labour slightly higher than government wages on road work, or fifteen bolivianos per day (thirty seven cents U.S). His skilled workers are paid 700 bolivianos per month, or $16.66.

Housing and living conditions among hacienda peons are among the most depressed of all classes of Andean Indians. This is partly due to the fact that, with rare exceptions, the patrón takes no responsibility for, and no interest in, the situation of his workers. Since the peon builds his own house without the help of a community and with the most meagre facilities, it is of the crudest construction, of insufficient size, and soon falls into a state of disrepair. The cottage of the average hacienda peon lacks the impression of thrift, rude comfort, and domestic activity of the homesteads of many of the free Indian farmers.

Some of the modern haciendas have built barracks or individual cottages for their workers. An English hacienda manager near Ayaviri, southern Peru, said, "When I first came here I built model cottages for the peons but they would not live in them. After a time I gave up the idea of helping my peons to improve their way of living and let them live just as they like".

The manager showed us the long adobe, grass-roofed building in which his full-time peons lived. It was divided into eight rooms, each ten feet square. No window relieved the grey mud expanse of the four walls. A four and one-half foot door opened into each room. One stepped down twelve inches to the sunken floor. A mass of filthy quilts was tossed on ancient sheep skins which covered a low mud platform comprising one half of the room. From three to six men lived in each room. The rest of the space was occupied by a crude fireplace of stones, a pile of dried cow-dung for fuel, a hunk or two of dried meat, half-picked bones and heads of sheep, a little corn, a pot, and one or two sections of logs cut for stools. The floor was deep in dust, litter and cow and sheep dung. On entering one of these dark holes, one was met by an overpowering odour of ancient, unwashed bedding, putrid meat, and the acrid smoke of animal dung; the impression given was that one had stumbled into a wild animal's den. There was provision for neither a smoke vent nor for ventilation, and at night the door was tightly shut to keep out the cold.

The manager of the hacienda had a low opinion of the Indian as a worker, but admitted he could not operate his farm without him and that, as compared with the cholo worker, he was "the lesser of two evils". The Indian operated all the power machinery and implements on the farm, but had to be taught again and again how to master the intricacies of each. "Over the weekend he even forgets the difference between the oil-valve and the gasoline intake, but the Ayaviri liquor shops are partly responsible for this". The manager complained that the Indian was an ingrate and had no appreciation of kindness or consideration. Further, that the only treatment by the white man which he understood was brute force and that he would not exert his utmost unless this was used.

"The Indian has to have just so much kicking, kneeing, and beating to get the best out of him. Unless he is manhandled by his employer, he is unhappy and feels that he is being neglected. My men stay with me many years at a time; in fact, too long, and the only way I can get rid of undesirables is to work them harder than they like".

The manager pointed to a strong-faced Indian, the foreman of his milk herd, and said, "That man is a thorough rascal. He has served several prison terms, but is very efficient. He gets a wage of 1.50 soles a day and everything else he can lay his hands on and makes a good living. Money makes no appeal to the average Indian except as a means of buying liquor and coca. When I raised the wages of my men, several of them came to work only two days a week: two days' wages was enough to live on a whole week and why should they do more? Coca has a very degenerating influence upon the Indian, but he will not work without it. When I locked-up an Indian worker for theft, the man fell on his knees and implored me to let him have a little coca and promised to work twice as long and as hard".

The numerical proportion of hacienda peons in the total Indian population is difficult to determine. The pattern of valley haciendas so common in most parts of the mountain corridors of Ecuador and Peru is frequently broken by large intervening blocks of private land owned by Indians, both small, independent farmers and communal groups or comunidades. In Ecuador, the hacienda peons probably account for one third or more of the highland Indian population. In Peru, the proportion is somewhat higher while in the Bolivian altiplano, which is too bleak and sterile for profitable large-scale farming, the proportion of Indians working as hacienda peons is probably not over twenty-five percent.

* * *

Mining in the Andes may be traced to prehistoric times as a traditional Indian occupation. Silver and gold were extracted in large quantities by the Incas and these precious metals formed the immediate goal of the Spanish conquistadores in their exploitation of the Inca Empire. Not a few of the ancient pits and galleries may be seen in Peru and Bolivia; some have been re-opened and, with modern mining techniques, have proved extremely valuable. The mining population of Ecuador is insignificant, a total of not over 10,000 men being employed. Peru's silver and copper mines, however, employ in the neighbourhood of 50,000 men. The many mines, smelters, transport and subsidiary occupations of the huge Cerro de Pasco Mining Corporation alone give employment to 30,000 workers. The principal Bolivian mines employ 60,000 men, but a very large number of small and unregistered companies probably account for at least half again as many workers. While the Indian is looked upon both in Peru and Bolivia as an indispensable source of mining labour, it is doubtful whether in either country he forms one-half of the total labour force; at least an equal number of the employees are mestizos and whites.

At the immense smelting plant of the Cerro de Pasco Company at

Oroya, Peru, one fifth of the workmen were Indians. The proportion of Indians who were taking out the ore at the mine face, however, was considerably higher. At the Aramayo Mines in southern Bolivia, the Commission was told that not over one-half of the men who extract the ore were full-blooded Indians.

Various reasons account for the general use of the Indian as a worker in the Andean mines: the proximity of many Indian communities to the mineral areas, the familiarity of the Indian with the mining process, and his need of supplementing his subsistence economy with the cash wages paid at the mine. But undoubtedly the capacity of the Indian to work hard at high altitude is a major reason for his popularity as a miner. Only a small minority of the older Indian mine labourers with their families remain continuously at the mines for a long term of years and so may rightly be called industrialised. A majority of the young men are temporary or seasonal workers, staying only until they have saved enough money to buy new plots of land or returning regularly to their farms to plough, put in their crops, and harvest them. Many Indian miners are contracted under this arrangement.

The Indians who settle permanently at the mines usually are skilled or semi-skilled mechanics who are employed in one of the ore-processing operations – smelting or concentrating, transportation, machine shop work, carpentry or in the power plant. The Commission met numbers of such men at the smelter at Oroya, visited them in their homes, and learned about the conditions of their work.

The first family visited had lived for twelve years in Oroya where the father was employed in the electrical division. He stated that he never came into contact with high officials but dealt only with the foreman and further that the men were disillusioned with the mines and all looked forward to returning home. He estimated that fifty per cent of the men degenerate while at the mines and squander their money on drink, gambling, and prostitution. Others save their wages and return home to improve their economic position. The younger men acquire new habits far more easily than the older workers; while at the mines they become accustomed to the use of modern amenities and carry a desire for them back to their homes. Most of the workers come to the mine as single men. This couple were members of the Methodist Church in Oroya and hope to return to their home in Huánuco. They plan to buy fifteen hectares of land and raise chickens and turkeys.

Another employee visited was a strong Indian type who had worked twenty-eight years in the engine house as an oiler, and was facing the question of whether to leave the company and work on his farm or to stay on at the mines until he is incapacitated for further work and then retire with a bonus. He had bought a farm for 6,000 soles which he had saved from his wages. He said that the miners keep in touch with their farms by going home twice a year for fifteen days. He complained of the injustice of the company rule requiring an employee to work until he is too old to get another full-time job before he is eligible for a pension. This man was a deacon in the Methodist Church.

Eight hundred families were living in barrack-like rows of houses, each barrack comprising twenty-four homes, twelve by fifteen feet. Many were supplied with beds and some were furnished in a pathetic imitation of European amenities. There was little or no privacy and children and parents usually occupied the same bed. One family had built an attic floor over a part of the room for sleeping space to which the children climbed by a ladder. These houses were each provided with a window and chimney for the cooking grate. One latrine sufficed for twenty-four families, and a row of cement laundry tubs ran down the middle of each area between the barracks. Two water taps served the needs of the twenty-four families. A large school was furnished by the company for the children of the workers and on payment of a small fee a "club" offered billiards, books, and refreshments to the men.

The Aramayo Mining Company of southern Bolivia is a member of the "Big Three" producers of tin, tungsten and antimony. The corporation is internationally owned and its operations are in the hands of American managers and engineers. During a week's visit to a group of the scattered mines of this company, a member of the Commission was driven by auto from Atocha where the main concentrating plant is located, through the mountains for fifteen miles to a cluster of four small mines located upon the upper slopes of two windswept Andean peaks. The concentrating plant, store, machine shops, and the homes of the American staff were crowded in a narrow canyon in the side of Tasna peak. Two hundred workers with their families live in long barracks beside the small stream, and on a ledge of Tasna, a thousand feet above, were perched the shacks of one hundred and seventy-five other miners. The company was replacing the antiquated barrack houses with modern, well-planned homes of two and three rooms, each with running water and its own cook-house, to accommodate families of different sizes. The company store sold everything that the mining family needed at fixed prices which did not fluctuate with outside markets. There was a small school for the children, but the beautifully equipped company hospital, situated fifteen miles away over the mountains, received only the more serious accident cases, and assumes no responsibility for illness among the families of the miners.

The highly-trained Bolivian doctor of this hospital stated that they took care of the families of the staff and skilled workers but, except for serious accidents, did not bother with their 5,000 Indian miners. At the time of the visit, only one of the twenty-five beds was occupied and that by the wife of a mestizo company bookkeeper. The six trained nurses who were in the employ of this hospital did not visit the mining camps.

The doctor in charge said that the great majority of the miners were "finished" by silicosis, or the infiltration of rock dust into the lungs, by the fifth year of employment and were discharged as semi-invalids. This lung condition results in a very high incidence of tuberculosis and other pulmonary troubles, to which the home communities are exposed on the return of the miner. Victor Andrade, director of the Bolivian Government department for Security and Insurance of Workers, is responsible for the statement that annually 3,000 of the 52,500 workers in the tin mines of the country become incapacitated through silicosis and other occupational diseases. This amounts to an annual wastage of 5.71 per cent of the tin miners.

A visit was made with the manager to one of the loftiest tungsten mines of the company on the icy, windswept slopes of the upper peak at a height of 17,000 feet. Squads of barefooted and bare-legged Aymará women with many layers of flaring skirts and shawls whipping about them and black felt hats tied to their heads, were mending the steep road and at the mine mouth were sorting over great piles of extracted ore. Indian men were tramming the ore from the rock faces far in the interior of the peak, using little push cars which ran on rails to the mine mouth. Other miners were at work with picks and hand-drills, while still others in teams of two men were operating the automatic air-drills in the hard schist and quartz rock. The stoical Indians seemed oblivious to the ear-shattering machines, the breath-taking altitude, and the cold, dust-laden air of the black, cramped galleries. They worked in eight-hour shifts and received a daily wage of from thirty-five to fifty cents a day. The women were paid from twenty to thirty cents.

Much of the ore was mined by contract as piece work – the miner employing his helper – and in this was increasing his income. It was apparent that this great company was employing few of the safety appliances, automatic water spraying, ventilating fans and other devices designed for reducing the dust hazard that Bolivian law requires. The manager admitted that his labour turnover from illness, accident, and death was unduly high, but considered that under the difficult conditions of operation, about all was being done for his miners that could be expected of the company.

* * *

The interior of a typical Indian home is a dark cavern measuring 12 by 15 feet, with four-foot adobe or stone walls from which the sloping rafters rise to a peak roof thatched with straw or grass. The floor is usually below the level of the land around it. There are no windows and no chimney or smoke vent and a tall man must bend double to enter the door. More progressive Indians and those who live in the neighbourhood of towns roof their homes with red tile. The floor of the house is of bare earth. It is usually littered with an assortment of trash and filth ranging from gnawed bones to sheep and cow dung, scraps of food, broken utensils, ragged bits of clothing and filthy bedding, deep dust and chicken, rabbit and guinea-pig droppings. Pegs are driven into the walls to support clothing, blankets, ponchos, tools and utensils, while long rows of varicoloured corn on the cob, red peppers, peas in the pod, and other dried grain and vegetables hang on ropes stretched between rafters. There is no bedstead, but a pile of sheepskins, blankets and ponchos piled in a corner by day are spread upon the dirt floor at night. Except on the altiplano, the family sleeps huddled together upon the open veranda with only a pent roof for protection.

The typical Indian hut has no furniture save possibly a stool or two with plaited leather seats. The broad top of the house wall serves as a catch-all shelf, while farm implements and tools are hung from the roof or stand against the walls. Some Indians prepare their food and eat it in the main hut of the homestead. More often a small kitchen adjoining the living hut is used and here the food is prepared, cooked and eaten. Many Indian homes are built in the shape of an L or a U around two or three sides of a courtyard. An almost universal feature is the open porch which serves as a vestibule to the living and working rooms and frequently runs right around two of the inner sides of the courtyard. The house plan provides for a maximum of sunshine in the courtyard and during the early morning and late afternoon hours the various family occupations are carried on, so far as possible, in the sun. The porch gives access to the various rooms, storehouse, kitchen, hen-house, workshop and the hut for the married son or daughter and is the centre of the family life. Here the pedal loom is usually placed and here the carding, spinning and dyeing of the wool is done, the plaiting of mats, the twisting of rope, and the score of other domestic operations in which the various family members participate. The inner rooms are used by large numbers of Indians primarily for storing their grain and potatoes in huge straw woven bins or hempen bags while the light and airy porch is popular as the family workshop and palaver place. Here the meals are eaten, the little children play by day and, except in the higher altitudes, the family sleeps at night.

The animal corral usually bounds the courtyard on one side and is an overcrowded and filthy pen laid up with low stone walls. Burros, sheep, cows and hogs are herded together at night, while the accumulated manure, straw, feed and trash are kicked all over the courtyard and into the various huts by the children, chickens, dogs and rabbits which freely run in and out. There are no bathing arrangements and the fields or courtyard serve for toilets. According to La Barre, the Aymará Indian never bathes, never washes his clothes and seldom if ever changes them. Jacket, skirt or trousers are worn until they disintegrate and drop off the wearer.

Clothes are worn day and night, adjustment to temperature being made by adding or taking off layers of skirts and other clothing. The legs and feet of the Indian man, woman or child, whatever the weather, are uncovered although many of the men wear sandals when walking in rough terrain. At Cuzco, during a day's snowstorm, hundreds of Indians trotted barefoot over the icy cobblestones and pulled their ponchos over their heads as protection from the freezing wind. The Andean Indian for many centuries has been inured to a bleak and bitter climate, to a struggle with high altitude and an unfriendly terrain and unproductive soil. This inheritance has toughened him and has given him powers of resistance and a capacity to live and work at altitudes which white men find impossibly exacting. Yet with this resistance to altitude, climate and hardship the Indian race is disease-ridden and, to an alarming extent, is susceptible to respiratory and alimentary ailments. The infant mortality ranges from 250 to 750 per thousand and the average life expectancy is from thirty to forty five.

Hookworm and parasitic diseases seriously reduce the normal vitality while dysentery, enteritis and tuberculosis weaken the worker. The respiratory diseases induced by working in the copper and tin mines annually incapacitate for further remunerative work many thousands of vigorous men. The incidence of tuberculosis induced by the silicosis in the mines is one of the highest in the industrial world. The inaccessibility of modern medical help tends to perpetuate the use of the native witchdoctor and condemns the Indian to a permanently weakened state of health.

The Indian race, as a whole, suffers from deficiency diseases and is ridden with largely preventable ailments. Were it to have access to the simplest of modern medical treatment, its health could not only be enormously improved, but its vitality and with it its working power and earning capacity could be strengthened and the whole economic position of the race could in time be altered.

The Indian is not only at the bottom of the social and economic order in the Andean republics, he is regarded as a distinct caste. In his contacts with the people of the towns and cities, he expects to be treated as inferior, to be served last, to take what is left and to do the things which are beneath the dignity of the white man. In travelling through the Andean corridor, wherever the Indian was in contact with the whites, there was evidence of this relationship. At Saraguro, southern Ecuador, during an unhurried visit with the owner of a general store, the treatment and behaviour of many Indian customers was noted. The storekeeper, a big, burly, flashily dressed white man, stood behind the counter with his hat on. The Indians were buying cotton prints, piece goods, salt, kerosene, cups, pails, needles, etc. A hill Indian timidly came in and priced some black alpaca cloth. He stood at the counter waiting for his goods to be measured and cut. The storekeeper roughly ordered him back. Later he came forward to get his unwrapped purchase and paid one and one-half sucres for it. An Indian woman came in to buy one sheet of white paper for which in payment she offered a five-sucre note; she was told to go out and get change before her purchase was given to her.

There are two schools in the little town – the government school for boys and a Roman Catholic school for girls. Only a few Indian children attend since they are needed for work on the farms. The local paymaster of the Loja-Cuenca highway construction company stated that the Indian pupils have a completely subservient position in the school. The teachers make them come early to sweep out the rooms and to do other menial work, in spite of their payment of the same fees as the white pupils. It is important to note that a majority of the Indians of this region are not hacienda peons but free Indians who own their own squares of land and are among the most progressive of any group with whom we came in contact. The haciendas are required by law to maintain schools for their peons, but the Government educational officers whom we met admitted that this law was largely a dead letter and that a majority of the estates did not even pretend to observe it. The only haciendas visited by the Commission which kept schools for their children were either Government owned or were operated by British managers or by missions.

* * *

The culture of a people must also furnish patterns of security by the aid of the supernatural in life. Up to a certain point in his activities, man recognises his own sufficiency but from that point on he must depend on the supernatural for existence. In an external world as adverse as his, the Indian's religion serves at times as a psychological escape and at others as a basis of security. It is, as all observers have noted, a mixture of the old religion and Roman Catholicism. When two cultures come together, the stronger endeavours to impose upon the weaker its way of life. It is not difficult for the weaker people to adopt the overt patterns of life of the stronger for these can be seen. However, the subjective elements behind these patterns, such as associations and values, are most difficult to transfer. This was true of the Indian of these countries. He adopted the form and ritual of the Roman Catholic faith and worked it into his old religious patterns. Old gods took on Catholic names; old shrines became new ones; the pomp of Catholic ritual was worked into old patterns. The former god of the community, village and town became the Roman Catholic saint and the Roman Catholic festival took the place of the pagan ceremonies. Nicolas Martínez says, "The religion of the Indian in outward form is Roman Catholic but in reality it is pagan. In this he follows his ancestors who worshipped the sun, moon, or an idol of wood and stone. Today the Indian worships a wooden image and gives it the name of some saint or virgin. For example, the Indians of Pasa worship a grotesque figure which they call Saint Fernand of Pasa Grande. They do not worship the saint which the figure represents; they worship a piece of wood, and when some priest tries to replace it by a better shaped or better dressed image, he finds the Indian "will not allow him to do so".

Thus Catholicism has not accomplished anything more than a change of idols. A prominent anthropologist told us that what the Spaniard tried most to destroy is the very thing which the Indian today has preserved almost intact, that is, his old religion. The Indian worships the sun and the moon or at least holds them in reverence. Each morning when the sun rises, he kneels and crosses himself. He has his house guardians who are revered because they prevent theft or loss of property in the home. He also has a class of evil spirits called Supoya which bring calamities upon men. He believes in place spirits which are of several types and ranks in hierarchy, depending upon their power for good or evil and upon their intelligence. Of greatest importance to the Indian are the spirits which inhabit the mountains, rivers and springs and the spirits of rain. These spirits can do good or evil depending on man's treatment of them. Among the most important saints is St. Manes, who is associated with the spirit of lightning and, in some cases, with Christ. They believe in the earth as the old earth goddess called with affection, Pachamama.

These spirits are to be placated with offerings of food, guinea-pig, coca and drink. Up on the high mountain passes, especially at crossroads, are to be seen rock piles called Huacas. The spirits haunt these places and the Indian as he passes must cast a small stone, spit coca and offer a little prayer in order not to become tired or sick on the way. The Indian seems in general to have some vague idea of the future destination of the soul. He believes in an evil being, corresponding to the devil, called in Peru shapsha. "The supernatural beings of the Quechua religion fall into various classes. There are the good and bad spirits, the terrestrial and the celestial, the deities as opposed to spirits, a Catholic pantheon and the pagan assembly of good, bad and ambivalent beings. God and Christ stand at the top of the Quechua supernatural world, yet they are so far removed from it that they play a minor part in mundane affairs".

According to Paredes, "The Bolivian Aymará has little faith in the deities of Catholicism but a great deal in his own idols; even now he does not know what the Catholics call 'glory'. The idea of eternal joy with God does not appeal to him nor does he desire it because he does not understand what the concept means. What he loves in the Catholic faith are its fiestas which give him the opportunity to drink and dance".

The Indian is profoundly pagan; Catholic doctrine has found no place in his spirit. He recites mechanically its prayers and obeys its precepts when they conform to his own beliefs and when in danger. The Indian has his own philosophy, his preoccupations, his morals, and his religion; and as long as he remains in the same condition as he is at present, it is useless to think of him as a Catholic or as a part of Western civilisation. His soul continues as that of his fore-fathers, rebellious to any change which might destroy his intimate convictions. Comprehension of Catholic dogmas is not found in the Indian and so he will continue until there is born in him some comprehension of them in harmony with the ideas and traditions which he has inherited and which do not violate his racial impulses today in attitude and instinctive responses.

Among the countless superstitions that play a large part in their lives are the following; when a hen crows like a rooster, it is a sign that someone will die. When a bat enters the home, it indicates that the head of the home is to die within a year. The sight of a white spider is a good omen. To throw a bone at the sheep or cattle will cause them to become lean. Lack of rain is due to the fact that a corpse is exposed on the surface of the land. In southern Peru, when dark clouds appear on the horizon, it is a sign of coming hail and the Indian begins to beat pans to make a noise and whip the dogs to make them howl so as to frighten the hail away. It is considered harmful to look at or point to the rainbow. To prevent harm coming upon the home through evil spirits, a cross is placed on the roof even before the house is completely built.

In various crises of life on the altiplano near Lake Titicaca, magic is employed to ensure security. When the sky is heavy with dark clouds and there is lightning, both adults and children go outdoors and begin to shriek, 'grandfather, grandfather, you old robber grandfather, pass over, pass over'. They also use bonfires to the same end. They often pinch their children to make them shout louder. This will continue for hours until results are obtained.

When the Aymará Indians begin planting, the weeds are cut and burned and the help of Pachamama is invoked. The future results of the crop are predicted by the direction of the smoke. Before the ground is opened by the plough, the Indian takes off his hat and pours whisky on the ground and prays for the help of the gods. He consults the almanac to find the most propitious day to begin planting and makes an offering of a guinea-pig, confetti, or coloured wool to Pachamama. If an eagle or condor were to fly over the field at the time of planting, it is considered a bad omen. When planting potatoes, in order to make them grow, the owner goes to the field with relatives and friends and makes a few holes in the ground. In these candy, chicha, alcohol, coca and pieces of coloured wool are placed. They are then covered in the form of a mound, and a potato plant, decorated with coloured paper, is transplanted on these mounds and a prayer mumbled. The people then give themselves up to drinking and feasting.

During the planting season the Indian is constantly on the alert for signs of hail, frost or drought which may ruin his crop. By day and night he watches the heavens for predictive signs. In the case of hail or frost, he turns to the brujo for aid. When drought threatens the crop, he kills a lamb and eats the meat but the bones, together with coca, are buried in the ground with the spirits of the mountain. Corn-meal is put in water and sprinkled around while one of the group says a prayer. If an abundance of rain threatens the crop, the Indian opens the grave of the ancestors so that their spirits will stop the rain.

When the potato crop is ready to be harvested again, a ceremony takes place in the form of an offering of first fruits to Pachamama. An offering to the ground is also made of a guinea-pig, coloured wool, confetti and candy, together with the embryo of a llama. At the harvest festival, the men take a girl and swing her by her legs and arms over the undug potatoes so that the crop will be large.

The Bolivian Indians believe that before being occupied a new home is inhabited by spirits which can harm the occupants. Thus before moving in they observe this ceremony. Upon the completion of the foundation of the house, an offering is made in the corners, and sometimes an animal is sacrificed. When the house is finished, the image of an animal representing the spirits is hung from one of the rafters and whipped. A sheep is killed and the meat given to the one who contributes this gift while the blood is thrown over the walls and sprinkled on the floor. This is done as a sacrifice and to give the house strength. The rite is accompanied by feasting, drinking and dancing. The typical dance is one in which the participants with lighted torches dance around the house and sing.

The Indians believe that all the fish are owned by a lake spirit which allows them to be caught if they are treated well. Thus, after a catch, the best fish is burned with coca and prayer offered to the spirit to continue to bless them in their fishing. In trading also, the Indian resorts to magic and divination to secure the best deal. When an Indian sets out on a long trip, he consults a brujo as to whether the trip will be successful. In case a brujo is not at hand, he will use coca as a substitute. Before parting, the family drink together and wish the protection of the spirits upon the traveller. During his absence, certain taboos are observed in the home to make his return safe. If the father is delayed in returning, the brujo is consulted. The latter will throw down coca leaves and if they fall upside down, it indicates that the traveller is sick. However, if only a few are inverted, then his delay is only temporary.

In nothing does his old religion give the Indian such a sense of security as in crises due to sickness. It seems to us that in the mind of the Indian, disease in general belongs to one of two categories, namely, those which can be cured with drug-store medicines and doctors, and those which can only be cared for by the Indian medicine man. One is led to believe that here again, in the realm of medicine, is an excellent example of what takes place when cultural contacts are established between two peoples. Here is a mixture rather than a complete substitution. Those diseases which require a cholo doctor or drug-store medicines are the ones which have come through contact with the white man and for which the Indian has no patterns of reaction. Consequently they follow the treatment of the white men. On the other hand, in dealing with their old familiar diseases, they follow the ancient Indian pattern for treatment. However, this deserves a detailed study which might well be extremely enlightening to future medical missions among these people. Those diseases which only the Indian medicine-man can cure may be due to the following causes: soul-stealing by evil spirits, witchcraft or the infringement of some taboo. As a rule among these Indians, white as well as black magic are all in the hands of one person. Each witch-doctor has his own peculiar pattern for curing and yet fundamentally there is much in common.

A witch-doctor at times malevolently causes sickness. He will take a wax figure, representing the person to be made ill, or perhaps an article of clothing belonging to the latter, and will prick it with thorns at the parts where illness will set in. At other times he may take an animal or a frog and prick it with thorns in a similar manner. Then the image is buried. To cause itch, for example, the witch-doctor takes a piece of clothing or hair of the person to be afflicted and buries it in a swampy place where there is rotten mud.

The curing process varies over the country with each medicine-man, but the general pattern is much the same. For example, when sickness is due to loss of the soul, the medicine man is called. Upon his arrival he takes a shirt or some other article of clothing of the sick man and goes outside of the home. There, holding the garment up before him, he calls the soul to return. When he thinks that the soul has had ample time to come and incorporate itself in the shirt, he goes inside and puts it on the sick man. Then the latter stands up while the former straightens him out by pulling his legs, arms and head.

When sickness is due to failure to observe some taboo, the medicine-man is called. All the members of the family await his arrival preparing coca, sweet wine and cigarettes. When he arrives, he takes great care to admonish all the members of the family to keep their eyes closed so as not to see the spirit of the mountain. If anyone should see it, it would cause great harm. Then the medicine-man works himself into a frenzy and groans, saying that the spirit of the mountain rests on his shoulders. He then tells the family that the illness is due to the fact that the sick person has not paid any respect to the spirits, having withheld the first fruits of the harvest. The witch-doctor advises, however, that if the sick one now makes amends he will get well. To effect the cure, the medicine-man will take an animal, preferably a guinea-pig decorated with coloured wool. With this animal he goes through the motions of cleaning the sick one. Then he takes coca, drink, tobacco, food and the guinea-pig and goes to the mountains where he presents this offering to the spirits of the mountain.

If sickness is due to witchcraft, the medicine-man, according to one informant, will take coca and offer prayer to the spirits to help him cast out the sickness. He then throws the coca on the ground. This procedure is supposed to reveal the location of the figure or animal, pierced with thorns, which is believed to have been causing the illness.

* * *

Hrdlicka says that prehistoric Indians did not suffer from rickets, tuberculosis, microcephaly, hydrocephaly, plague, cholera, typhus, smallpox, measles, lepra, syphilis, nevi, or troubles of the feet such as fallen arches, and that cancer was rare. Also that yellow fever, malaria, typhoid, scarletina and diptheria were doubtful. Their lack of resistance to typhus and other epidemics that ravaged the Indian population subsequent to, and indeed for centuries after the Conquest, would tend to bear out this statement so far as the infectious diseases are concerned. At least the diseases of the ancient Indians were sufficient to have stimulated him to the development of a most elaborate system of healing in which both medicines and witchcraft played important roles, which has not only survived but has become more involved as each period in his changing history has added to its lore.

Among the Andean Indians today, many are the beliefs as to the cause of disease. Goitre, it is believed, is caused by drinking water out of a spring containing a large frog. At Talavara in southern Peru, a Quechua barber who was also a medicine man told us, for example, that there were two kinds of tumours; small ones called 'Ocucha Chupos', and large ones known as 'Mau Chupos'. The former, it is believed, are caused by contact with a rat and the latter are caused by the large rock they use to crush corn. Rheumatism, they believe, is brought on when the bone of an ancestor is dug up in a graveyard. The spirits of the mountains are responsible for chills and fever, and typhus, they believe, is caused by the sun, or sometimes by drinking milk. Fright is the cause for many diseases such as certain diarrhoeas with fever and "soul loss", a common complaint in childhood, since it is believed a child's soul is very loosely attached to its body and therefore easily separated from it. Dysentery is believed to be due to heat or cold. Disease is often attributable to a sudden gust of wind.

While they ascribe disease generally to supernatural causes, their terminology in anatomy and pathology reveals a very extensive knowledge of the human body in sickness and in health. La Barre enumerates in what he admits is only a partial list almost ninety anatomical terms in the Aymará language, and over seventy names for diseases, including such a variety as cough, heart disease, epilepsy, toothache, migraine, dysentery, obstruction of the bowel, fracture, dislocation, goitre, tonsillitis, numerous skin diseases, paralysis of the arm, asthma, anaemia, blindness and deafness, etc. This rich vocabulary in anatomical and pathological terms was also found among the Eskimos of the Canadian Arctic and the natives of Cameroon, West Africa.

For each disease, and indeed for every symptom, there is a

particular remedy and often more than one remedy for the same disease. For example, we were told in one place that the cure for typhus was to take a black dog, split it open and quickly lay it on the body of the sick person. If this did not effect a cure, stale urine should be drunk, or soup in which a frog was cooked whole. Herbal remedies are used by adults in the treatment of most illnesses, and only when the condition persists is a medicine-man consulted. Their knowledge of medicinal herbs varies in different regions. For example, Tschopik feels that the ordinary Navajo Indian knows more about herbs than do the curanderos of the Aymará. To quote this same author on the Aymará remedies, "A great variety of medicines are taken both internally and externally. Most are vegetable, the roots, seeds, leaves, and flowers being taken for specific purposes. One or several plant species may be combined in a specific medicine. Remedies of animal derivation, next in importance, include various portions of mammals, birds, reptiles, fish, larvae, insects, starfish, sea urchins, and molluscs. Minerals rank third as medicines, mercury being used to treat syphilis and certain clays to stop internal bleeding. Last in importance ranks human flesh, desiccated bits of which are eaten to cure ghost sickness".

Usually, medicines when taken internally are in the form of infusions. Externally, poultices are used on open wounds and to reduce swellings, and one frequently meets an Indian wearing a coca leaf, fastened to the forehead, temple or jaw by spittle, for the relief of headache or toothache. Inhalations are used for cough and to drive away evil spirits.

At every Indian market the vendors of native medicines are many and popular, and in some areas have gained quite a reputation, notably at Loja in southern Ecuador, and at the famous market of Huancayo in central Peru. Peculiarly enough, these vendors are probably as well patronised by the mestizo as by the Indians. Besides all their own "native" medicines, the Indians purchase a variety of our drugs such as aspirin, camphor, iodine, cough mixtures, etc., at the many drug-stores in every Andean town.

For the most part, the therapeutic action of these medicines is little known to the Indian. We may conclude with Hrdlicka: "Just what real therapeutic virtue many of the plants used by the Indians for medicine possessed is uncertain. That some were valuable is attested by the large number of them that found their way into the white man's pharmacopoeia. And the Andean Indians may introduce us to still others when we get better acquainted with him".

Speaking of the Aymará, La Barre writes: "It is probably safe to say that no other primitive group known to modern ethnology has such a rich specialisation among practitioners of native medicine". According to this same author, the most famous of all the herbalists are the Colawayu, who are known all over the Pacific, Andean and southern South America. They travel great distances, mostly on foot, and are often absent from their villages for several years. To quote La Barre further: "I was seriously assured in the capital that 80 per cent of the Bolivian whites believe more in the Colawayu than in their own doctors, most of whose training is of an inferior kind. Fully 100% of the cholo population swears by the household remedies of the Colawayu, and indeed it would be ungenerous not to grant them some right to their great reputation for it was they who gave quinine, ipecac, and other well-known drugs to modern medicine".

It is a far cry from this chief of all the witch-doctors of the Andean Indian to the simple medicine man who, while tilling his own field, dabbles in native medicine to the extent of a few simple cures and spends all the money he earns on drink. In between are several classes of witch-doctors all of whom employ magic (since disease is attributed to supernatural causes) but who are recognised by their cures, by the diseases in which they are specialists, or by their methods of diagnosis. Some are fair surgeons, sometimes called "bone-setters" who treat fractures or other injuries due to violence. Trephining was done successfully in ancient times for compression fractures, headaches and epilepsy, the patient often living for many years after the operation.

Indeed, skulls have been found with as many as five successful trepanations, according to La Barre who adds, "which argues for a certain skill in the surgeon as well as for the vitality of the patient". Others are like chiropractors using massage, pressure and manipulation. Midwives often get the patient drunk so that they will not feel the pain of childbirth, at the same time getting drunk themselves.

Should a witch-doctor have two or three failures in a short period of time, it is believed that he is losing his powers. In some cases he might be forced to leave the community and in others he might even be put to death by an angry relative of one of the victims. In Ecuador, we were told there were two schools for witch-doctors, one at Otavalo and one at Cuenca.

Krogman writes about native Indian medicine and the witch-doctor as follows. "Aboriginal Indian medicine was a curious blend of fact, faith, fakery, flapdoodle, and who shall say whether this combination has ever broken down. Perhaps it is best that we conclude with Stone that, "the medicinal practices of the American Indian were marked by sincerity, confidence, and picturesqueness and were in many respects effective". At the back of all this relatively organised medicine, or perhaps better at the base of it, was the Shaman or Medicine Man. It was he most frequently who prepared the specified decoctions or dessications, it was he who most often administered them, and it was he who by the proper incantations and mumbo-jumbo, assured the patient of the soundness of the diagnosis, the efficacy of the treatment, and the hopefulness of the prognosis. The doctor-patient rapport was then even greater than it is now, for the medicine-man as intermediary brought the patient in rapport with the spirit world. To do this, doctor, patient, either or both, often invoked the vision-giving propensities of narcotics and intoxicants.

* * *

The State Church does practically nothing to improve either the health of the people or the sanitary conditions of the country. Indeed, one of the filthiest towns of the Sierra, with a most dejected and sick-looking population of sixteen thousand souls, had thirty two large churches.

Protestant missions, on the other hand, while not outstanding in their health achievements among the Andean Indians, have at least made a beginning. In Ecuador there are no Protestant medical missionaries in the Sierra, although several lay workers have rendered a most helpful service to the Indian in time of illness. A small clinic has some fifteen to twenty-five Indians coming daily for treatment. In northern Peru, with a sixteen-bed hospital one mission does fine medical work and major surgery is possible. The patients, however, are chiefly from the cholo and white elements of the population. Not far away, in the same region, another mission has a small hospital manned by two or three nurses who also do public health nursing in the homes.

Some years ago on a farm in southern Peru, a nurse opened a small clinic for the Indians. At first she had only six beds but after the arrival of a doctor – who, besides his London degree, obtained his Peruvian degree from the Medical School in Lima – the patients began coming in such numbers that the bed capacity of the clinic increased to thirty. There were usually between twenty and twenty-five patients hospitalised in the clinic at one time besides the large numbers that came daily for consultations. We were told that on any Saturday or Sunday there would be in the yard as many as ten cars with patients coming from all over that part of the country-side to see the doctor. While a great number of patients were Indians, a large number were from the cholo and the upper classes.

No elaborate building was erected but a few alterations to the large farm residence afforded a simple but very practical set-up. A large upstairs bedroom was made into a very serviceable operating room by adding a sky-light and here major surgery incident to such a practice was performed.

The untimely death of this young doctor, of typhus contracted from a patient, brought to an end this excellent medical service to a large and needy Indian population. This mission also had several nurses doing public health and maternity work in the homes.

A fine hospital of another mission in a town in southern Peru, at an altitude of over 12,000 feet, is an oasis of hope for the sick man from the Bolivian border to Cuzco. Here in an unpretentious, inexpensive, adobe building faced with cement is housed an attractive and comfortable apartment for the doctor and his wife – who is a nurse – a modern operating and delivery room, semi-private and private rooms for fifteen patients, a pharmacy and laboratory, a small X-ray unit, consultation and waiting rooms, and a large kitchen. Taking advantage of the warmth from the kitchen stove which has a fire in it twenty-four hours a day, a screened-in alcove has been built for a nursery. Running water and a plant adequate to supply light for the hospital and power for the X-ray complete the set-up. The doctor's wife is training young mestizo girls as nurses and she is hoping shortly to get government recognition for her training school. The doctor has a Peruvian diploma for which he had to pass nine different examining boards on each of which there were three doctors.

The town has about seven thousand people. Only about twenty percent of the hospital patients are Indian and most of them are from a large farm school run by the mission not far from town; others are employees of the railroad, the mines, and the oil company. A large Indian community surrounds the town (the Indians do not live in the towns) and they all come in to market but few know the value of the medical service available at the hospital. Yet at the Sunday service in the beautiful waiting-room of the hospital, by far the largest number of the small group were Indians. The location of this hospital in a town, therefore, automatically prevents it from rendering a greater service to the Indian population until they learn the difference between the treatment offered by a mission doctor and that of their own medicine-man.

* * *

Before proceeding to outline the work being done at the present time by the Evangelical Church in Ecuador, Peru and Bolivia, it is essential to give some of the religious background of the Indian population, though references have been made to it throughout this report.

One Peruvian writer has called the Spanish Conquest of America the "last crusade". Spain had emerged at the beginning of the sixteenth century as a powerful nation, unified after the long struggle against the Moors who had occupied the country for nearly eight centuries. Spain was in the grip of a counter-reformation. The crusading spirit aroused during the campaign against the Moors and the Reformation was transferred to the task of converting the heathen of the New World.

So it was a militant Catholicism which came to America. Indeed, religion was a part of the conquest itself. The famous pact of Pizarro, Almagro and Luque, preceding the conquest of Peru, was celebrated by a solemn mass in Panama.

Once the military conquest of the land was effected, the Spaniards proceeded to try and wipe out the pagan religion. The old gods of the Incas were smashed and the pagan altars torn down. Catholic churches arose in the ruins of the native shrines. Conversions were made on a wholesale scale. One priest boasted that he and another priest had baptised over fourteen thousand Indians in five days. The tragedy of the Andean Indian is largely to be accounted for by the fact that the ritual, the outward forms, such as processions, religious fiestas accompanied by drunken orgies, were what the Indian understood by Christianity. Its deep inner meaning for his soul, for his moral conduct, were never apparent to him.

So the religion of the Indian today is still pagan in essence and the ancient fetishism, animism and superstitions still persist, often disguised under Christian names. In many subtle ways, the Indian worships his old deities while paying homage to an image of Jesus or of the Virgin Mary. In Cuzco we were told, for instance, that the Indians put little mirrors in the crown on the head of an image of Jesus in order that they may worship the sun as its rays are caught. The Virgin Mary is the goddess of the earth to the Indian. The old religion still survives in the hearts of the Indians after four hundred years of "Christianisation".

In an article appearing in the Catholic magazine The Sign in April, 1944, Richard Pattee (formerly of the State Department) admits that the situation of the Indians had not changed in four centuries. Referring to the Indian population in the interior of Peru he says that it is, "poor and backward and, spiritually, not much beyond the initial days of the conquest".

Religion has not brought redemption to the Indian, human betterment and social uplift and an abundant life. It means that he is kept in subjection and ignorance. He is continually impoverished or in debt because of the many fiestas or on account of the demands made on him by the church. "Religion is very far from being supplied gratis in Peru", says Moisés Sáenz. Tariffs imposed for masses, baptisms, marriages and deaths are usually collected before the service is performed.

Even in modern times the Church has failed to grasp its opportunity for bringing health and education to these suffering, ignorant people. "The educational activity of the Catholic Church", says Sáenz, "with respect to the Indians is insignificant – it is limited to the teaching of dogma and can scarcely, if at all, be considered educational or cultural work". Moreover, Sáenz considers that the, "Catholic priest-class dominates Peru with even greater intolerance and arrogance than in other countries".

Evangelical work in the Andean republics has been difficult and progress slow, though there is evidence of greater development in Peru than either Bolivia or Ecuador. The reasons for this slow progress are several. The first arises out of the religious background which we have just outlined. The second reason is that the west coast of South America has been relatively isolated and cut off from European influence. Until the opening of the Panama Canal in 1914, it was not subject to any degree of liberalising influence from the Old World nor has there been any white immigration such as in Chile or Argentina. In the third place, the great natural barriers of these countries have impeded all economic, social and political progress. The towering Andean mountain ranges have isolated groups and prevented the establishment of communications to any extent.

When we turn to the Evangelical church itself, we find another reason which partly accounts for the slow progress of the Gospel among the Indian population, and that is, the approach that has largely been used by the missionaries.

The Indians have clung tenaciously over the centuries to their traditions, beliefs, superstitions, customs and ways of life, and when a foreigner appears among them and tries to make a purely ideological or doctrinal approach with his religion he does not, as a rule, get very far. It is difficult for the Indian to fully understand the new religion even if he wants to. Terms such as sin, salvation, faith and grace even when translated into the Indian language (if they can be) will not have the same content or connotation as they have for the missionary brought up in an entirely different culture. In some parts of Central America, it is impossible to sell white salt to the Indians because the salt they have made for centuries is grey. They have come to regard salt as grey and when a foreigner comes along with a carton of white salt and tries to sell it to the Indian he is not interested. Similarly with ideas and concepts embodied in a religion. We must do more than merely tell people about them, especially when those people are extremely conservative, as the Indians are.

One cannot fail to admire the devotion, sincerity and earnestness of any missionaries and workers in these countries, nor would it be right to belittle their achievements. But in many instances they themselves point to the meagre results of many years' labour as an indication that perhaps their methods should be changed or at least supplemented by other types of work. The effective presentation of the Gospel to such people as the Andean Indians is by no means as simple as it appears at first to be.

* * *

There are at present twenty Protestant missionary agencies with 130 foreign missionaries working in Peru. About one half of the missionaries are British, the largest British society being the Evangelical

Union of South America. Of the total number of foreign missionaries in the country, about one quarter are stationed in Lima. This fairly high proportion is partly accounted for by the fact that the Methodists have four schools in or near Lima and because most societies maintain headquarters or some kind of work in the capital.

The division of territory as agreed upon nearly thirty years ago by the major mission agencies has been more or less observed. New groups coming in have generally been allocated territory for their activities. The Methodists have devoted most of their efforts to educational work. Their four schools in or near Lima and one in Huancayo have undoubtedly made a valuable contribution as well as added prestige to the whole evangelical movement. Their evangelical work is conducted mainly on the coast, in Lima, Callao, and a few other points. There are congregations in Huancayo, Tarma, and several other places in the Sierra of central Peru.

The Free Church of Scotland maintains a large boys' school in the capital, evangelistic and nursing work in and around Cajamarca in the Sierra of northern Peru, and a hospital and evangelistic work in Moyobamba in the upper reaches of the Amazon system. In Cajamarca and Moyobamba the nursing work and medical work respectively have been a splendid approach to evangelistic work among the mestizo population.

The Evangelical Union of South America is an interdenominational missionary agency with headquarters in London. It is one of the oldest and strongest groups in Peru and has missionaries scattered throughout central and southern Peru though the aim is to develop native leadership as much as possible. The most promising work among Indians, we found, was on the altiplano in southern Peru, in and around Ayaviri. This work was started by the Evangelical Union of South America thirteen years ago in an area 250 kilometres by 125 kilometres in which there is a large Indian community. There are fifteen organised churches with nine others in the process of being formed, and it is estimated that there is an evangelical community of six hundred Indians. There is one missionary and the local churches are under the leadership of elders and councils of from three to five men. There are no ordained pastors but there are eleven lay preachers who move about among the churches. The degree of success obtained in this area is due to the development of Indian lay leadership and also to the holding of quarterly conventions for long weekends of fellowship, Bible study and worship. In a way these conventions also supply a substitute for the fiesta, in that they allow social mingling and contacts. Some of those who attend these conventions walk for six days, bringing their food and bedding with them.

The Evangelical Union of South America also maintains a large hacienda or farm of about 7,000 acres at Urco near Cuzco which enjoys a good reputation over a wide area. This mission has been largely responsible for the development of the Iglesia Evangélica Peruana which is a very interesting and outstanding example of a church built on the principle of indigenous growth. It was founded by missionaries who not only had no funds available for the development of the work but were not even assured of their own living. After preliminary visits to the highland regions of southern Peru, a monthly periodical called El Heraldo was started in 1911. This was the beginning of many inquiries and contacts. Invitations came in for persons to visit homes and tell more about the Gospel. Groups were formed around the study of the Bible rather than regular congregations and worship services. The groups were ministered to by some unpaid workers. There were no foreign workers employed as pastors but as time went on a few native workers served in this capacity. The supervision of missionary leaders and the counsel and inspiration that they have been able to give the scattered congregations have been important factors in the unification of this work. In time, the number of groups having multiplied, annual synods of delegates appointed by local churches began to be held.

At the present time, the Iglesia Evangélica Peruana is divided into two synods with twelve presbyteries. At one time there were as many as one hundred congregations in these two synods but a change in policy with regard to the organisation of the synod meetings has resulted in a decline. Evangelistic fervour among the congregations is not as great as it used to be, and book reading has become rare among local evangelical leaders compared with the early period. However, plans are now being made which will place new emphasis on the training of leaders.

The experience of this indigenous church movement affords many valuable lessons for the future development of the evangelical movement among the Indians of the high Andes.

The Christian and Missionary Alliance has twenty organised churches in Lima and the Huánuco region in the interior, and a number of other smaller groups among Indians. With the co-operation of the Evangelical Union of South America and the Free Church of Scotland, the Alliance maintains a good Bible institute in the environs of Lima. The course of seven years is divided into three years of preparatory work, two years of field work during which the student continues to study by correspondence, and two further years of training. The Institute has a good faculty composed of missionaries. At the time the Commission visited the Institute, there were fourteen students in residence.

Missionaries in the mountain areas expressed concern over the problem of training of workers as they felt that as a rule it was unwise to send students from a humble rural environment to be trained in comparatively luxurious surroundings in a residential suburb of Lima and then to return to make the adjustment to village life again. As a result of this difficulty, few Indians have been trained at this Institute.

– *Extracted from: W. Stanley Rycroft [Editor], Indians of the High Andes.*

Into the 1960s:
Dr. David and Nurse Netta on the Sierra

"WELL, DOCTOR, THIS SEEMS QUITE GOOD. WHAT BOOK DID YOU GET it from?" It was the last of my twenty-seven exams, for a degree in medicine at the university of San Marcos, in Lima, and the senior of my three examiners was looking at my thesis. It was written on some rather technical aspect of preventive medicine and he judged rightly that my masterly exposition of the matter was not out of my own head but taken straight from one of the best British text-books on the subject. He even enquired the name of the book and, for a moment, looked as though he would ask the loan of it and then he thought better and, after consulting briefly with his colleagues, he told me I had passed and we all shook hands. So ended a ten months' battle for recognition as a member of the medical profession in Peru. We call the process one of 'revalidation' and it is becoming more and more common for different countries, as they set up their own medical faculties, to require doctors from outside to gain recognition of their foreign degrees within the country in which they wish to work. This is the rule in Great Britain; and it is also the rule in all the South American republics. For me, it had been a hard pull full of delays and disillusionments.

At first they would not even let me start and I spent long hours waiting for an interview with the dean of the medical faculty. He was very much opposed to letting me go ahead with my revalidation and never did let me into his office. However, one day, I waited until he eventually had to come out, and then I accosted him. It so happened that he had known Dr. Ronald Payne when he was doing his revalidation in Lima and he had admired him greatly. I mentioned Dr. Payne and his untimely death from typhus so soon after starting his work, and used this to enforce my claims. Eventually he gave me his qualified and grudging approval and my trials began.

Then, just when things were going nicely, we awoke one morning to find that a serious revolution had broken out, with the army and the navy on opposite sides. It did not last long but when I went to the medical faculty for further instructions, the dean and his secretary had disappeared, being on the losing side. However the authorities seemed very anxious that I should not suffer because of their troubles and, eventually, this seemed to help rather than hinder. And so I had finished and the first important step had been taken towards work among the Indians of the High Andes.

The Indians of the High Andes is the title of a most capable survey by the Committee for Co-operation in Latin America on the Indians of Ecuador, Peru and Bolivia, and how romantic it had all seemed when I read it in London. Now I was ready to take my wife up to the mountains, or Sierra as it is called, to start work among them. We had met in Moyobamba, in the jungle of north-eastern Peru, when I went there to the Free Church hospital to work with Dr. Harold Lindsay. Netta was in charge of the nursing work and I repaid Dr. Lindsay's kindness by taking his nurse! The people of Moyobamba are Spanish-speaking and as warm-hearted as their tropical climate, and Netta had loved her work among them. When she first saw the poor, dirty Sierra towns and the Indians, to whom she could say nothing since they only spoke Quechua, she felt like going straight back to her beloved Moyobamba.

These Sierra Indians, who for the most part are descended from the serfs of Inca days, are both physically and morally a poor little people. They are dark brown in complexion, with thick, straight, black hair. Their features are nondescript except where you find a little community here and there whose features remind one of the typical faces depicted on their Inca pottery, and then they can be most striking, with full lips, slanting eyes, and a fine long nose. Their babies are born with a mop of thick, straight hair and the women folk look with wonder at our bald offspring. Characteristically, this thick hair grows from well down on the forehead and this mark of Indian blood is sometimes a matter of concern to those who would like to think of themselves as more of Spanish descent. School teachers who have worked both on the coast and in the mountains say that the Indian children are very dull and slow in comparison with their counterparts at lower altitudes and, though a sustained attempt is being made by the government to give the Indian children the benefit of a rudimentary education, it is slow, uphill work.

* * *

The scene now changes from Lima at the beginning of 1949, when I received my diploma of medicine from the university of San Marcos, to the Indian Bible Institute in Sicuani on 6th June, 1952. By now we had set up our medical work in Talavera, in the department of Apurimac. Mrs. Thompson and Gertrude McKnight (afterwards Mrs. Montgomery) were helping with the nursing work and Dr. Hugh Montgomery had come out and was in his turn doing his revalidation; it was time to think seriously of the future of medical work.

We were happy and busy enough in Talavera and the climate was ideal, it being at an altitude of less than 10,000 feet. But we were not quite satisfied with the spiritual side of things. The church in Anda-huaylas, to which we belonged, was well-established and somehow we felt that one of the great contributions of medical work was to form a spearhead into unoccupied territory, especially where living conditions are difficult, and contacts made by treating people can help so much in one's daily life. I had, on this occasion, left Talavera for a month to come and teach in the Indian Bible Institute, and we were having a meeting of our medical committee, consisting of Mrs.

Jardine, Leslie Hoggarth, and myself to discuss our plans for the future. We like to feel that Special Departments, such as medicine, are all very much part of the work as a whole, and for this reason these committees were formed. It was now, at our first meeting of this committee, that Santo Tomás was mentioned.

Santo Tomás itself is a town of around three thousand inhabitants, but is the road-head and market-town for a big area and the natural centre for anyone wanting to do work such as ours. It is the capital of Chumbivilcas but it is a derelict place compared with other such towns in the mountains of Peru and even the rich families, who have nice houses in Arequipa, are content to live there under very primitive conditions. The social set-up is still more or less feudal, there being very little between the landlord and the serfs. The former are known as misti, and this term now includes nearly all those who can speak Spanish and earn a reasonable salary; and the latter, for historical reasons, are known as Indians. Here again, in Santo Tomás we lag behind the rest of Peru. One of the most important changes politically over the last twenty or thirty years has been the emergence of a middle-class, but we have seen little of this and there is, of course, an important relation between this social set-up and the spread of the Gospel.

Santo Tomás lies at an altitude of over 12,000 feet, in a huge tract of country between the railway line from Juliaca to Cuzco and the western mountain ranges, known as the Cordillera Volcánica. In colonial days, it was important for the precious metals which were mined in the region, but its very remoteness and the fact that opportunities for work have opened up in other places, notably in the jungle of the Convención Valley, means that it has fallen on lean days. Nevertheless, it could still support a considerable population and the climate is healthy compared with that of the jungle. To us as missionaries it had always presented a challenge as having no consistent witness to the Gospel.

When, therefore, we went on furlough in 1953, our future was very much in our prayer, and figured prominently on my prayer list. After our return to Peru at the end of 1954, we did a year in the

Sicuani Bible Institute because of a shortage of staff, and then we got ready for our new venture. First I visited the churches of the Ayaviri region and went to the mid-year Convention of the churches around Cuzco by way of interesting them in this new development. Then we did a reconnaissance trip with a view to finding somewhere we could live. And so it was that, just after David's fifth birthday, at the beginning of October 1956, we were ready to start.

* * *

A sleepless night! At last we were ready to go into Santo Tomás and we were spending the night in Sicuani. The lorry was loaded. This had taken most of the previous day as I had had to threaten to take the owner to the police because, after I had paid for the whole load, he had arrived with the floor covered with sacks full of bottles: not a nice base on which to put our furniture and boxes! As it was, I was foolish enough to let him take one sack and this, with hours of bumping over bad roads, successfully smashed one of our best tables. However, threats had prevailed and we had loaded up and he had driven away with all our precious things, to return next morning before dawn to pick us up and set out on our journey.

But I did not sleep much. The responsibility of taking Netta and the boys into the unknown and all the possibilities of what might happen to our stuff during the night and to ourselves the next day were going round and round in my head. We had already been in to have a look round and we had got the promise of a house to live in, but such promises, as we were soon to find out, are very uncertain things to depend on; and the famous town of Santo Tomás, so renowned for its lawlessness, was little more than a collection of thatched huts. My chief worry that night was over our stuff. The lorry owner had already cast his eye on my rucksack and had asked for it and I was wondering how many more things would have disappeared before we got settled in.

As usual, my worries were quite unfounded and we lost nothing. The lorry did fulfil my worst fears by spluttering to a standstill a few miles from Sicuani. But it got going immediately and we had no more trouble. On its next journey, however, it was stuck for a week with a broken front axle, just to show what might have happened to us! In fact, our troubles came from quite a different direction, but fortunately it did not occur to me to worry that night about the question of our house.

* * *

We arrived at our destination late that night and the lorry owner, whom I had only the day before almost taken to law, informed me with a charming smile that he had telegraphed his wife and that we were to do him the honour of spending our first night in Santo Tomás under his roof. This is so typical of these folk, and indeed it would seem that the royal road to friendship is to start your acquaintance with them with a first-class row.

Next day I went to find the headmaster of the school, who had promised that we might occupy what was his apartment in the new school building which had just been put up with the help of American Aid under the Point Four Plan. We had already heard rumours and the worst was true. He did not now think that it would be possible to occupy the apartment as a new inspector of education had arrived. I asked where the inspector was and he said that he was away on a trip and would not be back for several days. In my desperation I began to try to read into his replies more than I knew was really there. I realised that though he would not say "no" bluntly to my face, this is what he really meant, and I had to reconcile myself to the fact that this was the answer.

We learned later that the matter had nothing to do with the inspector. The flat in the school was entirely at the disposal of the headmaster and he could have let us have it if he had so wished. He himself did not want to occupy it, his reason being that it had too many windows, and windows, in Santo Tomás, are considered the height of folly. When later the Medical Post was put up, also with American aid, our friend the doctor told us quite seriously that he would not think of sleeping in a room with an outside window; for it would be much too easy to shoot him! But so far as the school apartment was concerned, the headmaster had yielded to public opinion, which was that we were not wanted in Santo Tomás, so this was now no longer at our disposal.

I now had plenty of time for reflection and repentance and we tried to console ourselves with such formulae as, "the next time we do this sort of thing", etc. However, the fact of the matter was that, if we were to come at all to live in Santo Tomás, we could hardly expect things to be otherwise. A promise, even a signed contract, means very little to these folk, and we were beginning to learn this the hard way. So we left Ada, our maid, and the boys playing with the children of the house and went to look for a place to live in.

Now it so happened (blessed word this to missionaries in difficulties) that one of the principal men in the town had an inflammation of one of his eyes that was threatening to destroy his sight. It was touch and go as to whether it would spread to the other side and leave him totally blind. He was the one man who could immediately provide us with a room and he needed our help almost as badly as we needed his. Our search around the town had proved fruitless. We went first to the wife of the mayor, where we had stayed on our reconnaissance trip, but she was not interested. We examined a large and promising-looking building, but this turned out to be the prison. We had a look at another house but, though we later got possession of it, this was occupied at the moment and when we got back to our anxious little flock, the owner of the lorry was making noises that indicated that he wanted to unload, in order to use his car. So we decided to take the room offered us by the gentleman with the bad eye. We ourselves were anxious to get settled. We were by now more or less certain that the house in which we lodged was one of not very good repute and that, in fact, their small boys were only able to give time to playing with ours when they were not otherwise engaged soliciting for the family business. This was no place to have a girl of fourteen, to say nothing of our two boys, so we closed with the offer of the room and began to move in.

This room was quite the dirtiest we could have imagined. Most Indian huts have a floor of beaten mud but this was an upstairs room and the floor was pure dust, formed of the accumulated filth of ages. Any attempt to beat it would have done little more than deposit it all over the room below, as it was supported only on the branches of shrubs laid over the beams. And, by way of leaving us in no doubt as to what the dirt consisted of, there was a carefully preserved series of samples on some painted but shattered woodwork inside the door. We cleansed the paint, but the floor was impossible to clean, so we laid sheets of paper over it and did our best to forget it. However, the dust was unavoidable and our children woke up choking at night. David cried every day for our lovely mission house at Huantura, where we had been before setting out, and we all felt that we could not stand living under such conditions for very long.

John was six and David just five. We had had his birthday party in Sicuani with Dr. and Mrs. Montgomery and this had been a memorable and enjoyable occasion. We had brought the birthday cake with us and, in those first few days, when food was scarce and spirits were low, this was a great joy to us. However, one of our first patients was the lady who ran the chief eating-house in town. She was grateful for our help and became a firm friend and, in all our time in Santo Tomás, it was only on very rare occasions that she could not let us have a little meat when we appealed to her.

Food was always a problem for us. There was a market only on Sundays and at this fruit and vegetables but no meat and eggs were sold. For the most part, meat and eggs had to be bought from people coming in to the Sunday market. Such people had to sell on Sunday as they needed the money to buy in the market and go home the same day. Later we learned how to get in touch with people who arrived on Saturday night, but at first this presented us with an almost insoluble problem and we relied mostly on stuff which our folk in Arequipa, principally Brenda Chalker, sent up to us. Our weekly package from the city became the high spot of the week for us, containing, as if often did, letters and papers as well as food. It was a heavy burden for the Arequipa end but it was kindly and cheerfully borne and it meant a great deal to us. Such supplying of others is a very common chore in the mission field, but I know now from experience how much it can mean to the receiver and how appreciated it is.

We arrived in Santo Tomás just as the severe failure of the rains was making itself felt, and we only saw fresh milk on the rarest of occasions. There was indeed milk to be had not far from the town, but no one was interested in bringing it in for us. Both in Sicuani and Huantura, where we had been for the last eighteen months, we had first quality milk, which was excellent for the children and now we faced a diet more or less without this staple food. However, we were not very long established before the American Aid fat-free powdered milk began to arrive. This was to be given free to the school-children, but word soon got round that it wasn't good and very few would take it. For this reason it was put up for sale, and we bought as much as we thought we could keep. As the food shortage became more acute, and people saw how we were using it, they changed their minds and it was in great demand. Later, when we ourselves were distributing this milk, we were allowed to use it for our own needs, and so it was that the ravens remembered us again.

But, to return to our story, we treated the gentleman with the bad eye with cortisone eye ointment, which I happened to have with me, and it got rapidly better. We now found that the one house which would be at all suitable for us belonged to his brother and he was instrumental in helping us to get it. I was due in Huancayo, away in central Peru, for our annual Field Meetings a fortnight after we had arrived and we wanted to get into our new house as soon as possible, if only for this reason. But there was the question of the amount of the rent to be settled and this was a delicate matter which could not be hurried. After various promises and assurances on the part of the owner, which did not seem to be getting us anywhere, I finally went round and asked point-blank how much he wanted. This is just what he had hoped I would do, and he was ready.

He said seven hundred soles a month, which was, I believe, the price that Stuart Harrison was paying at the time for a modern flat in the centre of Lima! It was by all standards a ridiculous proposal but I was desperate and he knew it. I fought back, starting my offer at two hundred and we eventually agreed that we should pay four hundred a month for the whole house when it was finished and, in the meantime, sixty soles for each room as we occupied them.

This was the beginning of a long battle of offers and counter-offers, threats and counter-threats, attempts to take the house from us when we were on holiday, and finally a request for us to get out, to get more money out of us. We had only just arrived in time, as with the American Aid came officials, and houses which had been difficult enough to get hold of before, became completely unobtainable. This put the owners of our house into a state of perpetual mourning because they had not got us to agree to pay more and when I mentioned their flagrant breaches of contract they said quite simply that it was because they wanted more money. Eventually, I agreed to pay them five hundred soles a month for the out-houses as well and, having agreed on this, they almost at once let the out-houses to the girls' school, thus depriving us of the space that we had hoped to use for medical work. However, one just has to learn how to play this particular kind of game and we did eventually find ways and means of countering them.

And so it was that just before I left for Field Meetings we moved into the first two rooms of our new house. I put up a ceiling downstairs and a wardrobe upstairs, which are the two essential features if one has to live in a barn. This was to be our home for two and a half years in Santo Tomás. To the boys it was to become home, that vital pivotal point in the experience of a child, symbol of security in childhood and, in later years, of our eternal rest in God Himself.

* * *

We now had a toe-hold in Santo Tomás, but the physical strain of the next six months reduced us to a state of exhaustion which we have not experienced before or since. From a medical point of view, its effect was to produce a syndrome, which we came to call 'exhaustion syndrome', which consisted of severe bouts of vomiting and which responded perfectly to nothing but rest. When we went on holiday to the Pacific coast, it was ten days before we got back to our normal routine so far as sleeping was concerned.

Santo Tomás is at an altitude of over twelve thousand feet and, though this is nothing to climbers, it begins to tell when added to the other difficulties of life in primitive conditions. Our children soon adapted themselves to the altitude but, probably as a result of living in the dirty room, one of them had an infected crack in his upper lip for so long that I began to wonder if some permanent damage would not result. However, later, they were never better than when at home, since the primitive nature of our dwelling meant that they spent the whole day out of doors, and though they had all the childish illnesses they soon threw them off, and we were happy to see them well and thriving. The poverty of our diet did not seem to affect them. We trust that whatever parasites they may have come by are only such as can be easily got rid of.

I now had to leave Netta and the family and go to Field Meetings, which meant an absence of three weeks. We had realised, of course, that this would be the case, though we had not anticipated the difficulties over the housing question, and we had only been in our new house three days when I left. However, we had not wanted to delay any more starting out on our new venture and so it was that I came to leave Netta and the two boys with a fourteen year old girl in an indifferent, if not hostile, environment.

The house we were now in was a palace compared with the room we had left, but it was still little more than a barn. The thick mud walls had been left level at the top, where the roof fitted over, and this spacious shelf collected all sorts of debris and whenever the wind blew hard under the eaves, there was a shower of dirt into the room. There was no sanitation, but we were on the edge of the town and this was one of the great advantages of the house. Before, we had been in the main square, and the entrance to the house had been used regularly as a public convenience.

Perhaps the most trying of all was the complete indifference of the people towards us and their unwillingness to help. All water had to be carried by hand, but no one was at all keen to earn a little money by bringing it. This was one of the things that struck us most as time went on. The people might be face to face with the awful spectre of a drought and on the borders of starvation, but they were not at all interested in doing a little work to help themselves. In one of the out-houses of our new home lived a lady of easy virtue with her two children. She, of course, was too proud to do anything for us, but then so also was her schoolboy son. This is the first problem which confronts anyone who wishes to help folk such as these – their complete inertia. With the help of the U.S., the Peruvian government launched a well-conceived plan of relief for the whole region, but they retired baffled with the work uncompleted. Engineers came to examine the possibilities of irrigation projects but they too went away in disgust and have not returned. We want to help and we believe that the Gospel is the only power that can help, but even here it will be a long, slow work of faith and patience.

* * *

I had been away but a few days on my journey when Netta went down with what must have been something very near pneumonia. She lay in bed with a racking cough and nothing seemed to make any difference. Ada, our maid, looked after the boys but could do little else. Things seemed to be going from bad to worse and poor Netta's chief worry was as to who would bury her and what would happen to the children. At last she tried some Chloromycetin and this seemed to help her turn the corner. She was just getting over the worst when an urgent call came for her to go and see a girl who was dying after childbirth. At first it was impossible to consider it, but the case was so tragic and the call so urgent that at last, more dead than alive, she went. It turned out to be a poor girl who was so far gone that she could hardly see, but when Netta held her hand and spoke to her, she recognised a friend and cried pathetically, "Señorita, señorita, don't leave me, don't leave me!" Netta managed to sit with her for a while and then the Beatas came. These are women devotees of the Church who earn merit by good works and they had come to help the girl as best they could in her last moments. They had brought their books with them but none could find the place, for they only knew where to find prayers to the Virgin, and these were evidently not in order on such occasions. At last they gave up and asked Netta to pray, which she was only too glad to do. The ladies listened with wide-eyed wonder and were most impressed and poor Nilda clung to Netta's hand – perhaps it was her only way now of calling on the name of the Lord.

One of the people who wasn't there was the Government Doctor. He had been in many places in Peru and had eventually landed up in Santo Tomás. He must have been one of the last of a number of European refugees who were accepted by the Peruvian government if they would work in out-of-the-way places. Now Peru itself is turning out young doctors in sufficient numbers to supply its needs, and we were indeed glad to welcome one such instead of Dr. Fernando some months later.

Dr. Fernando was not present when Nilda died and there was nothing to be gained by his being there. He was present a few days before when we had had a case which ended in much the same way. Shortly after we arrived, one of the finest old ladies in the town had a strangulated hernia and I was asked to attend to her. I decided that, other methods having failed, I must operate and Dr. Fernando was asked to give the anaesthetic. We decided on an induction with an intravenous injection and the doctor brought out a large wrist watch and went ahead. Despite all my protests, he continued his injection until the patient was dead and there the matter ended. For me, it was indeed a mercy that I had not started to operate, for I should have had to shoulder the blame for my colleague's inefficiency if I had, but it was a tragedy that could have been avoided if I had known then what I afterwards learned about my opposite number.

Our first operation having ended so ingloriously, there was nothing to do but to sympathise with the relatives and attend the funeral. The family was one which afterwards became friends of ours, and they were very grateful for what we had tried to do for them. The funeral was a first-class one, that is, one that the Church provides for people who can pay, and the coffin was first carried from the house to the fine old church building. I waited outside, as I was afraid that I might cause offence if I entered. I learned afterwards that this would not have been the case. As it was, I found myself outside with a group of men who would not enter for various reasons, some of them at least because they were atheists. This was the case with the Doctor, who never lost an opportunity to scoff at the Church and its ordinances, and this was not a group with which I wished to be associated. I therefore separated myself from them and stood near the church door, examining the Biblical texts which had been incorporated into the stone-work. I feel now that it would have been better if I had entered and stood just within the main doors.

After this ceremony, the coffin was carried by stages to the cemetery and the procession stopped every now and then for an oration by some prominent member of the community. These were sincere tributes to one who had evidently been a great and good lady. As the procession wound round the little hill outside the town, the Beatas chanted and read responses and the Indian women set up a dirge.

These Quechua dirges, it would seem from early Spanish accounts, played an important part in the life and experience of the people in Inca times and they are most impressive. The Indians, both before and after the Spanish Conquest, have had their share of suffering but they have learned to express their sorrow and find an outlet for their feelings in such tragic and heart-rending songs, just as the Jews of old did, on a much higher plane, in the Psalms. We too had our moments of sadness in Peru and this is one of the lessons that I learned from such times.

After the funeral we had a reception and I sat next to the priest. He began to ask about Urco, as he came from the Urubamba Valley and knew a lot about the farm. I stayed as long as I felt I had to and then made my apologies and hurried back to the family. We were still, at this time, in our first room, but it was now our home and it seemed a heavenly spot after the scenes of incipient drunkenness from which I had just come.

This was my first visit to the cemetery and I learned, among other things, of their belief that if, after a funeral, you return to the town the same way as you have come, you will soon return feet-first. Under the stones near the main gate lives a black and red spider, whose bite is said to be fatal. Once, when I was away, a girl was brought to Netta, nearly dead with fright after being bitten. Netta put in a little morphia and the girl woke up a few hours later in the best of health. After this, everybody wanted to know our great secret but, for the sake of future patients, we kept it to ourselves. It is said, however, that horses have died after being bitten but that if you have been stung previously by a hornet, called a nina-nina, you are then immune to the bite of the spider.

Just above the cemetery is a relatively insignificant hill, called Sunaca, which is considered very sacred to the Indians. Here it is that the most solemn obligation of 'sending away' the soul of a dead person is performed in a special ceremony known as the alma kachar pariy. Details differ from town to town but the essential features are the coming together of the relatives, who prepare a special bundle known as the despacho, in which are included all the delicacies and foods of which the deceased was especially fond, and then burn it on the hill. The purpose of the despacho is to provide the soul with what it will require for its long journey, for it must then travel to a massive volcano near Arequipa, called Coropuna. Also, a dog is killed so that its spirit may serve as a companion on the way and help the spirit of the person concerned to cross 'the river of blood' – a stream which, by day, flows normally from the mountains but which, at night, becomes a raging torrent, impossible to cross except with the help of the faithful beast.

However, the cemetery featured chiefly in my later experiences as the place where I had to do post-mortem examinations. There was no mortuary in the town and when, for legal reasons, an autopsy was necessary, it was done in the open air in the cemetery. The body was usually carried there in a poncho (this is a square blanket, with an opening in the centre for the head, worn by men) and all interested parties gathered round. As each organ is exposed, there are grunts and comments from the audience and everything is helped along by the ever-present cheap rum. After it is all over, the body is wrapped in the poncho and dropped into the grave. On one such occasion, a drunken Indian was asked to finish the ceremony with a prayer. He offered an ex tempore prayer in Quechua, ending with the words: "And may the devil take the brute who cut him up!" referring, of course, to me.

I was once called upon, under such trying conditions, to examine the body of a man who was a workman on the road and who was said to have died as the result of a kick in the abdomen by a foreman. Forensic medicine has never been my strong point, and I was much at a loss to know how I should decide whether or not the man's death was attributable to the treatment he had received. I examined the body but could find little more than a large bruise in the solar plexus area and signs of chronic starvation. I was somewhat in doubt as to what to say, when a deputation from the friends of the accused man arrived to ask me to give a favourable verdict. This tipped the balances and confirmed me in my belief that the foreman was most likely responsible!

The result was that he was kept in prison for two years and then set at liberty on bail. How this came about is difficult to understand, as he should have been sent to Cuzco for trial within six months. However, in the light of our subsequent experience, it would seem to have been a sort of trial by ordeal, for any man who, at this time came out alive after such an experience could perhaps be considered to deserve his liberty. Justice in Santo Tomás goes more according to the person concerned than according to the Penal Code.

* * *

It was now drawing near to Christmas and I had brought back from Field Meetings a projector and film strips of various Bible themes, including that of the Nativity. I got permission to show these in the large stone building which served as the Town Hall, but we got away to an inauspicious start when, having made all the arrangements with the Secretary, we arrived on the first evening to find the whole place locked up. I was glad to have Netta with me for moral support, though the boys did not like being left alone with Ada, and we put up the screen outside and showed a few pictures to a handful of bystanders. However, next Sunday evening a boy, who had seen something of the show, volunteered to go and get the key and this time the Secretary turned up.

He stayed to watch and was always afterwards most helpful. In this way we reached a good proportion of the population and distributed Gospel literature to them. On Christmas Day we showed the Nativity scenes in our house and a good crowd turned out, including many of the matrons of the town, who are the hardest to reach.

We did, however, make a bad mistake with our Christmas tree. We had got this ready for our children and, among other things, had hung on it a lovely Christmas card of the Holy Family, which a friend had sent us from Canada. As soon as it became known that we had a tree, everyone wanted to come and see it and we were surprised at its popularity. Eventually a simple Indian, with whom we had become friendly, turned up and immediately knelt down before our icon and started to cross himself and recite some prayers. I was horrified and knelt down with him and, after he had finished, prayed in a loud voice that he might come to know the living Saviour. We were very shaken that so many had come to see our tree, thinking it another shrine where merit might be gained by the recitation of a few prayers, and we took it down and in future years kept it a strictly family affair.

* * *

It was one day soon after Christmas that a poor woman, with a child, was brought to the house by a pleasant man, dressed in black, and this is how I first came to know Erasmo Saldivar. He gave me unstintingly of his time and it was with him that, after examining the behaviour of some two hundred and fifty verbs, I wrote my first paper on the use of some Quechua particles. He was one of the group that Dr. Efrain Morote had gathered around him in Cuzco, who are dedicated to the study of Indian folklore. It would seem that the word folklore has been taken straight across into the Spanish, not without causing some difficulty to students. The first girl from whom I heard about Dr. Morote's work carefully spelt it out as "foreklore". The girl in question, who was a student under Dr. Morote in the University of Cuzco, was telling me of a practice that the Indians on their isolated farms still have of sacrificing to the hills. There are some small workings of metal ores and the Indians engaged in the work are so terrified of the presumption involved in thus robbing the hill concerned that they will at times bury a baby or an old person alive by way of placating the powerful spirit. As in nearly all mountainous countries, the hills are revered, and here the Indian believes that the spirit of one hill controls the fertility of his land, another his cattle, another the health of himself and his family, and soon.

Señor Salvidar taught me some very interesting things about Indian customs. The Indian still makes an absolute distinction between himself and those of Spanish descent, who are called the misti, and nowhere is this distinction more carefully preserved than in the question of their religious customs. Thus it was that Saldivar came to see me one day, very excited because he had witnessed, for the first time, the offerings that the Indian makes to his gods. The offerings consist of little piles of maize, spread out on a table. The gods were the spirits of the different hills, each of which has a name and a different status, and also included was Santiago, which is the name they give to the god of thunder and lightning. Santiago was the patron saint of the conquistadores and it was with the battle-cry of "Santiago" that these Spaniards fired the fatal fusillade which toppled the Inca Empire, when they kidnapped the Inca in the main square of Cajamarca. This may account for the fact that the Indians identified the god of lightning with the patron saint of the men who, in their muskets, seemed to have lightning at their command.

* * *

I returned to Santo Tomás alone, by way of Sicuani. Mario Moscoso, one of our Indian preachers, was dying of tuberculosis and I went to see if there was anything that could be done for him. He had succumbed to this final attack because of exposure while out on the Lord's work and he lay now in his windowless house, surrounded by his wife and four little children. It was a pathetic picture and yet there were bright gleams of triumph. Here was an Indian who had been faithful to the end. Many times his family had tried to persuade him to consider himself rather than the work but he had refused to look back. And now he was going to his reward. We sang together his favourite hymn and then I read from Second Timothy: "I have fought the good fight... henceforth there is laid up for me a crown of righteousness", and we said goodbye. On the day when those from every tribe and tongue gather before the throne, there will be a contingent from the Quechuan Indians and Mario will be there. As I left that dark hut thinking of the next time I would meet him, I felt something of the glory and solemnity of that great day.

* * *

One day a poor woman came along with a deep parotid abscess, the pain of which was just about driving her crazy. The only thing to do was to incise it but, as she was alone, I did not want to do it just on my own responsibility. I therefore went round to see her patrón (as the feudal landlord is called). After listening to what I had to say, he answered, "Of course, Doctor, do it as an act of charity"; which meant that he didn't mind very much what happened as long as he did not have to pay. The only suitable anaesthetic was an intravenous one but, for obvious reasons, I was not very keen on asking the Doctor to give it, so I asked the male nurse to help. All went well and, on waking up from the anaesthetic the woman said: "puñurusqani", which means, more or less, "Well, if I didn't just go off to sleep without realising it". This was the first time that I had heard this tense used in this person in Quechua.

These male nurses, or sanitarios, as they are called, are a great feature of the more out-of-the-way places in Peru. They are very ready to put in injections and, with an antibiotic and a sedative, they can cope with almost any emergency – after a fashion. They often attend confinements and, though they are an advance on the old gamps, who do the majority of such work, they are liable to become overconfident and do not understand when they should ask for help. Such was the case with Corsina, a neighbour of ours, who was due to have her first baby a few months before we were to leave. I was away at Field Meetings and the sanitario was asked to attend. He failed to recognise a Hand Presentation and when nothing seemed to be of any avail, a contest gradually took shape between the enlightened relatives, headed by the young policeman who was the father of the unborn child, and the old-fashioned faction, headed by the girl's aunt. Neither party would give in and the young man came in search of Netta. While she was getting her instruments ready, the Opposition called for the local Medicine-Men. Netta arrived to find that the sanitario had fled and the Medicine-Men were in charge. They had blocked-up the whole space of the door with a blanket to keep out the very dangerous Spirit of the Wind and were about to carry out a famous manoeuvre which consisted of tossing the patient in a blanket. If the mother's life was to be saved, there wasn't a minute to waste.

Tearing down the blanket, Netta kicked open the door. Inside were the two Medicine-Men and the old woman who was the chief instigator of the plot. The girl was screaming and the man was looking helpless and miserable. The witches were driven out and Netta got permission to go ahead. So far so good; but what now if she failed to save the girl? These cases can be difficult in the best conditions; they may be impossible in an Indian hut. The sanitario had been sent for and he and the man were the assistants. Ada was the anaesthetist and, after a moment of urgent prayer, the battle was joined. Preliminary manipulations left a high, difficult forceps. Time and again the instruments failed to get a proper hold and desperately

Netta re-applied them with efforts that sapped all her strength and left her stiff for days to come. At last, when dismal failure seemed the only answer, the tide turned and the baby was delivered. A stormy convalescence, and we had a grateful little neighbour who was always ready to help us and listen to what we had to teach her.

* * *

One morning I had a visit from the lady under whose roof we spent our first night in the town. She was in great distress as her brother-in-law was very ill out on his farm and she wanted me to go and see him. I had no one to help me to get my things together so it was mid-day before I was ready, but the good lady gave me a large plate of eggs and rice before I left. This stood me in good stead as I had twenty-five miles to go. I had taken some bread and hard-boiled eggs but it wasn't long before I put my hand in my pocket and found that the eggs were not hard-boiled, so that just left the bread. I should say that it takes a good fifteen minutes to hard-boil an egg at the altitude at which we work and I was missing the help and care of my family. It was dark by the time we got in and I was chilled to the marrow, but a good plate of hot soup revived me and I then examined my patient.

He was suffering from a meningitis which afterwards proved to be syphilitic and the acute phase had been provoked by his having got drunk and gone to sleep in the sun. By now he was literally climbing the walls so I did a lumbar puncture, which made him once again rational, and we all had a good night. I did not realise who the shadowy figures in the background were but they turned out to be the local Medicine-Men, whose chief was distinguished by the fact that he had a large goitre. They were greatly impressed by my witchcraft and by its dramatic result. It would indeed have been more up their street if I had extracted part of a dead toad instead of a colourless liquid, but at least I had produced something and had helped the sick man, so they retired to their dark corner of the kitchen and kept quiet. However, such meningitis is not cured by a lumbar puncture and in the ensuing days, as the headache persisted, they came back into their own somewhat, and I was able to observe their technique.

On the afternoon before I had arrived, they had performed the well-known treatment of the muda, which means the exchange. A dog had been killed and immediately opened up down the midline and then tied on the sick man's back, the head of the animal in a position corresponding to his head. After some hours, it was removed and the head was cut off and, with the brain exposed, it was left outside on a stone to rot in the sun. The theory is that the disease is transferred to the dog's brain and then disappears in the process of decomposition.

I had found my friend the sanitario there when I arrived but I don't think that he had anything to do with this famous form of treatment. He was putting in injections of Streptomycin and this was, by comparison, rather colourless and was not producing much in the way of results. The patient's headache persisted and so another form of treatment was resorted to. A large mud brick was heated thoroughly over the fire and then carried into the bedroom where putrid urine was poured over it. It was then placed at the patient's feet. The results can be imagined so far as smell and unpleasantness are concerned but it was impressive to the relatives and I felt that I was beginning to lose the initiative. I therefore insisted that the sick man accompany me back to Santo Tomás, and this he promised to do the following day.

That night I awoke at midnight. I was sleeping at the head of my patient's bed, this being the only bedroom in the house, and I was thus to witness one of the most solemn and secret of all their spiritist ceremonies, the calling-back of the spirit or alma waqyay. No 'unbeliever' is ever allowed to be present at such times, so for me it was a chance in a million. The male witches were all assembled at the sick man's side, and indeed they had never left him alone, except when I started to talk to him about God. They have an uncanny sense of time, these men, for they had no clock and yet, by my wristwatch, it was just midnight. I knelt on my bed, not knowing what was happening and watched, fascinated, as the leader proceeded with the ceremony. My intrusion may or may not have been noticed, but he could do nothing now but go on, as this and this only was the midnight hour and all had led up to this. He bent intently over the prostrate man's head, and rubbing something together in his hands, he uttered a low, hoarse cry and then waited. He moved a little down towards the man's feet and repeated the process and so on until he had been the whole length of the body. Each time he waited, as though listening for an answer, for he was calling back the man's spirit which was supposed to be wandering away from his body.

* * *

It is quite different working in the jungles of Peru, where malaria and hookworm take such a toll and respond so dramatically to treatment. In the mountains the chief plagues have been smallpox and typhus and these are responding to the government-sponsored vaccination programme and to the use of DDT. We have also had cases of typhoid, but this was mainly due to the drought making drinking-water so scarce. So far as medicine is concerned, the people themselves have their own remedies, some of which are quite good and some of which are pure superstition. They are very fond of the old Hippocratic system of classifying diseases, so that all ailments are divided into a hot and a cold class and similarly foods and remedies are said to be either hot or cold. Success in treatment depends on combining just the right hot medicine with the appropriate cold disease. There is a good deal of doubt among the people themselves as to which medicines are hot and cold and even more conjecture as to whether your illness is due to heat or cold, so that anybody can chip in and give advice. This is most satisfactory to everybody except the patient and he usually resorts to an old adage which says – "Anything not cured by a good dram of rum, won't be cured by anything!", and with that peace reigns. Their herbal remedies are good and I encourage their use and employ them for myself when I am ill. After all, Peru has given quinine and cocaine to the world and it is more than likely that among some of the household remedies in use today there are things that will be used later on by modern medicine.

* * *

The results of the drought were by now making themselves felt in earnest and our food distribution, which had begun as a quiet family affair, began to grow out of all proportion. Señor Torres had offered to let us have cereals and there was maize, wheat and oats brought in by the lorry-load almost daily. This was surplus food from the United States which the U.S. government delivered free of charge to Peruvian ports. The Peruvian government had it transported to the areas which most needed it and sold it to cover the costs of transport and storage. For us, this meant bringing it up on the southern railway as far as Sicuani and, from there, in by lorry. As conditions got worse, more and more people came to us for food and it was difficult for us as we were entirely dependent on Señor Torres. The townsfolk did not all like us having so much to do with the distribution as everyone was feeling the pinch and, if there was something going free, they thought that they should all be in on it. Especially did they object to the Indians receiving food from the CARE packets. This is the name of an amazing American organisation, supported by voluntary contributions, which spends millions of dollars buying first-class foodstuffs such as cheese and powdered milk, putting them in strong cardboard packets, and sending them all over the world. In all, we distributed many tons of this to the needy, and it can be imagined that even the better-class people looked at it a little enviously and were not backward in coming to ask for their share. We explained with sweet reasonableness that it was only for the poor, an argument that did not appeal to them in the least. We were sent slips of paper with the names of the people who had made such gifts possible, and indeed the world can hardly have seen such effective generosity on such a massive scale with such disinterested motives.

In this way, we had the privilege of giving cereals and CARE packets to many a poor family with starving children; of seeing grown men, useless through lack of nourishment, back on their feet and working again; of helping poor distracted mothers who had no milk for their children; and of giving to the sick to help them through their convalescence. It is true that some of those to whom we gave, exchanged their CARE packets for cereals, and this was often thrown-up at us by the townsfolk. The fact was that, to a starving family, twenty-five pounds of grain was worth more than seven pounds of cheese, and if they could make the exchange, who could blame them? Many were living on roots from the fields and anything that looked at all edible. One man I attended must have eaten a poisonous herb for he swelled and swelled and, despite anything we could do for him, he died. Many, many families must have sat before their little stock of seed potatoes and struggled to make the pathetic choice between sowing them in the hope of a harvest and eating them to keep themselves alive. Some, indeed, sowed them and then dug them up before the time of the harvest out of sheer desperation. It was a difficult time for us, having to turn away the hungry because we had not enough to give them. I did buy a little with money sent out from home, but it was very little in comparison with the need. And so the months dragged by until the harvest, and then things got better for a while and all distribution stopped.

* * *

Once again the time for our holidays came round and we had accepted an invitation to go and work in the hospital in Lamas, which is in the jungle in the north-eastern part of Peru. We were in a very different condition from the year before and we were looking forward to meeting friends in Lima and Moyobamba on the way through. It was to work in the Free Church of Scotland hospital in Moyobamba that Netta had first come to work in Peru, and there also that we had met and become engaged, so that it held many memories for us.

We left Ada behind with Brenda, in Santo Tomás and Hilda Briscoe had kindly come out from Cuzco to keep them company. This is something of a journey over the high moorlands, or punas, where the llamas and the vicuñas live, and it takes twenty-four hours if the driver keeps going the whole time. There is usually only one driver and he may, especially when carrying cattle, keep going without a rest. Otherwise, they will stop and sleep at intervals and though the passengers, especially those outside in the cold, get restless, they hesitate to encourage the driver to go on lest he sleep at the wheel and put his car over the precipice. Accidents are not uncommon; the lorry in which we had travelled the year before had turned over soon after we left it and just before we came away this time there was a bad accident in which several were killed.

I had, on this occasion, been called out to Sicuani to see one of our missionaries who was sick and so I arranged to meet the family en route in Yauri, which is about half-way on the road from Santo Tomás to Arequipa. Netta thus had all the responsibility of getting them on board and they were late in starting and made very slow progress. The driver stopped to sleep frequently during the night and the next morning, when we might already have been in Arequipa, we were just starting the worst of the punas. Then it was noticed that one of the two main beams on which the whole of the bodywork rested was giving way and it was clear that the whole thing might collapse onto the wheels at any moment. The cattle we were carrying were unloaded and we went to a nearby mine to see if they could help us. Here we left the lorry and got a lift on a truck carrying the mineral concentrate to the railway station at Imata. We arrived just in time to see the train steaming out of the station. All enquiries proved fruitless; there was no other train for two days and women and children were not allowed on goods trains, so there we were.

Imata is a bleak, wind-swept place and we gathered outside the station for a council of war. These journeys are hazardous and one expects delays, but we had all our connections booked and things looked bad. To make it worse, it began to snow. However, it so happened that a Señor Girladez, who lived nearby, had his pick-up there and for a very reasonable sum he agreed to take us some twenty-five miles to the main Puno-Arequipa road. We arrived there to see a lorry just passing and Señor Giraldez overtook him and stopped him, and there were seats for us all in the cab. It was carrying a load of plaster of Paris, and our bags, which had just been well contaminated by a sludge of lead concentrate, took on a layer of plaster, but this was nothing compared with the fact that we were in Arequipa by midnight. Such are our journeys, and with each new adventure we can raise anew our Ebenezer – hitherto hath the Lord helped us.

Later the same year, coming back from our annual Field Meetings, I was stuck at Imata for a day and a night, being three days and three nights on the journey. The miracle was, however, that it was just at Imata that the radiator came unstuck and a back tyre blew-out for the second time. Had it been on one of the lonely punas, who knows what we should have done. We were carrying no spare parts, not even a patch for the tyre, and we had to wait while the lorry returned empty to Arequipa for repairs. I happened to be carrying two blankets and Evangeline Payne had lent me a poncho for the journey as I was travelling on top. But what really saved my life, on this as on a dozen other occasions, was my duvet jacket. This is a coat, rather like the padded clothing worn by the Tibetans, but made of nylon and the finest down. It takes up hardly any room and, when worn, it puffs out with the heat of the body and is unbelievably warm. This one was given to Leslie Hoggarth by some climbers and he very kindly let me have it. It has made it possible to live and work in Indian houses without becoming a frozen lump of misery and I really begin to wonder what I did without it. On my last journey outward-bound on this route, the engine of the lorry caught fire at two o'clock in the morning. This time it was the courage and resourcefulness of the driver which saved us; little wonder that, at the end of such journeys, it is customary to shake hands with the driver and say thank you.

We had a most successful holiday, the boys flying for the first time when we crossed the mighty cordillera of the Andes into the luxuriant fairyland of the jungle. Both Miss Soper and Miss Gould were in Lamas and it was indeed a privilege to stay with these two intrepid ladies who had been responsible in the first place for opening up this whole region to the Gospel. In the days when the journey involved a fortnight on muleback over dangerous trails and through torrential rains, these two had come in here alone and God had honoured their work. They had lived to see the arrival of the aeroplane; not just the commercial aeroplane which had meant so much to missionary travel, but also missionary aviation through which the distant jungle tribes are being reached. And how they rejoice to see the speed at which things go forward! Yet it was because these two had come in on foot at the psychological moment that they had a place in the people's heart that is unique. While we were in Moyobamba we heard again from the lips of the folk there how it was the Señorita Soper and the Señorita Gould who had cared for them when they were dying like flies in an epidemic of dysentery and when their own ecclesiastical authorities sent no help.

There is something very significant in missionary work about being there first, whatever this may involve in hardships.

On our return, it was necessary to get ready for the missionary language school in Quechua, which was due to take place in Sicuani in August. Leslie Hoggarth was there doing his revision of the New Testament and he had suggested that we go, as his two helpers would make splendid informants for us. Ken Case was going ahead with his pedagogical grammar in the Apurimac dialect of Quechua and other material prepared in readiness. Our whole Quechua programme for missionaries working in the Sierra was gaining momentum and there had been a good response on the part of the members of the Field. We face the usual difficulties attached to living in an area where there is a strong Trade Language and to this is added the fact of the altitude, which seems to sap one's mental resources for anything but routine work. However, we owe a great debt to those who have gone before, and we trust that our laborious efforts will one day produce results.

We are not indeed the only ones in Peru who are interested in the study of Quechua. Both in the universities in Lima and Cuzco, there are Chairs of Quechua. There are also published from time to time grammars by priests, who are interested from their point of view, but these have not proved very helpful to us. In colonial days, the Spaniards committed to writing some old Quechua dramas and other matter, some of which have been republished lately and these make fascinating reading. There is also a band of men around Cuzco, one of the most distinguished being a priest, the Rev. Jorge A. Lira by name, who are really in love with their language, and who are doing an inestimable service in collecting Traditions, Love Songs, and Quechua sayings. The Love Songs, for example, have a quality quite of their own. The language is so expressive that we should need ten words to capture the shade of meaning that they can get into two, and the rhythm is the almost irresistible lilt of their dances. Jorge Lira has also written an excellent dictionary of modern Quechua and this is most helpful.

These men know Leslie Hoggarth and appreciate what he is doing, and they send him complimentary copies of their works. They are always interested in our approach and we hope someday to produce something that will be of use even to them. But Quechua is still a language without a literature and with almost as many dialects as towns in which it is spoken. To take such a language, the language of the kitchen and the farmyard, and to use it as a vehicle in which to express the whole counsel of God; and to produce, almost from scratch, a literary style in which to do so, is all a tremendous undertaking. Mr. Heriman's translation has been the basis for our work up to the present. Now the United Bible Societies have just published a beautiful edition, complete with illustrations, of the New Testament in the Ayacucho dialect of Quechua, done by Ken Case and Homer Emerson, of the World Presbyterian Mission of the USA. Leslie Hoggarth is busy on a revision of the Cuzco dialect version and so the work goes on. We also need to run our Bible schools in Quechua, to produce Quechua literature and to run a literacy campaign in Quechua, but we need more workers for all of this.

* * *

Our journey up the rocky path was slow and was interrupted by several patients who wanted to see me. On one occasion a woman came running down to take me to a house to see her husband. He was lying behind the door and away from the light, as all sick folk do here. As my eyes got used to the darkness, I found myself looking at one of the most repulsive sights I have ever seen. There was a poor creature, gazing up at me appealingly, with the whole of his upper lip and nose eaten away by infection. All that remained to connect the two sides of his face was a flap of skin under each eye and across the bridge of his nose. It looked like the last stages of cutaneous leishmaniasis that is well-known in the jungle, but it was too late to do anything more than give him what palliatives I had with me. Further on I was taken to see an old man who lived with his married son, and who wept like a child as he asked for help. He was paralyzed and was partially incontinent and his daughter-in-law did not take kindly to looking after him. He clearly needed institutional treatment but would have been very loath to go away from his home, even though, as it was, he would sink miserable and unwanted to the grave. Clearly there is room for Christian charity and kindness among these folk and we have a long way to go in teaching our believers their opportunities for showing forth the love of Christ.

* * *

Our road took us down to the Salqamayo and across the old colonial bridge at Santa Barbara. Here we saw the paved Inca road going eastward towards the jungle. They pointed out to us the pass over which we had to go and I was a trifle uneasy as they seemed to be pointing to the peaks on the skyline. We made good progress up past the homesteads where the potato planting was in full swing, on up past the shepherds' huts, and on again as the path got steeper and the air grew thinner. Netta became distressed and cold, so I got out the Duvet jacket. On again, step by step, and then we unrolled a bed and let Netta sleep a little, while I sent Evaristo for a horse. Now it was just a few paces at a time, and Netta was feeling sick and walked bolt upright, like someone under great duress. At last, yard by yard, we reached the first pass and took a longer rest.

Meanwhile Evaristo had arrived at his house in great distress, saying that the Señora would never make it and it was not his fault as he had never agreed that she should come. The only horse, which belonged to Cirilo Quispe, was away at a distant pasture, and he could find no other. After the first pass we made some progress, along a gentle slope downhill. We had not realised that there was still another climb before us, and as we started uphill again I really wondered whether Netta would manage. Our little guides were most concerned and offered to carry Netta but this would have been the last indignity. Night came on, Evaristo reappeared with a lantern but no horse, and we struggled on till at last we were on the second pass.

Now it was down, down, down, always hoping that we were nearing the end of the journey, always finding that there was just a little further to go. Finally we started uphill again and this was almost the last straw. We were assured that we were just arriving but we had heard this so many times before that it failed to raise our spirits. And then suddenly we saw the dim lights of houses and we were there.

The next morning Netta got up but was sick and had to go back into her bed on the straw. I was anxious and wondered, not for the first time, whether I ought to subject her to such journeys. Once vomiting sets in at such altitudes it can be very hard to stop and help was far away. I saw some sick folks and took a meeting and then went some distance to see a poor woman who had stuck an iron spike through her foot. She lived in a place called Vaca-ujyana, which means "the cows' drinking place", and to get there we wound our way through a fairyland of curiously-formed rock strata, which towered above us and in places had large cavities, like windows, on the skyline. I dressed the foot under mild anaesthetic, put in an injection, left some tablets and when I got back Netta had started a meeting and had all the folk singing. Later I joined her in the kitchen where our hostess was worried about four llamas that had got lost. We prayed about them and almost immediately a man came in and said that they had been found.

That night it snowed heavily and our hosts were very dubious about letting us set-out the next day as they were afraid of snow-blindness. We had a horse each and for two and a half hours we wound our way through untrodden snow over the mountain passes. Happily for us, the weather remained overcast. We had not realised the altitude over which we had come two days before, which must have been about 16,000 feet for we could see Ausangate behind us and in front of us the La Raya Knot and Kunarana. At the second pass we looked down on the panorama of the country around Sicuani and saw the triple sources of the Salqamayo.

We started down on the horses but soon had to dismount and slither down as best we could, the horses doing better on four legs than we did on two. We passed the snow-line but still continued on foot and at last we came to the large rock where I had started the fifty paces and two-minutes'-rest rule. I was amazed how far down we had come by now and I really wondered how Netta had ever climbed up over the two passes.

When we got to Sicuani a sick man from Langui was waiting to see us. Mariano had sent him to be cured by us, as his own wife had been. Before this time, Mariano, who is something of a herbalist, had had very little time for modern medicine and had said so quite openly. Now he was a friend and colleague and had sent this patient with a warm personal recommendation. Unfortunately the man whom he had sent to us was in the last stages of tuberculosis with involvement of the lungs, larynx, kidneys and bowels. We took him back home as there was nothing we could do for him and his presence was a danger to other people. I was glad to have gained Mariano's confidence, but there were many cases I would not be able to handle until we had better accommodations for them.

— Extracted from, David Milnes, Inca Stronghold, and Children of the Inca Stronghold.

Earthquakes and Evangelists:
Ronnie Christie looks back

MY WIFE MORAG AND I ARRIVED IN LIMA, PERU, IN THE EARLY HOURS of 2nd October 1968. Our daughter, Fiona, was born in San Isidro, Lima, in April the following year. We stayed at first in Lima to learn Spanish. We made a short visit to Cajamarca in November, 1968, and finally were settled there in July, 1969. Apart from a nine months' furlough, we had Cajamarca as our base until we came back to Scotland in January, 1977.

Peru falls into three natural regions: the Coast, the Sierra (the mountains) and the Selva (the jungle). The Coast is the strip between the Pacific Ocean and the Andes. It never rained there and this area was desert, with miles and miles of bare rock and sand. The waters of the rivers which came down from the Sierra were used for irrigation and so, at intervals, there were broad bands of agricultural land across the long strips of desert. In these cultivated valleys the big cities sprang up: Lima, Chimbote, Trujillo, Chiclayo and so on. On the eastern side of the mountains, was the Selva – a hot and humid low lying area with abundant trees and other vegetation. The Sierra was where we lived.

Here I am giving a description of our area, including places, heights and distances. This is to provide background for the stories that follow. It is also of use to any who may want to look more closely at the area. The Web will provide you with maps and photos of virtually all the places mentioned and you can trace the roads, as they now are, for yourselves, if you wish. The area I worked in consisted of parts of the Departments of Cajamarca and Amazonas. I usually described it as being an area the size of Scotland, but that requires some explanation.

Cajamarca is a city on the edge of a broad valley about 9,000 feet up in the Andes and when we lived there it had a population of about 50,000. In 1969, there was a small Presbyterian church there, one of less than a dozen evangelical churches in the city. There was also an English Academy, long since defunct, and "The Banner of Truth" Bookshop, which still survives. These were under the care of Hugh Varnes from Australia. Hugh and his wife, Roberta, lived with their two sons, David and Tony, in one end of the mission premises; we lived in the other end. We lived on the upper storey, the church building, bookshop and Academy being at street level.

Cajamarca was a service centre for a wide area around. The climate was moderate with temperatures in the low twenties centigrade during the day and between 5 and 10 degrees at night. Dairy farming was common especially in the valley of Cajamarca itself, and on the surrounding hill areas there were sheep and cattle reared and, where there was arable land, crops such as maize and potatoes were grown. That was the typical agricultural pattern of this area – except in the lower areas where a warmer climate allowed for the production of other commodities.

There are several routes radiating from Cajamarca and the distribution of the churches we visited can best be described in terms of these routes. The main route out of the Cajamarca Valley climbed up the hills for 1,000 feet to a pass which is the watershed between the Pacific and the Atlantic Oceans. It is called El Gavilán (The Hawk). The road then descended in great swirls and zigzags towards the river below. (It is said that the Italian engineer who constructed the road tried to write his name on the hillside). The river has a wonderful name: Jequetepeque. The road then follows the river valley westward to the Pacific Coast. Some 40 miles along this road from Cajamarca and at a height of only 4,230 feet above sea level is the village of Magdalena. In my time, it had a church building and a small congregation and the leading figure was Don Segundo Florián. At this lower level, sugar cane was the main crop.

Another road ran south eastward from Cajamarca on the edge of the valley and terminated in the village of Jesús. Here there was a very forceful leader and the church grew under his care. There were half a dozen groups meeting in nearby villages.

A further road ran in a more easterly direction from Cajamarca. Forty miles down this road and at a height of 7,385 feet was the town of San Marcos, the market centre for the surrounding agricultural hinterland. Here there was a full-time Peruvian pastor. There was a church building and a few groups in nearby villages. Beyond that the road turned in a more southerly direction towards the town of Cajabamba. But generally we didn't go that far. There was a church in the area consisting mainly of a group of related families. We had to cross a river to get there. Sometimes we could get the Landrover across the river; usually we had to leave it behind and cross on horseback. These families were originally from the hills (San Francisco de Cachachi) but had bought land in the warm fertile valley bottom (Tambería) and had developed it by constructing irrigation ditches. Tropical fruits were grown here as well as the ubiquitous maize. They were relatively prosperous and go-ahead families.

All these places (except Cachachi) could be served by short visits from Cajamarca – involving no more than a night or two away from home. If that had been all there was, I would have had a relatively compact area to deal with. But the next road to be mentioned runs for hundreds of miles. It crossed the Cajamarca valley in a north easterly direction. It climbed and dipped and climbed again to a height of 12,300 feet. Then it descended to the town of Celendín. It is 65 miles from Cajamarca and just a few hundred feet lower. This was quite a big town; like San Marcos, a major centre for the surrounding population. There was a mission house and church building on the Plaza de Armas (Main Square) and a good number of groups in the surrounding area.

From Celendín, the road climbed over another pass at 10,500 feet and then swept down the hillside to cross the valley of the Marañón River at only 2,800 feet. After the pleasant climate of the high hills, it felt hot in the valley bottom. Indeed, the next village along the road is Hornopampa, where horno means oven. But the road rose and rose again till it crossed a range of hills 12,000 feet high before plunging again into a valley – the valley of the Utcubamba River, where was situated the town of Leimebamba at 7,000 feet above sea level. In the ninety miles between Celendín and Leimebamba there were not too many people because of the nature of the terrain and just a few groups were accessed from that long route. In Leimebamba there was a church building and mission house, occupied by a brother who had had theological training and who ran the work in his spare time.

Following the river valley, there was a junction that led to Chachapoyas, up in the hills. It was a major city, the capital of the Department of Amazonas. There were extensive mission premises there but hardly a church at all – though there was a large evangelical cemetery with no one buried in it! But continuing to follow the river northwards, there was the small town of Jazán, the entry point to a distinct region, the Province of Bongará. It is sixty eight miles between Leimebamba and Jazán; there were no groups to visit.

From here we follow what was called at that time a new road. The area was just being developed. The government was driving a new road through the forested slopes of this area into the San Martín Department so as to link towns like Rioja and Moyobamba with the coast. The road was also being constructed from the San Martín side. The work progressed by fits and starts. When there was money, the road advanced. Otherwise it lay for months or years leading nowhere.

As the work developed, people moved in. They lived by selling the wood, until such time as they could carve out agricultural land for themselves. There were a few related families of Presbyterians who moved on as the road advanced and so left churches behind them in the places they had formerly lived in. So they had built a church in Pomacochas, 18 miles from Jazán – Don Domingo Vasquez was the leader there. These families were the nucleus of the church in Progreso some miles further on where Don Domingo's father-in-law, Don Sixto Solano, was a leading figure.

Some of the people had walked across the gap between the two roads and had opened up land on the Moyobamba side and held services there too. I think they called the place Aguas Claras. More connections of the extended Solano family were there. Away from this development area, there were groups in other places, notably in Jumbilla, the capital of the Province. All this made the Province of Bongará a specially significant area and there was generally a Peruvian Pastor settled there.

The road that I have described through Celendín and Leimebamba was our usual way of getting to Bongará but it was a difficult road and sometimes it was blocked by landslides or because a bridge had collapsed. In that case, we went a different way. We followed the road through Magdalena to the coast. We turned north and followed a good tarred road up the coast for a hundred miles or so. Then there was a road stretching for 180 miles, over the mountains to Jazán. It was much easier driving, though much longer, but there were no Presbyterian Churches to visit.

How then does this fit in with the idea that I covered an area the size of Scotland? Well, I discovered that adding up the distances, it wasn't anything like the size of Scotland. If we take Glasgow as being equivalent to Cajamarca, then going to Magdalena is like going to a little beyond Ayr; going to Jesús is like going to East Kilbride; going to San Marcos is like going to Edinburgh airport. As for the big journey, Celendín is equivalent to Perth; Leimebamba to Aberdeen; Jazán to Nairn and Jumbilla to Tain. To drive from Glasgow to Tain via Aberdeen is no big deal. So if we reckon by distance, it isn't correct to say I covered an area the size of Scotland. But imagine if these roads were all narrow and unsurfaced, and that the road didn't wind gently round the coast but crossed high mountain passes, one of them twice as high as Ben Nevis, then we get a different picture. Our average speed might be 15 or 16 miles an hour. Time-wise, it took fifteen hours minimum from Cajamarca to Jumbilla; from Glasgow to Tain via Aberdeen takes less than six hours. Stranraer to Portree in the Isle of Skye, via Wick, Caithness, and the north coast of Scotland, takes only about 13 and a half hours. We never thought in distances, only in time. At that level, it was like covering an area the size of Scotland.

Peru was, of course, a Roman Catholic country but, especially in the country districts, the religion was little more than baptised paganism. For many people, the centre of their religion was the annual procession of the image of their patron round the streets. The work was conducted against that background – a formal religion with little real knowledge of the Christian faith. It was imperative that sound basic teaching be supplied to new believers.

Throughout much of the area, the Presbyterian Church had been first in the field and had evangelised over a wide area. But other evangelical churches and sects had come into the area and taken over some of the work or threatened to do so. There was a need for deeper teaching to produce a more solid faith and a more mature understanding of the Scriptures in face of the welter of opinion around them.

Moreover, partly because of distance and partly because of other factors, there was a need to tighten up on the structures of the church so that each congregation had a body of suitable elders and that these elders would have the structures in place which allowed them to give and receive support from other elders. The transition from mission to church was only in the process of taking place. At the same time, many of the congregations had passed the stage of youthful enthusiasm and it was always necessary to provide input that would keep them fresh lest they stagnate or lose a vision for growth.

All this, of course, was the duty of the church as a whole – of the existing church leaders – not just of the missionary. But there was a lack of trained leaders. Two of the main centres, San Marcos and Bongará, had settled pastors who, in general, oversaw the work in their area. The other places depended on local leaders who, for the most part, had no formal training for the task. Amongst these there were excellent men – good men and natural leaders. Others were the best available in the circumstances, but without the same natural ability and gifts. It was obvious that leadership training was a primary necessity.

But there was another factor that needed to be taken into consideration, namely, that the Peruvian pastors were not permitted to administer the sacraments. I'll not say here what I thought of that from a theological point of view but from a practical point of view it meant that I was the only person that could baptise or administer the Lord's Supper. This was a big factor, because the question as to whether or not we should recognise the validity of Roman Catholic baptism was a contentious one. The Reformers accepted the validity of their Catholic baptism; and that, I understand, was the position of most Presbyterian Churches. But for people who had emerged from that background of baptised paganism, it was by no means obvious that their baptism as infants in the Roman Catholic Church was Christian baptism. In the Cajamarca and Amazonas region the general opinion was that such Roman Catholic baptism was not valid, therefore, almost all who had come from a Roman Catholic background were baptised evangelically, so to speak. That was a situation I was perfectly happy with, but it meant that in practice I alone could admit people to the church through baptism and build them up through the administration of the Lord's Supper.

So the work involved: (1) a ministry of teaching and encouragement to the church people in general, bearing in mind their religious background and the teaching that they were hearing from other groups who had come into the area; (2) the administration of the Sacraments and the promotion of a sense of corporate belonging; and (3) the promotion of leadership and the development of suitable structures in which the leaders should operate within their own area and for the good of the wider church.

I never did see how I could do justice to these various strands; I fluctuated between giving priority to one aspect and then to another; none got done adequately because I tried to do them all;

and in addition to that I fairly regularly struggled with the feeling that I wasn't the man for the job anyway.

To attempt all this, I travelled a lot. Sometimes I was away from home for two or three nights; sometimes for two or three weeks at a time. Sometimes I travelled alone; sometimes I took a promising young man with me – an apprentice, they might call him now. Sometimes we travelled as a family. I liked the country; the people were welcoming and generous. When we returned to Scotland, it was basically because of our daughter's education. And what memories we brought with us – some of which are still sufficiently vivid after fifty years that I can still write about them. Here's a selection of them. I am not giving a historical account of what we did nor am I attempting any detailed analysis of the situation. But these stories will, I hope, fill out the picture of what was involved in the ministries we were trying to conduct.

On one occasion I went to Bongará by the longer coastal road and I didn't bother filling-up with petrol until I got to Jazán. It was then that I discovered that the filling station there had no petrol – there was none be had in the whole area. I wasn't unduly concerned, because I had brought a five-gallon container and a large drum of petrol with me, so I continued with my preaching programme as planned.

In due course I came to Pomacochas. Don Domingo and others in the church were going to accompany me on the next stage so, to give them more space in the back of the Landrover, I added some petrol to my tank – plenty for the journey, I thought – and left the rest behind in Pomacochas to use on my return.

"The best laid schemes o' mice and men gang aft agley" – and there were two factors that contributed to my plans ending in disarray on this occasion. When we got to Jumbilla we discovered that the church people there were beginning to construct a church building. They needed large boulders for the foundation and they knew a place a few miles distant from Jumbilla where suitable stones could be found. These just needed to be lifted to the building site, and they were going to use something called an andalón, as far as I remember. It was like a big wooden sledge or a dray without wheels on which the stones could be loaded and a yoke of oxen could haul them to the building site. It would be a long and laborious process.

I suggested that the Landrover could do the work much quicker and cheaper. So the andalón was attached to the back of the Landrover and, using the horse-power of a Landrover engine instead of ox-power, in two or three journeys the foundation stones were hauled to the building site. It was a good idea, they said to me, but it made an unexpected dent in my limited petrol reserves.

Finally, we got to Progreso. As soon as we arrived at Don Sixto's house a passer by, who had come from the San Martín side of the gap, came and spoke with us. She reported that a couple of gringos (that is, fair-skinned foreigners) had walked across the gap from the San Martín side and had found no transport on this side. They were exhausted and hungry and wanted a vehicle to go and rescue them. I wasn't too sympathetic at first. I thought they were scaremongering. No Peruvian would pass by and let them starve; they would share their last piece of bread with them if necessary. Besides, I was busy – there would be a service held in the evening and I couldn't miss it. But when two or three other travellers came with the same message that the two gringos wanted rescued, I discussed the matter with the local people and agreed that one or two would go with me after the service to collect them.

The service was held when everything had been tidied up after their evening meal, that is, around eight o' clock. So it was that about 9.30 that evening – an hour when most Peruvians in country districts would usually have been in their beds long since – we set out to collect them. There, at the end of the road, we found them, sleeping in their tent. We will call them Harry and Iris: they were young people, hiking around South America, who had a few days before met by chance and, discovering they were both going in the same direction, had travelled on together. Harry was Jewish and from New York; Iris was an English girl, from a well-to-do background.

We loaded them into the back of the Landrover. I was having a laugh to myself because in the dark they hadn't realised that I was a gringo too, or that I spoke English! Back at the home where we were to stay, the travellers were welcomed. There was a light meal awaiting us, though Peruvians normally wouldn't think of eating at that time of night. I remember it yet – humitas, made from fresh maize, a favourite of mine; and I remember the look on the faces of Harry and Iris when they saw the food. Clearly they were very hungry. Thereafter we all slept on the floor of the house. It had been a successful "rescue" – but now my stock of petrol was severely depleted.

The next morning, we set out on our return to Pomacochas. I knew we wouldn't make it with the petrol I had, but we made a good effort. The first part was mainly downhill so I turned off the engine and coasted down. When there was a slight rise and the Landrover slowed down, Harry and Iris would jump out the back and push, and jump in again when it gathered speed. In this way, we reached the bridge over the river and turned uphill. We got to within three or four miles of Pomacochas when the petrol ran out. Don Domingo was dispatched to Pomacochas to bring me the petrol container that I had left there at his house and some time later he arrived back on his pedal bike with the container strapped to his back. And so we got to Pomacochas.

Harry and Iris stuck with me for what remained of my trip. They did their own thing during the day and came to the services in the evenings. When we got to Jazán, after having completed our programmes of visits and were ready for the long journey home to Cajamarca, we discovered that there was still no petrol there, nor was there, according to reports, any in Bagua, the next town we would pass through, so I spent half a day on the edge of the village, waving down every vehicle that came in from the coast and asking if they could sell me a gallon of petrol. By late afternoon, we had collected a few gallons but not enough. However, my patience ran out and though I knew we didn't have enough petrol, I set off trusting that everything would work out well. And it did.

Providence took the form of a policeman, who was thumbing a

lift to the coast. You can't say no to a policeman and so we took him aboard. He proved very useful – just the man we needed. First of all, it became obvious that we weren't even going to reach Bagua with the petrol we had. So when we saw the lights of an approaching vehicle, I would halt, our policeman would stand in the road and stop the approaching vehicle and commandeer a gallon or two of petrol. As I say, you can't say no to a policeman. In this way we got to Bagua.

The policeman had a friend who owned a filling-station there. He had no petrol either but he drained the dregs of his tanks and gave us enough to continue to the next filling-station that did have petrol. But it was dirty petrol and from time to time the engine cut-out because there was dirt in the carburettor. Once, indeed, it cut out as we were crossing a stream that ran across the road. I wasn't much of a mechanic but how to sort that problem was one thing I did know. I opened the door; climbed on to the bonnet and then onto the front bumper; standing on the front bumper, I opened the bonnet; disconnected the air pipe into the carburettor and, with my hand, covered and then uncovered the aperture while Harry turned the ignition key. This created a vacuum which cleared the blockage. I then got back into the driver's seat the way I had come out, and so sorted the problem without getting my feet wet.

Most of the journey was along a river valley where we made good time in the quietness of the night, but there was a range of mountains to be crossed to reach the coast. There we struck another problem. A line of trucks was parked in the middle of the narrow road: there was a landslide that they couldn't get past. We walked to the head of the queue to look at the landslide and I reckoned I could get through it, if it weren't for the lorries stopped in the middle of the road. I doubt if they would have moved if I had asked them but we had a policeman with us and when he woke up the drivers and told them to move over, they woke up and moved over. Thus we got to the head of the queue, squeezed past the landslide and made it to the coast.

By this time it was getting light and there was another difficulty to be faced. There was a world-wide shortage of petrol at the time, and in order to save petrol, the Peruvian government had decreed that all cars should refrain from driving on two specific days of the week. I had chosen Tuesday and Thursday as my days for not driving and I had to display a coloured disc showing which days I had chosen. It was now Tuesday, but I couldn't stop in the middle of nowhere for the whole day so I carried on for a while – after all, we had a policeman with us and that gave us some protection. But not for long.

There was a crack from somewhere around the front wheel and a jolt, and I pulled-up the Landrover on the verge of the main road. I looked under the vehicle and discovered that the U-bolt, which connected the suspension to the axle, had snapped. This happened from time to time, so it was another thing that I did know about – but it would take a long while to put right. At this point, the policeman departed on a passing lorry and we were left to our own devices. Never mind, he had served his purpose.

Harry minded the vehicle; Iris and I got a lift in a truck into the large city of Chiclayo – she in the cabin, I on the back. In Chiclayo, Iris went off to find a room in a hotel. I bought a couple of sets of U-bolts, got a lift on the back of a truck back to the Landrover, fitted the U-bolts and then rested for the remainder of the day – for we weren't meant to drive that day. But in the darkness of early evening we drove to the nearest town and had a meal. The Landrover doesn't have space to sleep two comfortably, so I left Harry to look for a hotel in the town, while I drove to a quiet place and slept in the Landrover. Next morning I picked up Harry – he hadn't been able to find a hotel and had persuaded the policemen to let him sleep in the cells – and Iris, who had spent the night in the comfort of the Royal Hotel in Chiclayo. I phoned Morag to let her know I was coming home with two extra people, and six hours later we got there with nothing significant happening on the last stage of the journey.

Harry and Iris spent a few days with us. They went to the tourist places, came to church on Sunday, took us out for a meal. One morning they departed on a bus to the coast, where they went their separate ways. We never saw them again. But we heard from them both. Harry had been staying in a hostel where there was a library. He saw a book on the Dead Sea Scrolls which he thought I might be interested in, so he took it and sent it on to me with his thanks. A couple of years later we were in Scotland and we got an invitation to the wedding of Iris to an army officer in England, but we weren't able to go.

I think of that journey a lot. It was different from others, no doubt, but it contained elements common to all of them: long distances, land-slides and break-downs; friendly brothers and sisters; help available when needed; everything in a Higher Hand – a cameo of missionary travel in those days.

Conventions and camps. I made various attempts at holding training sessions, gathering leaders in one centre for a week or ten days of teaching. The most successful ones were held in Progreso so we ended up going there once a year if we could. One merges into another so it is difficult to refer to specific incidents. There was teaching on Bible and doctrine, but there was also practical instruction, including, I remember, role-playing where a believer evangelised an "unbeliever" in an ordinary setting of daily life. They were really very good at turning a conversation about everyday matters in such a way that they could naturally introduce the Gospel in a fitting way.

One thing I do remember, which constantly happened at evening services in that part of the country, was the matter of lighting. There was no electric light and the meeting room would be illuminated by means of a pressure lamp and of course the preacher was expected to stand as close to the lamp as possible so that he could see his Bible properly. In these warm evenings, the windows and doors were wide open to catch whatever cool breeze there was. But it wasn't only a cool breeze that came in through the windows; the light attracted all sorts of flying creatures, that would circle around the pressure lamp. Some of them were quite fearsome looking, and it was only with some difficulty that I learned not to flinch or duck as these things zoomed past me.

The Youth Camps too merge into one another but because they were held in different places certain incidents stand out in the mind. The Camps were of importance for various reasons. At the time, couples tended to have large families, so a fair proportion of our congregations was composed of young people. The parents had for the most part been brought up in the country, with small bits of land, living in poverty and without a high standard of education. The children were getting an education their parents never had and many would become professionals or at least be able to move on from living in rural poverty. It was important that we should keep them in the church and make use of their better education to develop their understanding in spiritual matters. Hence the importance of these camps.

We have not to think that these were large or high-profile activities by Scottish standards. Maybe 15 or 20 teenagers and people in their early twenties, meeting for three or four days. Compared with the camp programme of the Free Church there was far more directly spiritual input, though there were other activities and games as well. At the camp in Celendín, I thought it would be good to take youngsters up to the top of the pass where they could see down into the Marañón Valley, 8,000 feet below. (This is, apparently, now considered a major tourist attraction rivalling the Grand Canyon). So we loaded everyone into the Landrover and set off to this great attraction. When we arrived, we unloaded everyone and they looked down at the Marañón far below and turned away, puzzled – why had they been brought all that way just to see that?

There was, however, a fairly flat grassy place at the top of the pass and we had a ball with us so they amused themselves by kicking the ball around. Someone kicked it outside the immediate field of play and it disappeared into a fold of the ground and a married male helper ran to get it. But one of the young girls thought it was a spring that the ball had rolled into and she shouted "es pozo, es pozo". And then she collapsed in giggles, because "es pozo" (it's a well) sounds just like "esposo" – and that means husband.

On another occasion, in Tambería, beside the normal teaching, a young man read a book to them in Spanish. It was a novel but with a good spiritual message and that went down very well with the older element in the group. The practical activities included for some learning to knit and for others learning to do origami. But the board-games we had taken from home were a great attraction. In the evening, we had a full-scale service with the local congregation and it was hard going preaching. It was hot, of course, and all the youngsters seemed tired-out; they were sitting there struggling with sleep during the sermon. But as soon as I said the "Amen" of the Benediction they were on their feet rushing for the games, as fresh as daisies, to have one last game before they went to bed.

The bookshop in Cajamarca was opened on the day we left Scotland to travel to Peru, so it was still very new by the time we arrived in Cajamarca. During most of our time, there was a missionary responsible for the management of the work – when we first went it was Hugh Varnes – and I might only be asked to help with the accounts or to stay in the shop for a short time, while the manager did something else. But one year I was responsible for its operation, though a young Peruvian man attended to the public.

It did not have a great range of books, partly because there was not a great range of evangelical and reformed literature in Spanish. Moreover, most of the people were not brought up in a reading culture; indeed, some of the older generation were illiterate. Anyway, the great attraction was the Bible and it was gratifying that interest was being shown in the Bible by people who had no evangelical connections.

One day we were in the back-shop speaking to Hugh, when a group of poor country-people came in. They wanted a Bible. We stood and listened as Hugh got a Bible and talked to them about it. Twice I noticed that a number of Bibles on a shelf had fallen over and I put them upright again. Eventually, the group left without a Bible – or at least without buying a Bible, for I discovered that the Bibles on the shelf had fallen over again, and one of them was missing. While some of the group had engaged our attention, another had stolen a Bible. We didn't know whether to be mad or glad – mad that they had pinched a Bible from under our noses, or glad that they wanted a Bible badly enough to steal it!

The literature work was not confined to the bookshop itself. Every year all the main towns held a Fiesta. It was centred on religion: the image of their patron saint would be taken from the church and paraded around the streets. Great crowds would gather and there would be a special market, bull-fights, fire-works and bands playing. Hugh obtained a moveable stall and went to some of these fiestas with Christian literature and established an evangelical witness in the market place. It was gruelling work in the bigger markets for the stall had to be manned 24 hours a day. We all helped as required, especially when the stall was in Cajamarca, attending to the public or sleeping in the stall over night.

When we stayed for a month in Celendín, I went with a local brother, Don Francisco Silva, to a day's market in a small town called Chalán at the time of their fiesta. There was no evangelical witness there, but there were some Seventh Day Adventist groups in the area. There was no road into Chalán so we had to walk the whole way. Don Francisco appeared at the mission well before dawn; we loaded the boxes of books on to a donkey that he had brought, and set out. There was a slow descent into a valley. By this time the sun was up. We crossed a river on a very narrow bridge with no sides and then it was all the way up for hour after hour. We arrived late afternoon at our destination. I noticed that there were fireworks in the plaza, where the main festivities were to take place, all rigged up, ready for going off. Don Francisco got us a room right on the plaza itself. We looked round the town, had a meal and got to bed early.

The next morning we set-up our books in the plaza. I asked Don Francisco when the fireworks would go off and he answered that they had gone off the previous evening! They had gone off a few yards from our room and I hadn't heard a thing! It had been a tiring journey!

The Virgin of the Rosary was the patron of the church here. Her image was carried round the square and mass said. I realised that it was quite a big thing for non-Catholics to remain with their hats on when the bell sounded, marking, as it was thought, the bread being changed into the body of our Lord. If I remember rightly, the Adventists gathered round us and we formed a small visible body of dissenters at that stage. I don't remember how much we sold but we certainly sold a lot of Bibles mainly to the Adventists, and we had good talks with various people. The fiesta was over by mid-afternoon, most of the traders moved off, hoping to break the back of their journey to Celendín before dark. This was a hit and run effort. We were never back there again. Nowadays there seems to be a road into Chalán and the little town has been transformed in appearance, but whether or not there is an evangelical church there now, I don't know.

Looking back, I don't think my work in Cajamarca at times displayed much wisdom. There were explanations of this, perhaps; there was an inadequate overlap with the previous missionary; there was a lack of training in specifically missionary work; and I was just a boy who had gone straight through school and college and whose only experience of mission work was summer missions where we preached and evangelised and left the work to someone else. As I say, there were reasons – or are they excuses? Anyway, this is not the place to analyse how this lack of experience or wisdom applied to the church work – but one or two episodes of a less clerical nature come to mind. These may help to fill-out the picture of the sort of things that happened to missionaries in those days.

Spanish is one of the easiest languages for Europeans to learn, especially if they were taught Latin at school, as generally happened in our day. Scots too were reputed to have better pronunciation than other speakers of English. But of course we made mistakes.

I had been just a couple of months in the country when I tried to give a wee talk to a congregation. I invited them to read in the Epistle to the Galatians. Now, the Galatians in Spanish are the Gálatas – easy to remember. The normal stress would be on the second-last syllable, but Gálatas has an accent which means the stress is on the first syllable – but I forgot that and I pronounced it wrongly.

Apparently, it sounded as if I was inviting them to read in Paul's Epistle to the Naked Woman. Of course, Peruvians were too polite to laugh at our mistakes. But there was one occasion when I had a wee slip of the tongue and instead of asking God to send labourers into his harvest, I asked him to send labourers into his maize. One teenage girl found it very amusing!

We once had a long tour through the area for which we were responsible, staying for a few weeks at a time in key places within my parish. At the beginning of October, we loaded up the Landrover with all our equipment: personal things, cooking materials, beds and bedding, Bibles and other literature, extra petrol – and Fiona's cot lashed to the roof of the vehicle. We spent four weeks in Celendín, living in the mission property there and meeting with the people there and the groups in the surrounding area. We then moved on to Pomacochas for three weeks; finally we stayed in Chachapoyas for three weeks or so. We got home again in late December.

In Pomacochas we did not want to burden the church families by staying with them – they were poor people with large families. Nor did we wish to stay in the hotel lest that would distance us unnecessarily from the people, so we rented a couple of rooms in the upper storey of a house in the village and we did for ourselves. Facilities were not of the best – I remember, for example, that we had no table. The church people, of course, were very kind and on one occasion we were given a chicken.

Now I remember, when I was young, chickens being handed in to the manse in Saltcoats, where my father was a minister, but they were ready for cooking. But the one I got in Pomacochas was alive. To prepare a chicken for the pot was outside my field of experience and I was not sure how to deal with it. I knew that you were meant to ring its neck but I had no confidence in making a clean job. I had visions of the poor chicken taking hours to die in agony, if I didn't wring its neck properly, so I decided that if I took a knife and chopped off its head, I would know that it was really dead. I also knew that if you immersed it in hot water, the feathers could be removed more easily. So we heated a big pan of water on the Primus stove; I wrapped the chicken in a cloth to stop it flapping its wings, and braced myself for the slaughter. With one or two strokes of the knife I severed its head completely. I loosed the cloth and dropped the dead chicken into the hot water – and it jumped out of the pan and ran up and down the verandah, flapping its wings and spraying us with water and blood. I didn't know chickens could do that without a head – but they can, for a few moments at least. So we got a good meal out of the chicken and I gained insight into things of which I had hitherto been ignorant.

That lack of wisdom didn't do any damage. But there was another occasion when, it could be argued, lack of thought did a lot of good.

We were having to rebuild the back wall of the big church building in Cajamarca. For that, a large quantity of cement was required, but at that time cement was in short supply in Cajamarca. Every time a consignment arrived it was rationed – one bag per person while stocks lasted. It was not a satisfactory arrangement for those engaged in large projects. But we made the best of it. On the day a consignment was expected, we would round-up all the youngsters in the congregation who weren't at school or at work. There were three couples in the congregation who had at least eleven children each, so there were always some youngsters available to help. I would give each one the appropriate money and they would all go and stand in the queue and in due course get a voucher which entitled them to one bag of cement. I would then collect the vouchers and claim the appropriate number of bags from the storeroom. It was a slow process getting the necessary building supplies.

But one evening I was visiting Magdalena to preach. I went early and visited Don Segundo's family beforehand and had a meal with them. In the course of conversation, I mentioned the problem we were having getting cement and Don Segundo remembered that one of the superintendents of a road building programme in the vicinity had offered him cement at half the market price any time he needed it. Don Segundo promised to try and get eight or ten bags the next time I was with them. And sure enough, the next time I was there for a midweek meeting, in the dark, after the evening service, I went with the superintendent to a locked storehouse, handed over the money requested and the bags were loaded into the Landrover. I was rather pleased with myself – a boost to our cement supplies – and at half price too!

In hindsight, of course, I had been very foolish. I had overlooked what was obvious; the superintendent had appropriated the cement from the building company's store and pocketed the money I gave him. Such a theft was easy enough to cover up; just mix the remaining cement with a higher than usual proportion of sand and no one would notice the theft. Sure, in a couple of years, a culvert or bridge might collapse because the concrete had not been up to standard. But who was to know? Bridges and culverts often collapsed under the force of the winter rains.

I hadn't consciously participated in theft – I had been thoughtless. Lack of wisdom – that was the problem. So, one way or another, the church wall got rebuilt, and it is still standing today even if partly constructed on a morally shaky foundation.

There was an old believer in San Marcos whom we got to know quite well. As a young man he had married and they had a son and then the wife died. When we knew him first he was with his second wife and they had several of a family. But this wife too died and in his old age he married for a third time – a young woman who in due course bore him a son. I was sitting in his shop on the corner of the plaza in San Marcos and he was discussing what to call his new son. As a joke, I said, "Do you know what Isaiah called his son?" He didn't, so I gave him the reference: Isaiah, 8:1. He turned it up in his Bible and he read it out and, instead of realising that I had been joking, he said, "What a nice name".

For those who don't know, the name is Mahershalalhashbaz. I tried to persuade him that it wasn't an appropriate name, but he wouldn't have it. He did compromise to some degree but a few days later I baptised his son Abraham Mahershalal.

Perhaps Abraham is proud of his middle name – perhaps not; but the lesson was obvious: have more common sense and don't joke in a foreign language!

It was a Sunday afternoon and we were taking a siesta. Morag was in bed; Fiona was in her cot; and I was stretched out on a lounger on the back verandah. It was 3.23 when the earthquake began. There was a general rumbling noise, things began to fall off shelves in the kitchen and some panes of glass broke. I got up immediately and took Fiona from her cot – she was just 13 months at the time – and we went to the front door. The whole street seemed to be swaying like trees in a breeze. The street was quite narrow and if the houses collapsed there was no safety in standing in the middle of the road so we went a few yards down to a junction and stood in the middle of the road there where, I thought, there was more safety. We stood there till the shaking stopped.

We then inspected the damage to the mission property. It was minimal. Apart from a few small panes of glass, damage was confined to areas of plaster-work that had fallen from the ceiling of the big church building. I then went round half a dozen families who belonged to the church to see how they were, but none of them had suffered damage to their homes. I was already prepared for the evening service but, back home, I quickly prepared a new sermon on Psalm 46 1-2: "God is our refuge and strength, an ever-present help in trouble. Therefore we will not fear, though the earth give way and the mountains fall into the heart of the sea". There were relatively minor tremors thereafter and one of them occurred in the middle of the sermon. I suspect that not many ministers have preached on that text to the accompaniment of an earth tremor. So that was our experience of what has become known as the Great Peruvian Earthquake.

We got off lightly in Cajamarca. The epicentre was well south of us and 15 miles out in the Pacific Ocean. The adjacent coastal area and the mountains around the Callejón de Huaylas were badly affected. The Callejón is an area of special scenic beauty with the snow-capped peak of Huascarán dominating the scenery at a height of over 22,000 feet. But in the earthquake, rocks and snow and ice were dislodged from the heights of Huascarán. Here's how a scientific website now describes what happened. "The single, most devastating event was the large debris avalanche that originated from the north peak of Huascarán, falling 12,000 feet and travelling 7 miles at an average speed of roughly 200 miles per hour to destroy the villages of Yungay and Ranrahirca. It is estimated that the earthquake took the lives of 70,000 people, caused 50,000 injuries, destroyed roughly 200,000 homes and buildings and left approximately 800,000 people homeless".

I never thought we could help in any practical way but, when we heard that an English missionary and an elder from the local Brethren Assembly, and two doctors from the local hospital, were going to the affected area to offer help, first Tim and Marjorie Donachie – Marjorie was a nurse – joined the expedition and then I got myself included. I don't intend to tell the story in any detail but to focus on the busiest Sabbath I spent in my whole life.

We left Cajamarca in two Landrovers and drove to the coast overnight. Down the coast it was slow going. We stopped in the large cities (Trujillo and Chimbote) and reported our presence to the authorities. As we got nearer to the area worst affected, we saw piles of rubble where there had been houses and we had to make our way through back-streets. The main road was closed because bridges were down, or the main road had simply been ripped apart by the force of the earthquake. At least we reached the headquarters of the relief effort, and were directed to a small town in the foothills of the Andes called Jimbe. The road to Jimbe was blocked by landslides but we drove as far as we could than evening. Some of the party were allotted Landrovers to sleep in. The rest of us slept in our sleeping-bags on the desert sands, under the stars.

The next day we walked into Jimbe. This was relatively straightforward but there was a point at which we had to wade through a stream – I think it had been diverted out of its normal course by the earthquake. The doctors set up a medical post in a temporary booth that had been erected in the central plaza. The following day, we split up to cover the outlying districts better. Two rivers join at Jimbe and the Donachies and myself made our way up one of these valleys with Marjorie ministering medicines where needed. We spent the night up on a hillside above the ruined little town of Lampanín.

Everyone was sleeping rough and the three of us slept together – Tim taking the middle berth, of course. The bedding was just laid on the ground but there was some metal sheeting erected as a roof over the sleeping area though there were no walls to this structure. I don't remember being uncomfortable. The only thing I do remember was that there was an earth tremor in the middle of the night and everybody sat up and prayed for mercy.

The next day was the Lord's Day and the busiest one of my life. We were on the road while it was still grey – just before six a.m. – making for a tiny village where people, we heard, needed medical attention. We travelled steadily for two or three hours; stopped for some refreshment and continued to our goal, El Aliso, I think it was called, for another two or three hours. There were two very badly injured people there: a middle-aged man with an injured leg – it had not been treated and gangrene had set in; and a young girl with probably a fractured pelvis and a fractured skull. It was obvious that they needed to be taken out for treatment and the only way to do that was by helicopter. I was given lunch and a horse and a boy to guide me and dispatched to get a helicopter. But I was happier on foot than on horse-back and I soon sent the horse and the boy back. It was all downhill, and sometimes it was difficult underfoot but easy on the breathing. Usually I walked, sometimes I trotted and I made good time, but it was almost six in the evening when I got to Jimbe. There were no helicopters there and there was nothing for it but to go on to the airport on the coast.

In the last of the light, I waded the stream and in the dark walked on for a couple of hours to where we had left the Landrovers. Then I drove down the main coast road, turned right towards Chimbote, and looked for the airport on the left. When I say airport, we are not to think it was like Heathrow. There were no commercial flights from it. In fact there were no concrete runways, just a strip of suitable flat ground amidst the sandy desert. There were no lights showing; no signposts indicating where to turn in. When I saw tyre tracks going off towards the left, I followed them until I saw the way blocked with soldiers with guns pointed at me. They asked what I was doing and

I explained my situation. The entrance, they said, was further on but the airport was closed for the night and I should come again in the morning. As I turned and drove off, I heard the click of the safety-catch of their guns being re-engaged.

I drove on to Chimbote, parked my Landrover amongst a heap of rubble in a quiet spot, stretched out on the front seat of the vehicle and fell asleep; it had been a busy day. From time to time thereafter, if I couldn't sleep at nights, I would run over in my mind the details of that day and wonder how far I had walked. I have persuaded myself that 35 miles is a modest estimate. I have always found it ironic that the greatest physical exertions I ever made were made on the day which in normal circumstances was a day of rest.

The next day, I went to the airport early. Organisation was not evident so I had to seek-out a helicopter pilot and put my case to him. He accepted, so off we went. But it was a small helicopter and the village was at a greater height than he had anticipated and he doubted if he could land safely. In the event, he did land safely, loaded-up the two injured people and then I realised he wasn't going to take me back. So, for the second day in a row, I had to make the long walk from El Aliso to Jimbe. I was so tired that I couldn't eat the lunch that was offered to me en route – a terrible insult, I fear, in face of their open-hearted generosity. The problem really was that I was dehydrated and when I got back to Jimbe I drank cup and cup of hot cinnamon tea, which I was particularly fond of, and a good night's sleep set me right.

A couple of days later, I walked and thumbed my way to the main coastal road: got a lift in the back of a truck: got off at the airport, picked-up the Landrover and drove home. That was the end of my earthquake escapade.

I found it very moving, how grateful most people were for any help they got at the time. I remember when we first flew up from Cajamarca to Lima, just six weeks or so after we had arrived in the country, Angus Beaton was meant to meet us at the airport. But he wasn't there – he hadn't heard the plane arrive – so we had to take a taxi. But half way to the town from the airport we met Angus coming to collect us so we changed vehicles and I paid off the taxi driver. Later I felt bad about it. Had he charged me for the actual distance that he had taken us or had he charged the full fare to the town? I was so concerned about this that I put the matter to Angus. He assured me with a quiet smile that there would be no doubt about it: he would have charged us the whole fare even though he had only taken us half way. Looking back, I know I was stupid to think otherwise. But when I climbed down off the truck that had taken me along the main road and dropped me at the airport, I asked the driver how much I owed him. Nothing, he said. I had come down from the mountains, I was going to the airport, I was obviously a helper of some sort in the earthquake relief effort, so he wouldn't charge me.

Indeed, years later I was doing door to door visitation in the city of Chachapoyas, miles from the earthquake zone. I had been invited into a home and was sitting with the gentleman of the house in a large and rather formal sitting room. Somehow the conversation turned to earthquakes and I said I had visited the area affected after The Great Earthquake. He rose, came across the room, shook my hand and, with great dignity, thanked me for my help to the Peruvian people in the time of their distress.

Yet I wasn't sure that I had actually done anything to deserve thanks. I never knew what happened to these people who got air-lifted to hospital. Perhaps they both died of their injuries. Then I wouldn't be very popular, for I had brought the helicopter that had snatched them away, so that they died amongst strangers far away from the highland home. Or perhaps they both lived and the man returned with crutches or perhaps an artificial leg and helped for the rest of his life, as he was able, with the agricultural pursuits in which for generations his family had been engaged. Perhaps the girl married and now, on May 31st each year, a day celebrated in Peru as Natural Disaster Education and Reflection Day, she gathers all her grandchildren and tells again the story of the helicopter that plucked her from certain death and took her to a hospital where her health was restored. Who knows, who knows?

When I look back, it is to reflect on how things have changed. The early missionaries would take perhaps 15 days or more on the back of a mule to get from the coast to Moyobamba. Then air transport opened up and they, generally speaking, didn't go overland any longer.

But as mentioned above, there was a drive to open up that area by constructing a road over the mountains and through the jungle to that area. On one of my last trips to the churches in Bongará, I drove to the end of the road, left the Landrover, and walked the gap to the road that was being constructed on the San Martín side. It then took three or four hours walking through the jungle to the road on the other side. We had been delayed in starting out and there was no transport on the other side of the gap. We had to walk another couple of hours in the darkness to Aguas Claras. I took a service there that evening and next morning got a lift into Moyobamba and paid a surprise visit to Andy and Margaret Fraser, who were missionaries there at the time. I was the first Free Church missionary for many years to travel there overland.

Nowadays, you can travel by road the 369 miles from Chiclayo to Moyobamba in about 11 hours and air transport is still available. You can get a flight that takes no time at all – what changes!

And with that, I wish to stop. What we have here are memories well over 40 years old. The roads have certainly changed; the way of life of the people also to a large extent; the church buildings that I have been able to identify on online maps have changed substantially as well. Some of the church work had also greatly developed. The rest I just don't know enough about to say. Our hope is that the seed sown years ago has yielded an abundant harvest.

Margaret Fraser:
Memories from Sierra and montaña

MY HUSBAND ANDY AND I EACH HAD A MISSIONARY BROTHER IN PERU – his brother was Alan Fraser of Colegio San Andrés and mine was Willie Mackay, also of San Andrés. They were all Free Church ministers. My uncle, Dr. Kenneth Mackay, had been the first Free Church doctor in Moyobamba and my aunt Margaret, from Achiltibuie, had gone out there to marry him. This was in spite of the fact that the Free Church Foreign Missions' Committee took no cognisance of her existence as a missionary's wife unless, and until, she misbehaved herself! It did, however, present her with an inscribed Bible which she gave to me, and which I gave to Petronila (Petita) in Moyobamba, because she did remember Dr. Kenneth's wife.

Ronnie Christie had told Andy that there were plenty of preachers in Scotland but many were needed in Peru. So, after his theological studies, Andy offered to serve the church (IEPP – Iglesia Evangélica Presbiteriana del Perú) there in Peru. We were married on September 6th, in 1974, and travelled to Lima on October 31st. There was a need in Cajamarca for a missionary to help with the bookshop, El Estandarte de la Verdad (The Standard of the Truth), when Hugh Varnes and his family would return to Australia. So it was decided that we should go there.

As Hugh at the time was in Lima, but was returning to Cajamarca, we accompanied him, leaving on November 13th. This was so that he could introduce us to people and places where there were fairs to which he took Bibles and Christian books to sell, using the "puesto" (bookstall) which belonged to the bookshop. We would be there from May 1975 to February of the following year.

That journey was a real introduction to Peru! The bus broke down in Pacasmayo, which added three hours to our journey. We were somewhat worried by the sheer drops at the side of the road in the mountains. Hugh kept saying, "wait till you see the view from the Gavilán". That is the high point from which you can look down on the beautiful valley of Cajamarca – but it was covered in mist and there was nothing to see! We arrived in Cajamarca (which seemed pretty dirty) the next day at 4.30 p.m. We were very tired, but were given a lovely welcome by the Christies and the Varnes.

Next day we went to see the Policía de Investigaciones del Perú (PPI), to whom foreigners must report when they travel around. Then we did some sightseeing – the Belén church and former hospital with beautiful stone carving, where the missionary nurse Sarah MacDougall from Glenurquhart started her work in the 1920s, the street named after her, and the monument to her on her grave in the cemetery. Though she was Protestant, her funeral was one of the largest ever in Cajamarca. Next day there was a tea for us to meet the church folk, and later another tea to meet church leaders from other denominations – Assemblies of God and Brethren. We also met Alexandro Huaman from the Nazarenes. He was once a colporteur for the early Free Church mission. My aunt Margret said that if he were a Nazarene now, he must be a Presbyterian one! She also said that he had been a very good brush-maker.

Hugh took us on an interesting journey over the jalca – what is called the altiplano in the south. It involved a day's very bumpy travel to Bambamarca. We passed through Hualgayoc, a depressing mining village, where men were using coca with lime which they kept in a small gourd with a pin in the stopper which they licked and used to pick up the lime in the gourd. In Bambamarca, the women wore distinctive blue and white shawls as they jogged along with a baby on the back and a spindle in front. We met boys who tried out their English – "good afternoon, thir". We later met the schoolmaster, who had a lisp. We were given a great welcome by the church people and one old lady, Señora Angelita, brought us camomile tea to calm our tummies: the sheer shaking on the bumpy roads upsets the body.

A pastor told us a very sad story. When anyone travels a distance, others will ask them to carry items to distant relatives, etc. Un paquetito – a little packet – often turns out to be a very big parcel indeed. The pastor was asked by a relative to take some cheese to Lima. It was checked by the police on the way and turned out to be drugs. He was imprisoned for years, and for a long time could not forgive.

In Chota, a village famous for its weaving, we lodged with Pastor Nunara and family. Hugh had warned us that they had one guest room where we all three slept on one large bed (decorously arranged, of course!) They were extremely kind and gave us a wedding present of a wall-hanging. Travelling on from Chota, the passengers of a bus which had broken down came to our one, complete with chickens, etc. From time to time the bus stopped and the driver's assistant came out to knock the leaf-springs under our seat back into place. The road was narrow with lots of bends and deep drops, and often we seemed to be hanging over nothing. We were not reassured when the bus stopped for the driver to light candles where another bus had plunged down the abyss killing its passengers!

We reached the coast at Chiclayo and returned to Cajamarca by the road which we had originally thought terrifying on first acquaintance but now thought luxurious compared to our recent travel. Andy was shown how the puesto was put up, and various matters about the bookshop, which also sold general stationery, jotters, pens and so on, for scholars. There was also stock-taking and advice about bad debtors. Roberta Varnes killed a rat in the house: Morag Christie's cat was not interested. We visited Atahualpa's room where the conquistadores told him that he would be saved from death if he filled it with gold and silver. They decided to kill him anyway, but said they would strangle him rather than burn him alive if he converted. Sensibly enough, he agreed to that.

There had been a big earthquake shortly before our arrival, which took down houses in Lima. We experienced an aftershock soon after we arrived there – each of us thinking the other was shaking the bed, and leaping out of it simultaneously. We experienced another tremor in Cajamarca, which was felt in other parts of Peru too.

We returned to Lima (just 16 hours and three quarters this time) where we were given warm hospitality and shown around, and we learned more about the early history of Peru and its various cultures. We were to study Spanish at the Universidad Católica, despite many delays, strikes and riots. One day the police went on strike and the government brought the army to the main police barracks not far from us. There was a long and fierce gun-battle in the early hours of the morning. Unwisely, we went to class next day but, as the smoke of battle drifted over, the class was shut-down, as did all shop doors, and we dodged tanks and burning cars on the way home. There was a curfew for a week or so after the trouble. We got to meet folk in the church in Lima, many from the Sierra and the montaña, and other missionaries from the Evangelical Union of South America, including Dr. David Milnes, who gave us our tetanus booster!

We did some English teaching in Colegio San Andrés and had some private Spanish lessons but in this frustrating time we were so thankful to God that we had seen the Sierra with its interesting people, amazing scenery, beautiful birds and flowers. This, we thought, was the real Peru – though this was not the opinion of my class-teacher Fanny. She was a very fashionable Limeña, who thought that all serranos were savages!

We had experienced Peruvian travel with its delays, filthy toilets (or none), learned to carry soap and toilet paper (no wet-wipes available), experienced dirty flea-ridden "hotels" and upset tums, so we were not starry-eyed, but were still keen to return to Cajamarca. This we did on May 21st. 1975, in time for Cajamarca's big fiesta – Corpus Cristi. After the rains, the countryside was green and beautiful, and the view from the Gavilán of the fertile, dairy-rearing valley was stunning. We were no longer so worried by the twists of the road and Cajamarca had just been washed cleaner. The puesto – three by two and a half metres with metal struts and striped canvas cover – was erected, and books and so on were sold over ten days, including during the very noisy religious procession on the 21st.

We had one day's outing to a fair at Sorochuco, a small village a bit off the Celendín road, along with Nelly Lopez, a young girl from the church. We just had a tarpaulin on the ground to sell our Bibles and books, and had some interesting conversations. There were quite a few Adventists there. The drunkenness from the aguardiente (burning water, or sugar-cane brandy) or beer was quite something. Couples were dancing round the plaza, but barely able to hold each other upright.

In July, we had a nine-hour journey to Bambamarca, where we set up the puesto in a street, slept in sleeping-bags and cooked on a Primus stove. A church family nearby allowed us to use their water-tap and hole-in-the-ground in the corner of the yard, for which we were truly grateful. One day, I noticed bits of meat hanging on their washing-line and asked what they were. They were skinned and gutted guinea-pigs. Later on, one of their girls arrived with a plateful of cuy and rice with a delicious sauce for me. Andy, being a veggie, did not partake. Peruvian cooking at its best is amazing. Their fiesta day was July 16th. Nuestra Señora del Carmen – different images of Mary, often from different places in Spain – are paraded around in competition with each other. There was a bullfight as part of the fiesta, but evangelicals did not attend.

We packed-up on the 21st., and left on a lorry at 11.30 a.m., arriving in Cajamarca around 9.30 p.m. The cold on the jalca was intense, even with anoraks with ponchos on top, and we were frozen. In the Sierra night falls at 6 p.m. but even in the day you can step from intense heat on one side of the street to pretty chilly in the shade due to being near the Equator but 9,000 feet or more up. The country women deal with this by wearing many petticoats under their wool skirts, but bare legs.

On top, they wear bright silky-type blouses with lace at the neck and edge, long enough to cover the first ten inches or so of the skirt, which is cotton at the top and has a slit for opening to put on, or expanding for pregnancies. Over the blouse they wear a shawl which can carry a baby or other load. The men wear heavy woven ponchos, russet or brown, and trousers which, if home-woven, may stop half-way down the calf, and sandals made from car tyres. The women, more often than not, go barefoot, but may have sandals. The hats are tall and wide-brimmed, are flat-topped and made from straw or similar material. The men also carry alforjas – saddle-bags – which are long strips of woven material turned over at each end to form pockets. They can go over your mule or your shoulder.

Two days later we left for Celendín, about a five and a half hour journey, and set up on a rough street beside other puestos. There were lots of Seventh Day Adventists who always asked for the Antigua Version of the Bible as it uses the word Sabado (Saturday) instead of dia de reposo (day of rest). There were also Jehovah's Witnesses who came to argue but, at first, would hide their point of view, and people would crowd-round to listen. I don't know how we managed as our Spanish was pretty basic. Some wee girls had bought little gospels earlier, and brought them back saying that the cura (priest) had told them it was a sin to read them. There was an Iglesia Evengélica church in Celendín and a house belonging to the church. I suppose we must have got water there. Certainly, there was electricity as I remember a light-bulb in which one could see a red filament – but it gave no light.

Sometimes, if it was quiet, one of us would go for a walk. Andy, going up San Isidro hill at the back of the village, found fossilised shells – cockles, mussels and sea potatoes – just like present ones. Imagine the upheavals that brought the sea-floor up to make the Andes! The early morning mists on the hills reminded me of Scotland and made me feel a bit homesick at times.

In September, we went on a holiday to Arequipa and Cuzco where we stayed with Bill and Alice Mitchell of the Bible Society. We celebrated our first wedding anniversary in Machu Picchu with them but unfortunately Andy fell ill with glandular fever and ended up in the Urcos clinic – so we did not manage up the Sacred Valley. We did meet David and Netta Milnes at Bill and Alice's.

In October, we had students from the Seminary in Lima evangelising for a week, and then we set off with Ronnie Christie for the Amazonas area. The route was via Celendín and then the zig-zag down to the Marañón at hot and sticky Balsas, and up the other side. I seem to remember Ronnie deep in the Landrover engine, as dusk was falling, while we were high up near Saullamur. But he must have sorted-out the problem,as we arrived at Don David Landa's in Leimibamba around 8 p.m. He was church leader, medically trained to some extent, father of Dr. Apollos Landa. There was plenty of wildlife – raccoon, green parrots, butterflies and, as we travelled along the Utcubamba river, lots of forget-me-nots. The houses changed to thatch-roofs and, towards Jazan, there was more coffee, bananas and oranges to be seen, fewer straw hats and more hankies on heads and often things carried on the head. Rice and bananas figured more in the meals. I remember young Hermina Calongos, with a baby on her back, carefully holding my hand while fording the river and then making us a meal of cuy and rice before dark. Ronnie had a service in Jumbilla and various other places in the evening, with lamps into which a variety of large insects blundered. We were following the new road to Progresso to its end, after which there was a track through more jungly forest with moss and ferns which would eventually become the road to Moyobamba.

We back-tracked to Domingo Vasquez' chacra near Pomacochas where he grew bananas, cane and vegetables and had a small sawmill. His small son, Samuel, aged about three, was very skilfully cutting something with a large machete and I couldn't catch the name of the toddler son. "Nayeel", repeated Domingo, "Nayeel – como el astronauta" (Neil – like the astronaut). His wife rather embarrassed me by removing my socks and shoes and washing my feet, which was very nice of her, presumably following Jesus' example. We slept in their house and the pig got loose in the night so there were shouts to older daughter Elizabeth to catch it. There was a service in the church in the evening and next day there was the all-age Sunday School common to most of the churches, which allowed for more informal teaching and questions and answers. Ronnie had emphasised that all teaching had to be shown to come from the Bible, and Andy followed that ever since. The church had a tin roof and, unfortunately, there was a very heavy downpour so, for a while, little could be heard.

We visited various people, one of whom lived across a river which one balanced on a log to cross. After the service, we slept the night in the church at Suyubamba. Throughout the trip we were well fed with fish, eggs, etc. Still, boiled eggs, on one occasion presented a challenge as they were very lightly boiled ("pasado" through the water) and we were given them unshelled and dessert spoons to eat them with.

After a push out of the mud (not for the first time) we headed for Chachapoyas which is a good-sized town up on the hills, more like a Sierra town, poking out of the warmer areas below, rather cloudy. There we visited a church family and Ronnie had business to do regarding church property. Then, back to Leimibamba for a service. Next morning, heading home, the brakes had to be bled at Saullamur and again at Celendín. We brought bananas to Don Hermogenes Correa, the leader there. We got home about 10 p.m. The roads were very hard on vehicles (and drivers) but it was very interesting to meet folk that Andy would be visiting when Ronnie was away, and it was a very interesting part of Peru, sort of half-way between Sierra and montaña.

Back in Cajamarca in November, I tried to get my International Driving Licence converted to a Peruvian one. Morag Christie accompanied me to the Ministry of Transport umpteen times over some weeks, the official making excuses every time (even, "I'm up to here with people!") He was just wanting a bribe. Eventually, he gave me a test with another new guy in the back seat. Because Morag had spoken for me, the official thought that I couldn't speak Spanish. As I was doing a hill-start, the other guy said, "she can drive fine". The official agreed, but said, "she doesn't understand Spanish, I am going to fail her anyway". That is the power of officialdom in Peru, and it made me understand why people have to pay bribes and tell lies in order to get any official stuff done.

The upkeep of vehicles took an inordinate amount of time due to the awful roads (many of which are tarmacked now) and the vast area which the missionary had to cover. There were garages in Cajamarca with skilled and innovative mechanics, but they did not keep car parts and someone had to hang around and go and buy these (after learning their names). The same was true for tradesman's work in the house – householders had to find the materials. The missionary also had to learn to be a mechanic himself to do emergency repairs in isolated places and, besides learning theological Spanish, to know mechanical and practical Spanish. I remember trying to explain to Luciano Raico, our excellent bookshop assistant, that I needed to go and buy a paint solvent. "Ah!", he said, "you mean tinner".

Andy was gradually eased into preaching as there were various groups near Cajamarca who wanted services, as well as the Cajamarca church – the all-age Sunday School (one hour) followed by service (one hour). The ladies wore mantillas and the Lord's Supper was in the evening, with unleavened bread baked by Señora Lopez, an elder's wife. There was also a midweek prayer meeting, and a youth group, and Morag Ritchie introduced me to visits to the women's prison.

In February 1976, the Mission sent us to Moyobamba, because Bill, Isobel and David Scott were to go on furlough. We flew from Chiclayo on the north coast as there was no road in yet, only from Tarapoto in the selva. We stayed at first in the old hospital at the edge of the plaza, with its high airy rooms, along with Bill and family. It had running water and electricity but the toilet was in a "wee house" in the grounds with a seat and a long drop – very clean and hygienic. If one went out at night, there was an energetic serenade by frogs. There were extensive grounds with hibiscus, roses, bougainvillea, a chicken run, an orchard with oranges and bananas, but we knew this idyll would be short-lived as the PIP were buying the property. The original Annie Soper building was in a poor state and would have to be taken down, but the Kenneth Mackay and Harold Lindsay buildings were fine.

We were moved to a house owned by the manager of Aeroperu in the town. The sitting-room and dining-room were in the old building of adobe and tile, and then there was the new long concrete building of kitchen, shower-toilet and bedrooms with corrugated iron roof. After a bad earthquake the order had been given that new-builds should be in "noble material", though actually adobe houses are much more comfortable in the heat. I see in Uncle Kenneth's memoirs that they thought the climate ideal and cool at night, but when we were there even the Moyobambinos were complaining that it was too hot to sleep and was getting like Tarapoto.

The congregation was a good size with elders, Sunday School classes, women's meetings, youth groups and men's class. Manuel Moraes preached often when Andy was away. He had been one of the first young men to be sent to Costa Rica to train as pastors. He was quite rough and ready and could be very brusque but was actually very soft-hearted, especially with children. When we were back in Cajamarca and about to host the National Assembly, and our baby crawling about into everything, he came into the kitchen and washed a big pile of dishes which was most unusual for a Peruvian man! When we visited Moyobamba later, in 1981, he was still telling people off for coming into church late with dirty clothes and smelly armpits! There were services in surrounding villages – Soritor, Calzada, Rioja (where there was a young pastor), and also in new hamlets out along the new road that was being built to meet up with the Amazonas road – Aguas Claras and Aguas Verdes.

Bill and Isobel gave us good advice, and "bequeathed" us Juana, a serious teenage girl who helped in the house in the morning and studied in the evening. She was able to give us much information and advice. She later became a special-needs teacher and advisor and has four girls, all doing well after attending the Annie Soper school and further education. It was a great help having her, as cooking was a slow process with just two kerosene burners which you couldn't adjust very much. (There was a hearth for cooking over an open fire, but I never tried it). Sometimes water was limited to certain hours, so we had to fill buckets and have them ready, and I remember being shocked to see a long black thing swimming in a bucket. I took scissors and cut it in two – and was even more shocked when both parts swam away! (It was a flatworm). Sometimes, electricity would be limited to the hours between 6 p.m. and 6 a.m. Washing was by hand, and our fridge was kerosene-powered.

There was a market open every morning around 5 or 6, to which people brought in vegetables – mainly cabbage, beans, squash and corn before they went to work on their chacras outside the village. I can't remember if there was fruit – probably different varieties of bananas – red, cooking or tiny "ladies' fingers". Most people had fruit trees and you could see oranges rotting on the trees. The variety was amazing – chirimoyas and anunas (differently-flavoured custard apples), little guavas, passion fruits of different kinds, pineapples, papayas, lemons, melons, avocados. There were a few trees near the plaza which they called "poma rosa" which had apple-sized fruit the colour of radishes. They were very delicious but only had a very short season. Dr. Lindsay had planted a grapefruit tree, and the owners of his former house used to bring some to the missionaries.

Juana showed me how to plant beans beside maize so that they would grow up together. We tried tomatoes but they were poor, as were potatoes. There were sachapapas, a local variety of tuber. There was a meat-market once a week but you had to queue in the midday sun. I didn't bother as Andy is a vegetarian, but when I became pregnant I was desperate for protein and Don Manuel kindly volunteered to get me some meat as he was buying anyway. There were various general merchants but their range wasn't great. It was quite exciting to see what you could find: I remember being thrilled at finding some dried broad beans!

The only cheese was unpasteurised "crowdie" type, though in Tarapoto you could buy tinned cheese. Milk was mainly evaporated and we bought packets of powdered milk from Lima. However as our (Bill and Isobel's, really) Lassie had eight puppies and not enough milk for them, they all thrived on the powdered milk. We did ultimately find milk from cows, which had to be boiled. It had a strange taste which was similar to some armadillo meat which a farmer had brought me. He said the milk tasted odd because of the plants the cows fed on. We did get a present of a hen for eggs, which we tethered to a palm tree but it got itself tied up and we passed it on to someone who would treat it better! The palm tree was eventually chopped down and we were given some of the interior – I didn't know that you could eat trees!

There was a lot of interesting wildlife. Even at the Bañoshot springs, we shared the swimming pool with frogs. Juana brought in a small, furry tree-anteater which was called an intipelejo. It had long claws but it didn't seem to mind being held. Once folk found that Andy was interested in snakes, they brought in any they killed on their chacras. He pickled them in aguardiente and sent them off to a lady in Lima museum. There were some very poisonous snakes in the selva, such as the shushupe (bushmaster) and the jergon (fer de lance). Once they brought one in alive that was called a curamama. It looked double-headed, blunt at both ends with tiny eyes. It was not poisonous, but was said to have a dirty bite. They also said that if you killed it, you would get a sore back.

Insects were abundant, and some of them were very strange. Cuy-machacue is a caterpillar the size and colour of a canary whose hairs can sting. Chicharra-machacue is an insect about three inches long with a double-nose like an unshelled peanut. (The word machacue signifies ferocity). The normal chicharra (cicada) makes a noise like a circular saw, and when it would blunder into the mesh of our window, the dog and the cat would rush to snap it up first.

Humans eat a certain type of ant which comes out in October after rain. Toasted it is okay to eat, and I suppose it would provide some protein. Otherwise, ants tend to eat humans, apart from the leaf-carrier ants you meet on the paths, or pollillas (termites) which eat your furniture and drop beautiful little wings in piles at a certain stage. The river Mayo yielded little bony fish which were deep-fried whole and were quite tasty. Sometimes, fishing involved a little dynamite which brought bigger fish belly-up. With fish, your chips would be banana chips. There were sometimes slabs of salt fish, paiche, which was a huge fish from Yurimaguas, further down the Amazon river system.

Butterflies were amazing, some with figures of eight or other numbers, beautiful swallow-tails very often drinking at puddles or on cow-pats, and huge blue Morphos whose bodies are not so big, and therefore flap occasionally and glide, fire-flies and glow-worms, mosquitos and other nasties too (bed-nets required). Cockroaches were aplenty – they have the advantage that they can fly, swim and scuttle through the smallest cracks and investigate your food cupboard during the night.

People in general were very friendly, which was a legacy of former Free Church missionaries, beginning with Dr. Kenneth Mackay. Several people remembered that he had started the tennis club. The doctorcito (little doctor) could be rabioso (furious). He did have red hair and I could imagine his twinkly blue eyes blazing if he met with lies and obstruction. Evidently, Dr. Renwick had told him not to do anything rash. I have a letter that Margaret wrote to my mother for "Bengers" that she had sent. I think it was a food supplement, as the twins were quite sickly. She said that the local folk were quite surprised that they survived. The cemetery workers were also losing-out on trade since the doctorcito had arrived. The retired school-mistress, Señorita Margarita, had a photograph of Uncle Kenneth on her wall in 2006 when my niece Catriona Clubb worked with the Asociación San Lucas as a doctor. Those in the church were especially kind, though there was some anti-gringo feeling among the young folk, especially about there being no instrumental accompaniment in the church. I remember Jorge Vasquez behind me singing very loudly in Psalm 33, "Cántale sin arpas ("without" instead of Sing to Him with harps) to make the point.

In both Cajamarca and Moyobamba they sang only psalms in church, though in other meetings in Moyobamba hymns and choruses were sung. In Lima, they also had a hymn book along with psalms. Aunt Margaret asked if anyone sang the Evangelical Hymn for us. Evidently it had started with a record of the Eriskay Love Lilt that they had, and that the Moyobambinos loved. They are good singers.

A Canadian hippy family turned up in Moyobamba and caused some confusion to the brethren. They did come to church but they smoked – definitely not done by evangelicals. They thought Moyobamba a paradise, fed their kids pretty much on bananas only, but after a few months they returned to Canada.

Many of the townspeople had crofts (chacras) outside the town and – much further into the jungle – there were Aguaruna Indians who occasionally came into town. I remember being in a shop when a couple came in. The woman wore a dress and had long hair tied back like any other woman, but he had long hair with a fringe, a bare torso, and a wrap-around below. The shopkeeper spoke very rudely and arrogantly to him – "Are you a woman?", and that sort of thing. Moyobambinos and village people didn't wear any typical clothing – just light western clothing and didn't wear hats much. Some carried umbrellas for rain and sun, especially if carrying babies, but often just did not come out, even to work, if it was raining, as they might only have one suit of clothes. They were excellent tailors and could make very smart dresses out of scraps of material put together, and they were good at crochet too.

Señora Esperanza Linares brought a very poor couple to church. The father had been badly injured after falling off a lorry when returning from hunting out on the new road. When we visited, we found that they had three older children plus two-year old twins, Marilou and Maribel, and a month-old baby boy. One twin was smaller than her baby brother, with stick-like arms and legs and a big tum. Her twin was more normal in size, but with an even bigger tum full of worms. Along with the oldest sister, I took them to the police doctor who didn't charge for the consultation. He gave samples of worm medicine to us, and told me to use my money for protein powder, calcium and vitamin shots. The poor wee soul had hardly any buttock to put the needle into and little strength to cry. She was not by any means a neglected child and evidently ate everything. However, that didn't mean they were keen on the medicines and tended to spit them out, or be sick. The parents had earlier given us some yucca which they had a big shed of, and we were glad we had accepted a little, because it obviously made it easier for them to accept help. We had to return to Cajamarca six weeks later, and they wept when they came to say farewell. We did leave some money with Señora Esperanza for further needs, but they evidently moved away and nobody knew what happened to them.

Worms were widespread and everyone regularly dosed. People often took their dose on Saturday and it was quite understood when they weren't in church on the Sunday! We dosed the puppies too (yeuch!) before we gave them away. People spoke about Uncle Kenneth's "tonic verde" (green tonic) but when I asked about it fifty years later, people couldn't remember. They thought it was for iron depletion – the result of walking barefoot and getting hookworm. I can remember walking barefoot myself (more comfortable) on the path to Yantalo to visit a dear old Christian lady, Doña Ernestina. You had to cross the river Indoche in a hollowed-out log canoe to get there – evidently, now there is a road and a bridge. When we said goodbye, I remember her saying matter-of-factly, "well, we'll meet again, en el más allá" (in heaven). Yes!

There were always tijera chupas (scissor-tailed kites) wheeling above that track. We were returning along the road into Moyobamba once, very hot and red-faced, when a gentleman invited us in and gave us oranges to refresh us. He turned out to be the father of one of the young men in the church who was a Sunday School teacher. Although the father didn't go to church himself, he was delighted that his son, Juan Ruiz, was "heart and soul in the gospel" – which he still is.

Andy's transport was a motorbike, as the Mission Landrover had come to the end of its life and had been sold. Many Moyobambinos had scooters on which the whole family rode. I was forbidden by the doctor from riding once I became pregnant because of the bumpy roads outside of town (and some inside). As a result I didn't visit the villages much, but Andy had services and visits, very often at night, and very often it was difficult keeping the bike upright on muddy roads, especially when tired.

We went on an interesting outing with some of the church folk to elder Don Roberto's chacra about a ninety-minute walk on the other side of the river Mayo, which we crossed in a dug-out. The horse swam across. Some other narrower rivers had a box with a pulley, or a raft. Don Roberto had a tambo there – four props with a roof with a closed-in bit to keep things dry, so you could stay overnight if necessary. We were introduced to cocoa beans. The pods grow directly from the trunk on a short stalk. Inside are rows of beans in a sweet jelly. To remove the jelly one sucks the beans and spits them into a pail. They are then roasted, so that's okay! Don Roberto showed us his machine for squeezing the juice from sugar-cane, known as a trapiche, and where it was boiled-up to make chancaca syrup and then poured into moulds the size of a pudding bowl to set. The housewife then chips off a bit and boils it with water to make syrup.

There was another church trip to the chacra which, of course, was originally cut out of the jungle. This was a working party to make humitas. You stripped the corncobs, ground the grains with onion and garlic, wrapped a spoonful in the maize leaf and boiled them. Andy didn't manage on that trip, because he was too busy. But he did go on an outing with the young folk when they climbed the Morro, the volcanic plug in the middle of the plain.

He had a lot of frustrating work obtaining the titles for the Mission hospital. Since August he had to chase-up lawyer, notary, registrar, council, court, engineers, etc. – latterly almost every second day and, though each actual process might not take long, it interrupted other work. His legal training probably helped so that he could check-up on each stage. Nobody would tell you something was wrong until afterwards, leading to great complications. He was able to post off the titles to George Thomson on November 17th and take a much-needed night off. He should have been at Aguas Claras, two hours away, but the bike needed a part which had to come from Tarapoto and, as he had already cancelled the men's classes, he was free!

The postal service was quite good but there were no telephones.

Urgent messages to other parts had to be sent by telegram. I had to go to Lima to have a breast lump checked and was unable to send (good) news back to Andy because it happened to be The Day of the Telegraphist – ie. they were having a holiday! We still received mail for the Scotts, Florrie Donaldson, George Thomson and even the Lindsays. Things were beginning to change when we visited Moyobamba again with the children in 1981, staying with the Dutch missionaries Hans and Jeanette de Groot, from the Dutch Reformed Church Zendingsbond which had co-operated with the Free Church and the Iglesia Evangélica. Jeanette was a doctor and the Iglesia Evangélica had set-up the San Lucas Clinic in which Dr. Apollos Landa was involved, so Moyobamba was in a better position medically than it had been, though I don't think Jeanette could work officially because of revalidation rules. Manuel Reano, a former pupil of the San Andrés school in Lima also worked there, later on.

The de Groots lived in the former mission doctor's house, the other half of which had Dr. Lindsay's grapefruit tree. I peeked in at the old hospital. The huerta – the garden – had been razed but the building kept up, though there was a bad crack down the Mackay building. It was all PIP families who lived there. We were glad to have had the privilege of staying there and experiencing the old Moyobamba, where nobody locked their doors, where there was little crime, and we only saw one drunk man in the street and he was from the Sierra. Now there is a road in from Chiclayo which brings its own problems, but also goods and services. When Juana's husband needed an eye operation a few years ago, it was to a hospital on the coast that he went – a long journey, but on decent roads. There is a new all-day market and lots of new things including a new church building, and the work of the gospel goes on though with more competition (Adventists and Mormons).

We were sad to leave Moyobamba in December 1976 after only eleven months, but had known that we would return to Cajamarca to allow the Christies to go on furlough. When we came back to Cajamarca, Ruthi Lopez (aged about five) said, "you can more or less speak Spanish now". We thought we could before going to

Moyobamba, but probably the slower speech of the montaña had helped us to pick up more. Ronnie introduced us to a new member of the congregation, Alonso Ramirez, an agricultural student from Jaen, further north, who was keen to learn all about his new faith in the Bible. Also, there was a lad from Moyobamba who had started trial as an assistant in the bookshop. But Ronnie had found that his level of arithmetic wasn't sufficient, as the shop had a big turnover after the Mission Board had invested more money in it. This meant he had to return to Moyobamba, which would be very difficult for him, and, we think, caused some resentment there.

A new recruit came from Suyubamba, Vladimiro Chukimbalki, a lad with green eyes, who later worked in the Colegio San Andrés as a janitor. Quite a few people from Celendín had green eyes, thought to come from the Spaniards, including Don Aladino Escalante's wife, Cristina. Peruvians are very good at sourcing names from around the world – Nelson, Napoleon, Wenceslau and Ludovina. Classical names too – Hermogenes, Heraclito, Romulo and Teofilo. I suppose we Scots also have Hector and Alexander which the Peruvians use too, but less commonly. We also gave them a Calvin in Moyobamba, presumably from the Free Church missionary John Calvin Mackay. They also use foreign adjectives as Christian names – the pastor's son in Bambamarca was called Clever. There were later two bookshop assistants – Orlando and Juvenal.

Andy was the only missionary there until early 1978, so he had both Cajamarca morning adult Sunday School and service, and an afternoon service in Magdalena (a two hour journey) and the evening service in Cajamarca, though after some time Alonso was able to preach. I remember one time, when Andy stepped up from the floor, where he interacted with the Sunday School, to the dais for preaching, there was some miaowing from underneath the tablecloth covering the pulpit and our cat Minnie, who thought she had found a safe place for her kittens, started removing them from there! Minnie was required because of mice and rats, but one day a rat came straight up the stairs from the front door on the street, was not put off by my trying to shoo it down, headed for the back stairs, and Minnie was not interested. However, later, when she had her kittens in the garden, I noticed a bare tail in among them, so she wasn't as useless as she seemed.

We came down to Lima in mid-January for the Field Council which was the annual meet-up for all Free Church missionaries. Our bus, leaving at six a.m., took only 13 hours, beating another which had left at four a.m., even though we had to creep over the Gavilán because of mist. It was a race between drivers – somewhat scary! We returned to Cajamarca a week later, after farewelling the Christies, on a normal 16 hour bus ride.

My brother Willie Mackay and family came at the end of January for a short holiday during which two delegates from the Dutch Reformed Church Zendingsbond also arrived. One of them promptly slipped on our stairs and broke his arm – which curtailed Landrover journeys for him. Willie took me down by car to Lima for the arrival of the Scottish delegates, the Rev. Archie Boyd (later, Principal Emeritus of the Free Church College) and Professor James MacIntosh, plus Irene Thompson and the Baileys (their visas had taken ages, which was very common). Andy left Cajamarca with the Landrover on February 11th. He took three Peruvians and Willie's son with him. The Dutchmen went by air. So all were present for the National Assembly which ran for five days from February 12th. It was agreed that the Dutch Reformed Church would co-operate in Peru, and they made up for the lack of Scottish missionaries in Moyobamba, Pomacochas and around Lima.

I stayed down in Lima, awaiting the birth of our baby, while Andy took Archie north in the Landrover – they experienced a burst radiator hose and landslides, and had to tow a car, which had broken down in a place where the saturated earth was trickling down a 45-degree slope, to Cajamarca. Then there were problems with telephone communication with Lima. Andy showed him round the area, then they passed eight landslides on the way down to Chiclayo where Willie met them. Andy barely managed to take Archie on to Chachapoyas due to more landslides, but they did travel a bit in Amazonas. Then they went back to Chiclayo where George Thompson met them, to accompany Archie by plane to Moyobamba. This all illustrates the problems of Sierra travel and, although the road surfaces are now much better, you still can't avoid landslides.

Andy arrived in Lima in time, and set about getting me a safe-conduct in case I had to go to the clinic in the night, as there was a curfew in place. He was directed to the Ministry of War, where he was told that he had to produce the evidence – ie. me! Elspeth Anne Fraser arrived in the world on March 11th. We returned to Cajamarca in the first week of April, where the new baby was approved-of by Señora Juana Raico – "dark hair, dark eyes – better!" I had help from Señora Juana's niece, Edelmira, and from the Lopez family, especially Esther, when she was not at university. Andy has asked a carpenter to make a cot and a high-chair, working from a Mothercare catalogue. He produced the goods, chunky but serviceable. The serranos were very clever with their hands, whether weaving, knitting, copying a garment without patterns, or sewing.

Andy continued visiting the villages. When he visited one village while the leader was away, he found that the leader had been teaching that the Trinity was not Biblical. He was a very strong personality and usually sound and a very gracious man who, not finding the word in the Bible, took it to be un-Biblical. He did come to understand.

I continued to visit the women's prison, sometimes alone, sometimes with a lady from the congregation and – once Elspeth was a bit bigger – with her. The prison was like a Sierra house with rooms around a central yard. Señora Maria, the wardress, and the prisoners welcomed our visits. They were all country-women, some had babies or toddlers. One went out to the hospital for three days to have a baby. I asked if it was a first. She said that she had another ten at home! I took a kitten there for the rats and the mice. Some of the prisoners' crimes were very violent. They put up with a lot of hardship and abuse, and would suddenly crack. One douce-looking woman told me that she had found her husband with her niece, so she just picked up a rock and that was the end of him. I remember reading them a portion about when the boy Jesus stayed behind in the temple in Jerusalem, and how Mary and Joseph didn't really understand what Jesus said about His Father. One lady was offended, saying that the Mary she knew, whose image was in San Francisco church, was perfect and all-knowing.

Walking back from the prison in February was perilous, as Cajamarca prided itself on being the Capital of Carnival. This gave free reign to teenage boys to throw water balloons and buckets of water at mainly passing females, sometimes to their injury. This behaviour lasted over a month and towards the end dye, paint and flour were added. Singing and drunken dancing in the middle of the night with drums and whistles was not appreciated by the parents of babies! Towards the final few days, there were daily processions, and our church service was held at seven in the evening. This was to avoid problems later in the day.

There was a British Agricultural Mission to help farmers in the area. Just as we returned from Moyobamba, a new vet arrived. He was Andrew Newitt, an Anglican who worshipped with us, and we rendered each other much assistance. He showed us some nice big liver flukes in the laboratory that they had. Flukes don't usually affect humans, but around Cajamarca their incidence was so high that they did. The valley was mainly devoted to the production of milk destined to become Carnation evaporated milk, and there was also some very good Swiss-style cheese. We had plenty of milk, but it had to be boiled.

The fields were fenced with penka cactuses – big spiky aloes which put up a slender trunk, and flower once in a while. The country-people used the spike, which would come off with a fibre attached, as needle and thread. The leaves, when chopped into lengths, would be used as tiles on the top of earthen walls. Some hedges were of tuna – prickly pear, fruitful if spiny. The countryside around is bonny with a lot of eucalyptus – an introduced plant – as well as some conifers. My Aunt Margaret remembered the scent of eucalyptus cooking-fires in the evenings, and it was still so in our time.

I had English-speaking company in Maureen Puga from the

United States, who had been a Peace Corp volunteer and who had married a Cajamarquino. She had joined our church and wanted to study the Bible with me and we started, but her husband objected. Her little boy enjoyed playing with Elspeth, as did the Lopez children. Andrew Newitt introduced us to others from the British Agricultural Mission. He also accompanied Andy on some journeys including one to Saullamur where the village school was balanced above the abyss and the school teacher needed an injection which the vet applied! Alonso also accompanied Andy on journeys.

Cajamarca had a good all-day covered market, with more sales activity spilling out onto the streets around, and a great variety of fruit and vegetables was on sale. Strangely enough, potatoes, which belong to Peru in all their variety, were sold only as white or yellow, though there were other tubers such as olluca. Something we loved was cancha, a type of maize roasted and cracked. We did not like mote, which was maize boiled endlessly with lye to remove the hard shell until it was tasteless. Maybe it was a way to use-up stored maize. The meat section was rather smelly and the meat a bit tough. Bread rolls in different shapes were sold in the market and at various bakeries, and there was a mini-market which sold sliced bread and various packets and tins (some of them imported). Also, we had our own chacra, made from a collapsed adobe house in the mission grounds, which grew courgettes, beans, peas and so on.

Every Saturday we made soup which was given at the bookshop door to the poor. They were almost all men from the countryside with their "mates" which were half-gourd bowls. This soup was a tradition. One time we were just back home and in a hurry, so I just used packeted soup with a little addition of something. When I looked out of the window, I saw them tipping the soup into the gutter! The country-folk were, in general, despised by the town folk, and I can remember being approached for help with some forms in the Post Office, because they knew that foreigners would not reject them as postal officials would. You did get some alcoholics or coca addicts sleeping it off in the streets, but most were hard-working and had a hard life relieved by chicha beer.

We had a constant stream of visitors from town, from the villages round about, from further afield, from brethren needing to visit the hospital, the doctor, the council, folk from Lima, our own missionaries and folk from other missions in need of a holiday. It was lovely to have them but cleaning the house, even at times when I did have help, was a never-ending task because of the huge quantities of dust. If your brush handle knocked the wall, then earth and straw would fall out. The floorboards would have been laid in earth, and then the gaps collected more dirt, which was very interesting for little fingers, once Elspeth was on the move. After she had a very serious tummy upset we bought something rare and expensive – a hoover. It was amazing, properly removing the dust, instead of just moving the dust around with a brush. But it had to be emptied all the time, because it lost suction quickly.

Donnie Smith arrived in Peru in 1977 after delays to his visa and he and Catriona Urquart travelled up to Cajamarca in July to visit. Catriona was a representative of the Free Church Women's Foreign Missionary Association (on a private visit) and a niece of J. Calvin Mackay. He was, of course, the earliest Free Church missionary in Cajamarca, where he was known as el caballero Cristiano – the Christian gentleman. Catriona was very interested to meet the people who remembered him. Andy took them both via Celendín through Amazonas. Then they walked the path where the new road would go through and meet the road from Moyobamba, thus travelling through all three provinces – Cajamarca, Amazonas and San Martín. Donnie and Andy later did a camp in Suyubamba, with meetings for adults at night. By January 1978, after his language study, Donnie was resident in Cajamarca and able to preach and help with the bookshop.

We hosted the 1978 Assembly, which had only two delegates from San Martín, two from Amazonas, two from Celendín and four from Lima, but it was a beneficial Assembly. There were also day-visitors from Cajamarca. Señora Lopez, along with a daughter, did most of the catering and cooking for up to twenty people, and I assisted along with a lady who picked out the sticks and stones from the lentils and rice – though it turned out that her sight was not so good. The men were organised into a rota of pairs for washing-up. It was a scream to hear some of them discussing how to go about this unaccustomed task!

Illness was a problem, with diarrhea and vomiting very common, causing delays to planned journeys. Also respiratory infections, common in Lima, though you would have thought the fresh air of the Sierra would have lessened this. There was tuberculosis, scarlet fever and hepatitis. Donnie contracted this later when he was on his own, and his life was saved by the Lopezes and Andrew Newitt getting medical attention for him. A family from Malcat near Celendín stayed with us a couple of times as the husband, Ernesto, was suffering from severe epileptic seizures. (There was a doctor in Celendín, but he wasn't interested in poor people). Two of Ernesto's brothers came to help because the fits were violent. One was called Antonio and Priscila, his wife, was greatly amused by Elspeth's attempts to say his name which came out as Tonto (which means stupid). Their baby was wrapped in swaddling bands (to keep the back straight). Priscila told me that the men's mother had spaced-out their births by breast-feeding each until the age of four – but that doesn't always work, though.

There was a hospital in Cajamarca, where Elspeth had her inoculations and weight-checks, but you couldn't rely on it. For example, when Priscila went with the baby with a terrible cough, the hospital was closed due to a strike. There was also a laboratory in the university, but when I took a sample to it, they couldn't process it because the water was off, which it often was because of serious drought. People in the valleys might source water from streams and those in the heights might have a misty climate, but those on the middle slopes were in desperate straits. Andy took supplies to some but, later, a project called PROESA was started in which Donnie and Alonso were involved, and with the TEAR Fund to promote better ways of farming to conserve water.

In April 1978 we had a holiday in Lima with a short trip up to Huancayo in the central Sierra. Elspeth became ill and we packed up rather quickly. At Ticlio (15,807 feet), Andy pulled out a bag from behind his seat and a little later began to feel dizzy. Knowing it was soroche – altitude sickness – he began to take deep breaths to get more oxygen but could feel paralysis coming up from his feet and his hands, but he continued thinking this was the soroche getting worse. (Later, we found out that this was caused by hyper-ventilating). But God was looking after us because, when I flagged down a car, it stopped (unusual) and it had two drivers, a mining engineer and his driver, who hopped into the Landrover and drove us to a mining clinic a bit further down the road where the nurses gave Andy oxygen. But the paralysis kept creeping up to his chest. Eventually a doctor came and said sharply, "Stop breathing like that": which he did. He had been over-breathing, which had flushed carbon dioxide out of his system, causing alkalosis. (For future reference, the cure is breathing into a paper bag). The driver very kindly stayed with us and took the Landrover to the outskirts of Lima. Andy had gradually improved and managed to get us back to where we were staying. We were shaken but very thankful. In the early morning we were shaken again – but this time by an earthquake! We returned in a few days to Cajamarca.

In May, there were price rises which led to rioting. Lorries were being stopped and their contents looted. Andy and three students set off for Amazonas via Chiclayo, but there was no fuel to be had. On the return journey, road-blocks were being set-up in coastal towns, but they managed to get through (though in one town a brick was thrown at the Landrover). But on the road up from the coast, they were stopped and money was demanded. Those involved were workers who were unemployed. Andy refused at first but, since they were in real need, gave them money. Two days later he tried, with Alonso, to get through via Celendín but country folk on the way decided to copy the trouble on the coast, and had dismantled a plank bridge. Nine days later, Andy and Alonso got through via Chiclayo.

In July Andy started a series of daily teachings in Hualqui, ninety minutes by Landrover and a very steep thirty minute walk away. On the last day, climbing up to where the Landrover was, he felt his strength just draining away. He drove home and collapsed. A doctor diagnosed physical and mental exhaustion and he was forced to rest. He preached in Cajamarca for the last time on the sixth of August, and we sadly left for Lima the next day. We had to do the paperwork for Elspeth's passport and finally left Lima for home on the seventh of September.

But we returned to Lima in the October of the following year, where our son was born and where Andy ministered in a church of mainly serranos in the Las Flores district of the city, and taught in Colegio San Andrés for a while. He also travelled to Cajamarca, Amazonas and San Martín to get the title deeds to mission properties, which had been taken out in different names, sorted-out in order that they could be passed on to the Iglesia Evangélica. We visited Cajamarca again in 1982, and arrived in time for the wedding of two church young folk and the graduation of the bride and of Esther Lopez. We had a lovely time catching up with the folk and our Jamie celebrated his second birthday with church children. Esther came back down with us for a wee holiday. Much later she married Alonso Ramirez. He later studied in the Free Church College in Edinburgh, where their son Samuel was born. Later, Samuel's sister Analiz was born in Jackson, Mississippi, where Alonso did further studies. They have done a power of work in Cajamarca and further afield in Peru. We have kept in touch with them ever since.

Now Esther's brother Dr. Nicolas Segundo Lopez pastors the original church and runs the Sarah MacDougall Health Centre Project. The Sierra missionaries were always too thinly spread. But when we finally left Peru in 1982, the Sierra was much better served. Donnie and Julia Smith were in Cajamarca, along with Charlie and Daphne Douglas in the bookshop. David and Olwen Ford were in Celendín, Corrie and Bert van Donkersgood in Pomacochas, and Hans and Jeanette in Moyobamba. In San Andrés, Alejandro Tuesta, early mission lad from Moyobamba, was the pastor.

Bookshop and Bibles:
Charles Douglas remembers

LET ME START WITH HOW MY WIFE DAPHNE AND I WERE CALLED TO Cajamarca in Peru. In a 1977 edition of the Free Church missionary magazine, From the Frontiers, a photograph appeared which showed all the missionaries who were working in Peru at the time. However, as many of the missionaries were due to come back to Scotland that year, another photograph was printed underneath showing only those who would remain in Peru. There was also an appeal, asking for others to come and join those who would remain.

At around the same time, there was an appeal for help in running the Christian bookshop in Cajamarca, which was called La Librería Estandarte de la Verdad (the Banner of Truth Bookshop) and which had been set-up by the Australian missionary, Hugh Varnes. So both Daphne and I felt called to apply. I had some experience of books and was used to administration. We were accepted and presented to the 1977 General Assembly and given a Bible from the then-moderator, Professor W. J. Cameron. Due to visa problems, however, it was not until the summer of 1978 that, with our two small children, we left for the Peruvian capital of Lima.

While in Lima we lived in flats right next door to Colegio San Andrés. All the missionaries who worked in Lima lived in that building. I was studying Spanish at the university, while Daphne studied at home. Shortly after our arrival, Clive Bailey invited me to go with him to a Scripture Union class in a place called Kimo, which was in the jungle. It was there that I really started to learn Spanish, as it was difficult to learn the language while living so close to other English speakers.

In 1978, there were serious problems in the Cajamarca province due to the lack of seasonal rains. The Free Church sent out £1,500 from its disaster-fund to help. However, there were no missionaries at that time living in the Cajamarca area, so Daphne and I were asked to go. With the money donated, seed was purchased and – accompanied by Pastor Juan Silva – we headed up to Cajamarca to distribute this to the needy. It was our first experience of the Andes. We arrived at an empty mission house but thankfully Andrew Fraser had left some furniture locked away in a back room. We dusted the empty house and, with our two small children, settled into the large building. Downstairs was the bookshop I had come to administer, the church, some other rooms, and the garage. A student at the local university, Alonzo Ramirez, stayed in one of these rooms. He and I became great friends, and he was a great help to me.

In Cajamarca, there was a British Diplomatic Mission and one member of that Mission, Andrew Newitt, came to our aid. He was of great assistance to us when Donnie Smith was very ill. Andrew was full of advice about living at altitude and what foods to avoid and so on. He came with us to show us around Cajamarca province, as he thought it better that I did not drive our mission Landrover until I became accustomed to the altitude and the dangerous roads. So, with Pastor Juan Silva and Andrew, we visited the surrounding area, reaching as far as Leimibamba. This was to evaluate who should get the seed.

It was my first encounter with some of the local church leaders. We met Don Napoleon Lezama in San Marcos – to my amusement, his wife was called Josephine! Don Napo, as he was called, became a good friend as we got to know each other over the years we spent together. His father-in-law, Modesto Romero, was also an elder in the church. We travelled to a town called Jesús and met Don Fidel

Aldave. I came to admire him for his leadership skills in the local church, and the respect he had from the local community. He was very familiar with the Bible, on one occasion telling us about Jacob's twelve children. But then he added that while Jacob had four wives, he had just one – though she too had borne twelve children!

In 1978, Cajamarca city was a fairly quiet place. Although the mission house was so near to the Plaza de Armas, the main square, there was not too much traffic. Our children enjoyed the freedom of the city. We managed to introduce ourselves to members of the congregation. The large López family was a tremendous help to us. Esther López became a great friend and help, especially to Daphne. I go to know their father, Don Nicholás, well. He used to come with me to visit some of the nearby places. I remember him coming with me to Magdalena, a town down the mountain from the city. He also undertook a lot of practical work around the mission building. Sadly, he died while we were on furlough.

With the mission house being so close to the main square, and with so many political problems at the time, many demonstrations passed in front of our house. Our children being so young used to join-in with their chants – el pueblo unido jamás será vencido (the people united will never be defeated). Opposite our building was the department for education and, since there were many teachers' strikes, a lot of demonstrations took place there. One one occasion, as I looked from our balcony, a load of soldiers climbed down from their truck and – preparing to confront the protesters – started lining up opposite our house. They then took out their rifles and made ready to face the oncoming protest.

After evaluating the distribution of the much-needed food, we returned to Lima to finish our language training, although being up in Cajamarca with very few English speakers for a few weeks was a great help. We were eager to return as quickly as possible. So, having managed to get to the required level of Spanish, we left for Cajamarca in February 1979, and were encouraged to continue our studies there. We arrived just as Carnival was starting – Cajamarca is the capital of Peruvian Carnival. It was in full swing when our lorry full of furniture came, which made for a memorable arrival in the city!

Now that we were settled, my main task was to manage the Christian bookshop. With the shop being directly below our house – well, that was very handy! Unfortunately, the employee of the shop at that time had to be asked to leave, and my first task was to find a replacement who would help run the shop and whom I would eventually train to become manager. I was introduced to a young man called Juvenal Pando, and we developed a good working relationship. Along with running the bookshop, we were starting to get involved with the church. Thankfully, a few months into our work David and Olwen Ford arrived with their children David and Elizabeth. They stayed for about a year in the mission house just next door to us, while Donnie Smith was getting over his serious illness. David along with his family then moved to Celendín. By that time Donnie had arrived back with his new wife Julia.

With David taking the Landrover to Celendín, the Mission Board sent money to allow us to purchase a new car. Donnie bought a double-cabin Datsun pick-up. This became very useful for distributing supplies to the needy. That car served us very well. Throughout our years in the Andes together, the Douglas and Ford families often arranged visits to each other. David worked well in the area of Celendín along with Don Mermogenes. We visited Celendín a few times and stayed with the Fords. David had started a Bible teaching school so a few of us from Cajamarca went to one of his courses. David even taught Hebrew to the locals! I still have a certificate, signed by him, saying that I had attended.

This was part of another project that Donnie set up, called the Timothy Project. It started in Cajamarca and we would invite church leaders to the city from the villages nearby. Julia was in charge of cooking for the brethren who arrived. Preaching skills and Biblical truth were taught to the participants. Donnie took on the preaching duties within the church and I used to lead the Bible classes before the service, which I enjoyed. They sang using the Psalm book that had been produced and various people would take part in the service, reading the Scriptures, taking the collection or leading in prayer. It was good to have participation from within the congregation. There was also a Sunday School, which our boys attended. We also had contact with an organisation called SEPAS and through it we were able to obtain sacks of rice that were donated by the USA. As we continued to distribute the food, Donnie Smith was starting to realise the need for a development project.

The bookshop was the only Christian one in the whole of the province of Cajamarca. The legal transfer of the title of manager to my name was completed with the help of a local lawyer, Señor Terrones, who also finalised the accounts to pass on to the relevant government office. I was responsible for checking stock and keeping the paperwork required by the government. As well as Christian books, the shop stocked stationery. To help distribute the much-needed literature within the province, there were a few pastors who took books and Bibles on a sale or return basis to the villages further up the mountain. A pastor called Balcassar was one of these helpers who was keen to get the literature and Bibles to the believers in remote areas.

Our stock all came from Lima and from time to time I travelled down to the El Inca bookshop and the Bible Society and other distributors to make personal contact and to get any discounts that I could. On one of these occasions, Juvenal went with us so that he could be seen as the new face of the bookshop. We had a good working relationship, and he proved to be a fast learner. I tried to leave him at the shop front, although at times I also was there. However, I was too sympathetic and tended to give too much of a discount. Juvenal on the other hand knew how to deal with the locals better than any gringo!

The stationery side of the business helped to offset the overheads. Just after arriving in February, the Campaña Escolar (school campaign) was about to start. The pupils were required to purchase their own textbooks, jotters, pens and pencils. So, we quickly placed an order and they arrived just in time. Business was brisk. Realising that the sale of stationery was a great way to offset expenditure and allowed the shop to have a good stock of Christian literature, I started to contact offices within Cajamarca to see if we could gain a contract to sell them stationery. The local hospital became one of our best customers, ordering great amounts of paper. That helped the bookshop to gain a good reputation with a few other government offices. However, as I grew to know the various officials in different offices, they began to chat with me. They found out that I was with the same mission as the late Sarah MacDougall. She was so well remembered in the city that folk were very sympathetic towards our shop.

Around about this time the Women's Foreign Missions Association of the Free Church sent a very helpful donation to the bookshop which enabled us to improve stock and the furnishings of the premises. Within the shop we had a mimeograph machine – this was before the age of computers, of course. Stencils were made and put through the machine. In the past, it was used to produce all Biblical literature including a publication of a Psalm book in Spanish. In our time, we rented-out the machine to students and others who wanted to run documents off. This was another way of producing income for the shop.

At that time Bert and Corrie van Donkersgood, from Holland, were working in Moyobamba and a message arrived that they were in need of Christian literature, especially Bibles. So I set off in the Landrover with Alonso and another friend, Wilber, with a vehicle full of books. Alonso was from Jaen so rather than go via Celendín we made our way down to the coast, heading for Chiclayo. By the time we headed up from there to Jaen, it was getting dark. Suddenly, out of the corner of Alonso's eye, he saw something falling off the roof of the Landrover – which turned out to be the spare tyre. Providentially, a lorry was just behind us and stopped to help, with the aid of flashlights. The tyre was retrieved, and we made our way to Jaen. It was good to meet Alonso's parents.

The next day we headed for Amazonas, but soon the dirt road became almost impassable. The rain had caused the surface to become soft and heavy lorries had made deep trenches in the soil. We made our way as cautiously as we could. With daylight fading, we sought somewhere to sleep for the night – ironically, the village was called Progreso. A local family opened-up their home for us, and we spent the night on the floor.

Arriving at the military checkpoint, I only had copies of my documents, as the originals had been sent to Lima for renewal. The soldiers at the checkpoint ordered me to go to the local police office. It was then that I was accused of being a spy! (Looking back, I think they were trying to extort a bribe). Anyway, I showed them our Bibles and offered one free to the officer. Thankfully, Corrie came to vouch for us. Bert and Corrie were delighted with the Bibles and Christian literature. Sadly, after moving from Moyobamba to Pomacochas a few years later, Bert died. We received a telephone call from Lima, and Donnie and David went to see how they could help.

We enjoyed worshipping with the large congregation in Moyobamba, and visiting the bank of the local river, where they were selling bananas not by bunches but what they called heads of bananas. I also purchased boxes of oranges to take back to Daphne. These she made into many jars of marmalade. Before making our way homewards, I was worried about the state of the road. But luckily, the army had gone on ahead and had repaired it, so our trip back was much faster than I had feared.

I previously mentioned Sarah MacDougall. She was a nurse who served the Free Church in the early days of the work in Cajamarca. She was so well respected in the community that a street was named after her. And when she died, the authorities erected a monumental bust to her in the cemetery. When we received visitors from the Foreign Board, they always appreciated a visit to the cemetery to see her grave.

She was also awarded a gold medal in recognition of her years of service among the people of Cajamarca. The citation read (according to a report in From the Frontiers for November 1952): "To Señorita MacDougall, whose work for social welfare as a nurse and obstetrician is fully appreciated by the people of Cajamarca. In thirty years of consecutive service, she cared for the different social classes with a spirit of dedicated self-sacrifice, and with the exceptional love and tenderness which marks her out as a person of outstanding merit and personal worth, deserving of the greatest honour that the citizens can bestow on their benefactors, on the anniversary of the Nation's Independence".

A leading lawyer, Dr. Velasquez, as recorded in a number of reports in the Monthly Record, said that, "attending to the spiritual as well as the bodily needs of the people was at one and the same time fulfilling the human and divine mission of our Lord, and this was daily being practised in the evangelical mission in Cajamarca. Señorita MacDougall carefully attended to the physical needs of her numerous patients and found many opportunities of directing them to higher things". When she died in 1955, John Alexander Mackay wrote that, "her work of ministration to the sick and indigent in the Cajamarca district proved of the greatest value in breaking-down prejudice towards the missionaries, and in making hearts receptive for the gospel message".

This was so true that the community still remembered her twenty years after her death. When I was working in the area, the authorities removed the bust from the cemetery and placed it in a kindergarten, which was to be named after her. I was invited to the grand opening ceremony, when authorities from all departments gathered to honour her memory. Furthermore, while I was still in Cajamarca, the hundredth anniversary of her birth was celebrated. A special service was held in our local Presbyterian Church, where again all those in authority, as well as representatives from various churches, came once more to show their respects to this lady who did so much for them. The fact that I could say that I belonged to the same church and country opened many doors for me in the various government offices and departments. Often, they would say, "Ah! You are from the same church as Sarah MacDougall so how can I help you?" This was to prove very useful as I began to integrate government resources for the project called PROESA (project of education, health and agriculture).

As well as working in the bookshop, I used to visit some of the Presbyterian congregations throughout the province, in the evenings. I really enjoyed worshipping in Spanish and contributing to the services in these rural areas. Don Fidel was the main leader in Jesús, and the elders in the nearby villages came together on a Saturday morning to worship there. However, during the week, they had their own services in Chuquita and other villages. The only way to reach these villages was to walk, as there were no roads in these parts. I enjoyed the informal way that folk would ask questions as you preached. There was plenty of opportunity to teach basic Biblical truths. At first, I just went to visit but – seeing a missionary in their congregation – they always asked me to speak, so I learned to go prepared.

I also enjoyed going to San Marcos, where Don Napo, along with his father-in-law, Don Modesto, always welcomed me. Often, Alonso came along with me. One time, we were asked to cross the river to a village called Saporcon where some brethren met together for worship. Usually, at that time of the year the river becomes completely dry. So, we crossed the dry riverbed to visit the brethren. However, without warning the rains came – and when it rains there, it certainly rains! The river became fairly deep, wide and fast-flowing, but I wanted to get back to Cajamarca, and so we crossed anyway. Thinking back, it was not a wise move, but at the time I just wanted to get to the Landrover and get back home.

However, it is my conversations with Don Fidel that I will never forget. We enjoyed many a meal together in his home and he, like others, would remind us of some of the missionaries who used to work in the area. The church in Jesús was always full, and he usually asked me to speak. After any invited speaker preached, Don Fidel would speak afterwards as well, to emphasise a truth that was worth repeating, or to correct any misunderstandings. He often spoke about his vision of improving the church building – and much of that vision did in time become a reality.

Julia's uncle Florencio Durán formed part of an organisation called ALFALIT. Its aim was to help people to learn how to read and write. As children grew up in the countryside, they were required to work in the fields so had no chance to obtain an education. So Julia arranged for her uncle to come to Cajamarca to present a course to volunteers who would then go to help. Daphne and I enrolled and ended up going to a small village nearby where we started classes. Daphne, being a teacher, focussed on the reading and the writing side and, being more numerical, I focussed on the arithmetical side. We grew very fond of that group and when it was time for our furlough many were sad to see us go. We had formed a good bond with them.

Another task that required attention was to begin to prepare the transfers of properties that were owned by the Free Church to the Iglesia Evangélica. Andrew Fraser, being a trustee, drew up papers giving me permission to see to this paperwork. I was surprised how many pieces of land and buildings were owned by the Free Church. With the help of Señor Terrones many of the documents were filled in ready to start the process. Unfortunately, due to various bureaucratic difficulties many of these properties and pieces of land have still not been transferred.

We were due to go back to Peru after our furlough, but the Falklands War broke out and our time in Edinburgh was prolonged. Peru was very sympathetic to Argentina in the conflict, and it was thought that it would be better if we stayed at home for a bit. One advantage was that our oldest boy, Alistair, completed Primary One, and our second boy, Iain, had a chance to attend nursery school. Kenneth was born on the tenth of January – which was registered as the coldest day that Scotland had ever had. Sadly, just days after Kenneth was born, Daphne's father, the Rev. Duncan Beaton, died. We finally returned to Peru, along with David and Olwen Ford, and our three children, in 1982.

Early one morning I woke up suddenly – Daphne was still asleep. At first I did not realise what was happening. But then it dawned on me that there was an earth tremor under way. Then Alistair came through to our room complaining that someone had been shaking his bed. I recall that news had reached Celendín and David and Olwen had heard that Cajamarca had been badly hit by an earthquake. Thankfully, however, it was no more than a tremor – though that is still a frightening experience.

At first Alistair attended the local primary school and Iain went to the local nursery in Cajamarca. However, Margaret Mackinnon, a former missionary, volunteered to come out and help with the teaching of the Douglas and Ford children. Margaret soon recommended that we home-school the boys, and a classroom was set up and Daphne's teaching skills were put to use. Thankfully, we did have help in the house, which allowed Daphne to spend time in the classroom.

On the whole we both kept fairly well, though there were a few times when Daphne was unwell. The most difficult time was when she was expecting our fourth child. Since the hospital in Cajamarca did not have a good reputation, she travelled down to Lima to undertake a thorough test. The doctor there advised her that the condition of our baby girl, anencephaly, was such that she could not survive, so it was decided that Daphne should undergo a caesarean. Our baby daughter, Ruth, died a few minutes after her birth. On returning to Cajamarca, Daphne found great comfort and help from the ladies within the church, many of whom had also experienced the loss of babies or young children. Strong bonds of friendship were formed, many of which remain to this day in spite of the distance which now separates us.

Throughout our seven years in Peru, we enjoyed receiving many visitors from Scotland. I will just mention a few of them. Professor James Fraser came as a representative of the Foreign Board. As I have already noted, the mission house was close to the main city square, La Plaza de Armas. One day he left the building on his own and went for a walk to see something of the city. On arriving back, he proudly announced that he found his way by asking, "dónde está La Plaza de Armas?" (where is the main square?). He was pleased that he could use this Spanish phrase.

In his moderatorial year, Professor Archie Boyd visited us. I still have the picture he gave us of him wearing his robes of office. He also gave me his Greek New Testament, and this was an incentive for me to learn that language. He wanted to visit the villages where the Mission had been working. John O. Sutherland also stayed with us, and he wanted to visit the work in Hualqui. This was the centre of the PROESA project, and we had started to build a communal house. As soon as he set eyes on the building he quoted Deuteronomy 22.8: "When you build a new house make a parapet around your roof so that you may not bring the guilt of bloodshed on your house if someone falls from the roof" – and this was because the communal house did not yet have a roof!

The Rev. Fergus Macdonald also visited. I remember taking him to the Cuarto de Rescate (ransom room). This was where the Inca ruler, Atahualpa, was taken by the Spanish and ordered to fill it, to the height he could reach, with gold and silver to redeem his life. It did no good, as they killed him anyway. There is a mark in the room that shows the level to which the gold and silver reached, and Fergus reached up to the mark. We also had a visit from the Rev. John MacPherson. He reported to the 1986 General Assembly and paid tribute to the various workers for their contributions. Not only did he see that there were practical benefits to these communities but also that there was growth and new life in churches. All these visits were a great encouragement to us, as the visitors listened to our experiences. It was a great encouragement to have the full backing of the Foreign Missions Board and the General Assembly.

The church leaders within the city decided to form a united effort of Evangelism and I was invited to attend. Pastor Carlos Palacios was the Baptist minister and we were good friends. The children of both families used to get together, especially for birthday parties. The chairman of this gathering was Pastor Julio Suyon and he had plenty of ideas. A good number of leaders were involved as we met to discuss evangelistic events. Three of these stand out in my memory.

Bible Day is marked with great enthusiasm in Peru, so on one occasion we arranged for the Bible to be read by various helpers in the main square of the city. We gained the relevant permission from the authorities and started to read various passages from the Bible with loudspeakers in place. As well as reading the Bible, we would preach in the square, and good numbers gathered.

On another occasion we decided to have a march and invited all the evangelical churches in the area to participate. In our planning, we started to look at some of the practicalities of the matter. How many would we have in the march? Would we go ahead with two hundred? This was a bit like Abraham's prayer. Perhaps we would go ahead with a hundred and fifty – or even a hundred? Let's say we get fifty – we would still go ahead with the march. So we prayed about this event, and we asked God to bless these plans. On that particular Bible Day, the leaders encouraged their members to come out and march along one of the main streets, finishing up in the square. What we never expected was that news spread and Christian churches further up the mountain also joined the march. Then most of the community of Porcon came too. The numbers grew and grew. As we finished the march and gathered in the main square, the Word was preached.

Porcon is a Christian community high up the mountain. As you drive up towards the village, you passed Biblical signs which corresponded to the scenery. Psalm 23, Psalm 121, John 10, among many others. They have evangelical gatherings and I was invited to go to speak at one of these. So, I spent time preparing and with Juvenal set off for the event. The event was crowded out and God was clearly present. After the meeting, a long cloth was rolled out on the grass, and all the congregation then sat along both sides and ate together.

The third occasion I will mention was when we received news that the O. M. Logos ship had docked in the port of Trujillo. Operation Mobilisation was the name of the missionary company which ran the ship. We managed to get permission to take a group of six Christians from the ship. So I drove down to collect them. It was great to visit the ship which had many visitors that day. One of the main ministries of the ship is the sale of Christian books, and it was very encouraging to see so many titles on display. As you travelled around the ship, the stages in the life of the Prodigal Son were displayed with words underneath re-telling the story. I then went to a conference area where many had gathered to hear God's word being preached. There was simultaneous translation into Spanish.

In fact, the translator spoke with more enthusiasm than the original speaker!

After spending time on the Logos,the group of six joined me on the journey back up into the mountains. Arriving in Cajamarca, it took time to get to know them all, as they were from different parts of the world and spoke various languages. However, this was no barrier to how God was going to use them to bring the different evangelical churches together. I recall our visit to the Pentecostal church, where one of the group preached in English and I translated. I recall at the end Donnie saying to me, "you preached a different sermon, but better!"

When we arrived back in Cajamarca in 1982, Juvenal had been running the bookshop on his own for a whole year, so it was evident that my presence there was not needed, as it had been in our first term of service. However, by that time Donnie had produced a document outlining his plans for a project that would help develop the poor villages nearby. An old proverb says, give a man a fish and you will feed him for a day, but teach a man to fish and you will feed him for life. So, with the experience we had of distributing seed to alleviate immediate problems, plans were put in place for a longer-term solution. The new project, which was called PROESA, needed an administrator, so I was asked to take on that task, with Donnie leaving me to oversee the practicalities of finance, accounting, supplies and co-ordinating the team.

We used one of the mission rooms on the ground floor as our base. The bookshop was just along from that room, so I could keep an eye on that too. But Juvenal was quite experienced by now, and mostly able to manage it on his own. The new project was seen as a practical way of demonstrating the Lord's love. So steps were taken within the Iglesia Evangélica to take time to understand the practical improvements that could be made within the existing environment.

The final document set out the basics of the project, the problems the villages faced, a plan of work, possible activities and resources. It amazed me, as administrator, that the full budget of £46,700 had been spent on the work during the first phase – so was this expenditure worthwhile? We had received funds from the TEAR Fund and the Free Church. Other sources of funding came in from contacts in Canada, Ireland, Holland and Australia. A group of committed personnel was found, and the project got under way. All the teams were members of churches in Cajamarca, and were qualified in their particular fields. The initial team was made up of Olonzo Ramirez, an agricultural engineer; Dr. Nicolas López, a medical doctor; Esther López, a sociologist; Elsa Aguirre, a nurse; and Victor Cardenas and Dorti Rojas, trained in literacy work.

The team lived together in Hualqui. To reach Hualqui, we drove the Landrover which we had inherited from the late Bert van Donkersgood towards the village, which was past Jesús. Another helper, Don Demetrio Rojas, was hired to drive the team to and from the village. However, there was a landslide and the Landrover could not reach the community. The team had to walk the rest of the way, carrying all their equipment until they reached the community house. This took a great deal of dedication. The team was quick to learn to listen to the people. It was a question of perseverance, as the villagers could get easily discouraged. I remember one occasion when frequent visits and meetings had to be held so that a drinking-water project could get under way. I then visited the community to encourage them to continue. This involved a climb to the source of the underground spring. It was so encouraging, once the system was fully operational and families could have running water near their houses.

One of the main problems within communities like Hualqui is that, for long periods, the men in such villages travel to the coast to look for work. This means that the women and children are left to care for the crops while the men are away. Children are often taken out of school to help with the various chores. They travelled down to the nearest river to gather water, or took their animals to far-off places to find pasture. So, this meant that many in the community were not able to read or write.

Victor and Dorti were trained in the use of ALFALIT material, and spent time in trying to improve the situation. All the work was coordinated through the church, so Bible-based material was used.

While using this material, opportunities opened up for discussion. Again, the ladies within the Free Church helped with funding and raised money to help with this literacy work. PROESA was an integrated development project, so all three areas of education, health and agriculture were connected. So, as we will see, there were educational programmes within the areas of health and agriculture as well.

Dr. Nicolás along with nurse Elsa attended to the health needs, as they lived in the community. One of the first tasks was to construct a medical post. From this centre, they started a programme of training health promoters so that, in time, the community itself would be able to deal with the treatment of basic health issues. One other main area was that of prevention. So, immunisation and nutrition programmes were started. Small vegetable gardens were planted, in coordination with Alonzo, the agronomist. Then, coordinating with Victor and Dori, a course in basic hygiene was held. Infant mortality within these communities was high, so much time was given over to checking-up on expectant mothers and baby-care. Later on, a nurse from Belgium, Marie-Christine Lux, joined us, and she faithfully served in these communities, enduring the hardships that that entailed.

Alonzo saw to the training of some members of the community so they could learn basic techniques that would improve the size of their harvest. Terraces were constructed on the steep hillsides so that more land could be used for the planting of various crops. He also helped increase production by teaching the use of fertilisers and fumigation techniques, to help with pest control. He was well-respected within the community. When Alonzo left the project, another agronomist, Almanzor Fernandez, came to help. Since many of the women in the village were responsible for the upkeep of the crops, while their husbands were away working in other areas, it was decided to employ Miriam Urrunaga. She too was a qualified agronomist, and much of her initial work was to organise the planting of potato crops.

After administering PROESA for about a year, Donnie was due to go on furlough and I was put in charge as director, with Victor López assisting me. His sister Esther, the sociologist, also stayed in the community and undertook a detailed study of the needs of the villagers. Her document helped to guide us to what their needs were, and not what we thought best for them. It was evident too that the project could do with a full-time vet, as the people placed a high value on their animals. An advertisement therefore went round the churches, and Don Napoleon, from San Marcos, recommended a vet called Luis Cabrera.

Soon Luis got to work, and one of his first plans of action was to introduce a new breed of hen into the area. Families were provided with a number of hens that would produce nutritious eggs. Luis also sought to improve the various breeds of other animals. I was so taken with the hen project that we took ten hens into our back garden, thus providing us with a supply of fresh eggs. After Luis left, we employed David Chuquipoma, whom Donnie knew from his contacts in Lima. I vividly recall David transporting a large hog – a pedigree Yorkshire White – into the village, so that a better breed of pig could be produced.

The project also tried to diversify income sources. Tools were purchased so that a carpentry workshop could function better. A local man, José Matara, headed-up that project. Local industries such as weaving and basket-making were also encouraged. Gonzalo Salirrosas was employed as a civil engineer to help with the various building and irrigation projects. We also had a volunteer from Holland, Timen Eilender, who was a great help, not only with his engineering skills, for he also drove the team back and forth from Hualqui. I remember, on one occasion, the Landrover broke down – not an unusual occurrence – and Timen ended-up buried below the vehicle, sorting out the problem.

We still used the Datsun pickup to visit the project and on several occasions Donnie and I would go to see what improvements had been made. The community also invited us to celebrate special events. Often, the children of the local school would put on plays for us. There were openings of buildings to attend, and other events to go to as well. On one of these occasions, our wives and children also went along with us, though Donnie's son Alex was too young to come.

At the end of the celebrations we set off on our way back. But the rains had come and there was severe flooding on the road. Water got into the engine of the vehicle and we ground to a halt. There was no way through for us, but Donnie and Julia managed to make their way back to Cajamarca. We managed to restart the vehicle and tried to make our way back to Jesús as Don Fidel's youngest son, Benjamin, was with us. But the car ground to a halt once again. Benjamin warned us not to get out of the car at that time of night, as it was too dangerous. So with our three boys we spent a cold night in a damp car. The next morning, we eventually got assistance and arrived back in Cajamarca, tired and wet, but safe. God had clearly protected us through that experience.

When Donnie was on furlough, the TEAR Fund visited us, and I helped them to make a film of the PROESA project. Our first stop was Jesús, where we visited the church. It was a Sunday and, as usual, the church was full. Don Fidel again asked me up to speak. However, this time I translated Don Fidel's sermon into English. Don Fidel realised that the visitors from England would not be able to follow the service. Once we had finished, Don Fidel then explained to the congregation that this was what meant by speaking in tongues. Pentecostal influence had grown within the area, and he wanted to show the real use of tongue speaking!

From Jesús we made our way past Cebadín and as we went along, the TEAR Fund crew stopped to speak to local families and gather information for the film they were making. The project had also erected a medical post in Cebadín, and helped several families there with agricultural and educational problems. From there, we had to carry all the film-making equipment to Hualqui.

Once Donnie came back from furlough, he employed a new director, Humberto Bullón, and I continued to oversee administration until just before returning to Scotland for good. Shortly before I left, the project employed a Peruvian to oversee the administration, so I had handed over both of my tasks, the bookshop and the project. After all, missionaries are meant to work themselves out of jobs so that local people can take over. It was most satisfying to have been used by God within these various areas – an experience I will never forget.

In working alongside the community in a practical, material way, the project demonstrated that the church was interested in their physical needs as well as their spiritual needs. By serving in this way, we show that we have a message with continuing relevance. By transforming the outward circumstances, a proclamation will be made through the very acts that are carried out. What we need is a theology of mission that is distinguished by a faith that acts. As it says in James, 2.26. – as the body without the spirit is dead, so faith without deeds is dead.

On returning to Cajamarca in 2003, the city had completely changed. Gold had been discovered in the mountains above it. The city had expanded at least four-fold, and the traffic was almost as bad as it was in Lima. We were thankful that we had the opportunity to serve there before all this came about. I cannot imagine how a young missionary family would cope with the city as it is now. God's providence is a great thing to ponder. Also – and this was really encouraging – Juvenal was still in charge of the bookshop. It had a new name, Casa de la Biblia (House of the Bible), as Juvenal had managed to arrange a partnership with the Bible Society.

It was great to meet up with old friends and revisit the villages we used to go to, including Hualqui. On arriving there, we found a group from North America being given a tour of the village by José Matara, a local man whom we knew well. He was amazed to see us when we came round the corner, as he had just been explaining to the visitors about the improvements that PROESA had made.

The mission work in Cajamarca started in 1921 with John Calvin Mackay so 2021 will be its centenary, and plans are being put in place to celebrate that event. One hundred years on, and the evangelical work still continues to meet both the material and spiritual needs of these communities. It is a record of missionary endeavour in the Andes with which the Free Church of Scotland can be satisfied – and I am happy to have been part of it.

A very short afterword

IT IS CUSTOMARY, WHEN CONFRONTED BY ANY FINISHED PIECE OF work, to suppose that the idea for it fell from the sky fully-formed. And that indeed may often be the case: but it was certainly not the case with this book, which came about in the following way. In the autumn of 2019, my second cousin Hilda Clow and I drove round the North Coast 500 route. At the end of the trip we stayed in the Priory Hotel in Beauly. Hilda's mother's people came from Ruilick up on the Braes above the village, as did my mother's people, from Rheindown. We got to yarning about the history of Beauly and the people of the village and the Braes above. We recalled that the district had produced two Andean missionaries of the Free Church of Scotland – Flora Matheson, a daughter of the local Free Church manse, and Netta Fraser from Rheindown. But that – more or less – was all that we knew. It seemed obvious, of course, that the story of the Free Church in the Andes was in print, somewhere or other. I assured Hilda that I would find everything in print, and would send it to her when I had found it. And then I started to search...

Of course, there was nothing to find in the historical or religious journals – or nothing that I could find, anyway. So I took myself to the Mitchell Library in Glasgow (which has a complete run of the Free Church's Monthly Record) and worked my way through a century's worth of the periodical. As a matter of habit, more than anything else, I took a note of anything that pertained to the Andean missionaries, and in the evening – again as a matter of habit – I typed-up the notes. At length, there were no more notes to take, and no more keyboard-bashing to detain me. I had, at least, with very little conscious effort, written a skeletal account of the Free Church missionaries in the Andes – who, what, where, when and why. But it was a curiously hybrid sort of account. It was not exactly a fully-sourced piece of writing for some sort of academic journal, although it could have become that. Actually, it was more of a "memorandum to self" – a start to something, though it was not clear what that something would be. After a couple of weeks, I woke up during the night and saw the solution to the matter with perfect clarity – what I had written was (with a lot more work) an introduction to a book on the subject. And so – this is that book.

Does it represent the last word on the subject of the Free Church in the Andes? I very much hope not. But for the meantime it will have to do. There is not much more material available at the moment. There may just be some more material hidden in cupboards and lofts: though that is probably unlikely. This is a pity. The reader will have observed that though women were a large part of the missionary cadre in the Andes, they have not (with the exception of Margaret Fraser) written any part of this book. But that is because they left no written record behind them. And yet they must all – men and women – have written home regularly. Where might such letters now be? And might there still be some letters, or photographs, or diaries, or draft memoirs, for the likes of J. Calvin Mackay, to be found? (Perhaps urgent efforts should begin at once to search for such material, to collect it at a central point, and have it curated to archival standards).

Books like this, after all, represent the art of the possible – and are themselves sometimes open to set back. On the morning of Easter Monday, 2020, my e-mail account was hacked in connection with some online scam. The hackers, perhaps by way of calling card, emptied my inbox and outbox. That destroyed hundreds of e-mails relating to the research for the book. They would certainly have been of interest to any doctoral-level researcher who might someday take the story of the Free Church in the Andes as the subject of his or her thesis. It is to be hoped that in time that sort of academic attention will be brought to the matter, perhaps under the title of missiology. That is why "sources for further study" is as detailed as it is.

But for the meantime, this is all there is. At least the book snatches from the jaws of oblivion an honourable corner of Scottish history in the 20th century. At least it remembers a missionary effort of which the Free Church of Scotland can be justly proud. And it pays tribute, I hope, to some extraordinary people: people possessed of intelligence, determination, fortitude, ambition, vision – and above all, of course, religious faith.

Finally, an explanation for the dedication of this book. The frontispiece shows Netta Fraser with her sister, mother and brother. The photograph dates from the 1940s, shortly before Netta's departure for Peru. But in the previous decade there had been another member of the family. He was called Hugh. He was, by all accounts, an extremely good shot: with the rifle, and at targets only. One day he missed the target altogether, and continued to do so. Tests showed that he had multiple sclerosis. It was aggressive, and would be terminal. Netta left her midwifery training in Perth and came home to nurse her brother. One day, my mother, studying Latin and mathematics at Aberdeen University, came home too; by train to Inverness, by bus to Beauly, and then the long, and surely lonely, walk up the hill to Rheindown.

That was the week that the world changed for ever on the Braes of Beauly. After all, people had farmed up there for centuries, for millennia, with no traction power but themselves and their horse. But that week, the first tractor arrived at Rheindown. My uncle drove it round to the front of the house, and left it running. He then carried Hugh out (for by now he could not walk) so that he could see and admire the new tractor. He assured everyone that he could see and did admire the new tractor: but everyone knew that this was not the case, for by now his sight had gone too. But at least he could hear her running, and smell the exhaust smoke. He died on his 28th birthday. So the dedication of this book sits next to the photograph of his own family. I have, if the reader will allow, symbolically re-united them all. Of course – it need hardly be said – such a gesture, for the likes of Netta and her mother, at least, was and is and always will be completely and utterly redundant.

– *Iain Fraser Grigor*
  iain-fraser-grigor@hotmail.co.uk

Sources for further study

THIS BOOK TAKES A MULTI-AUTHOR NARRATIVE-DOCUMENTARY approach to the story of Free Church evangelism in the Andes. There are, therefore, areas of knowledge and theory with which it does not directly concern itself. Under the general heading of missiology (or intercultural-theology), these might be thought to include ecclesiology, sociolinguistics, Bible translation and cultural anthropology: not to mention the shifting sands of Peruvian national politics. These might also include questions about the most effective distribution of scarce resources ("opportunity cost") on the part of a Home Church; the significance, if any, of gender in missionary work; such relation as missionary endeavour may have with issues of colonialism and imperialism and matters of class and cultural oppression in the countries in which it works; the question of missionary orientation to the redistribution, by state (or other) agency, of individual or collective wealth by methods such as "land-reform" and redistributive taxation; the question of strategies of "integral mission" – primary versus secondary evangelism (in the form of medical, educational, economic-development and other projects); and the issue of publishing (evangelistic communication), on an individual and mass scale, in the age of social media. And of course there is the issue of which social stratum any missionary effort might primarily concentrate its efforts on, in a given territory. Any scholar who wishes to explore these issues in a Peruvian context might find some of the following sources to be of utility.

BOOKS ON THE FREE CHURCH IN THE ANDES

The only title in English which touches on this subject is, J. B. A. Kessler, A Study of the Older Protestant Missions and Churches in Peru and Chile. Netherlands, 1967. Kessler devotes just three pages to the Free Church in the Andes.

BOOKLETS ON THE FREE CHURCH IN THE ANDES

J. Kennedy Cameron, Peru and its Free Church of Scotland Mission, Inverness, 1921 (70 pages)

Free Church of Scotland Missionary Enterprise, Edinburgh, 1949 (18 pages about the Free Church in the Andes)

David Milnes, Inca Stronghold, London, 1950.

David Miles, Children of the Inca Stronghold, London, 1959.

UNPUBLISHED BOOK

Margaret Kemp Melanson, (Editor), Memories of Peru, Christchurch, New Zealand, 1984

BIOGRAPHIES AND STUDIES OF JOHN A. MACKAY

John Mackay Metzger, The Hand and the Road, Kentucky, 2010. (Metzger was a grandson of John A. Mackay).

Raúl Chanamé Orbe, La Amistad de dos Amautas – Mariátegui y John A. Mackay, Lima, 1995. [The Friendship of Two Wise Teachers – Mariátegui and John A.Mackay]

Tomás Gutierrez Sánchez, Protestantismo y Política en la Vida y Obra de John A. Mackay, 1917-1936, Lima, 2014. [Protestantism and Politics in the Life and Work of John A. Mackay]

John H. Sinclair, John A. Mackay, Un Escocés con Alma Latina, Mexico, 1990. [John A. Mackay, a Scotsman with a Latin Soul] (Sinclair's father had come to the United States from Caithness).

ONLINE MATERIAL ON MACKAY

There is an essay on the relationship between Mackay and Mariáregui at:

jesusenaccion.blogspot.com/2012/05/mackay-y-mariategui.html
See also:
oizquierdo.blogspot.com/2014/07/john-mackay-mariategui-y-haya-de – la.html

ACADEMIC JOURNALS

As noted in the Introduction, there is nothing on the work of the Free Church in the Andes in a range of Scottish and church-affairs journals. There is Gavin D. White, Scottish Overseas Missions – a select critical bibliography, in the Records of the Scottish Church History Society. But there is no mention of Peru.

See however:

Samuel Escobar, The legacy of John Alexander Mackay. International Bulletin of Mission Research, 1992. For a time, Escobar taught in the Free Church school in Lima.

Raúl Chanamé Orbe, La Relácion de Mariátegui con John A. Mackay, Textos para la acción 3, no 3. January, 1995. [The relationship of Mariáregui with John A. Mackay] (Cited in Metzger, the Hand and the Road).

W. Stanley Rycroft and John H. Sinclair, Collision (and Conversion) in mid-air, 1918, The Journal of Presbyterian History (1997 –), April, 2008, vol. 86 (1)

John H. Sinclair and W. Stanley Rycroft, W. Stanley Rycroft, Latin American Missiologist, American Presbyterians, July 1987, vol. 65 (2)

Stanton R. Wilson with William O. Harris, John A. Mackay: Bibliographical Resources for the Period 1914-1992, Studies in Reformed Theology and History, vol. 1, no 4, Autumn,1993

PERIODICALS

The Monthly Record of the Free Church of Scotland, and its associated missionary bulletin, From the Frontiers, along with its magazine for children, The Instructor, are essential sources for the story of the Free Church in the Andes.

PERSONAL PAPERS

W. Stanley Rycroft Papers
Presbyterian Historical Society, Philadelphia
These papers, inter alia, contain two or three decades of correspondence between Rycroft and John H. Sinclair, relating to the latter's biography of John A. Mackay.

John A. Mackay Collection
Princeton Theological Seminary
There are letters from Mackay to José Carlos Mariátegui at:

Correspondencia, 1915-1930, Tomo I, Biblioteca Amauta, Lima 1984, 102-524.

Archive of the Evangelical Union of South America
Centre for the Study of World Christianity, Edinburgh University.
(Thomas Chalmers' papers are also held in Edinburgh University).

McIntosh Missionary Archive
National Library of Scotland
This is a collection of material relating to work in Peru by the
Presbyterian missionaries George Stewart McIntosh and his wife
Janet. They were not, strictly, missionaries for the Free Church
of Scotland, but their work overlapped largely with that of Free
Church missionaries. McIntosh and his wife went to South America
in 1965. The following year, they went to the north east of Peru,
to the areas of Cajamarca and Moyobamba, with the Peru Inland
Mission. Their second daughter, Ruth, was born in Annie Soper's
hospital in Lamas – the last missionary child to be born there. Later,
the McIntoshes worked with Quechua speakers in the southern
mountains of Apurímac. In 1977, they moved to Lima, where
McIntosh taught in the Lima Evangelical Seminary. He also co-operated with the Evangelical Presbyterian Church of Peru.

Free Church Records, Edinburgh.
The Foreign Missions Committee/Board of the Free Church
supervised missionary operations in the Andes for the best part of
the 20th century. During that time, it is likely that it accumulated a
large amount of documentation. It may be that in that documentation, there is as-yet undiscovered memorial material.

Iain Fraser Grigor Papers
Sabhal Mor Ostaig

A file of material relating to the research for this book is held in
these papers. The file includes a manuscript index to the Monthly

Record from 1914 to 2014 with reference to Free Church involvement in the Andes. The file also contains a copy of Dr. Kenneth Mackay's memoir: a single-spaced typescript of 118 pages and close to 50, 000 words.

Two teachers at the Free Church school in Lima, who also travelled extensively in the Andes, were V. R. (Vere Rochelle) Browne, and James MacIntosh. It is not presently known where any personal papers for either of them might now be. Nor are any personal papers of the Rev. J. Calvin Mackay or Neil A. R. Mackay known to exist. But, who knows, who knows? It is just possible that, someday, something might turn-up.

BOOKS

Ladislao Barreto, Apuntes Históricos de la Iglesia Libre en el Perú, Morococha, 1942 [Historical Notes on the Free Church in Peru]

Pedro W. Merino Boyd, Historia de la Iglesia Presbiteriana en el Perú, Lima, 2016 [History of the Presbyterian Church in Peru]

Stewart J. Brown and Michael Fry, editors, Scotland in the Age of the Disruption, Edinburgh, 1993.

Stewart J. Brown, Thomas Chalmers and the Godly Commonwealth in Scotland, Oxford, 1982.

Ramón Cawston, Iglesias Nacientes, Trujillo, 2015. [New Churches] This title contains information relevant to the story of the Free Church in the Andes.

Noble David Cook, Born to Die: Disease and New World Conquest, 1492-1650, Cambridge, 1998.

Wade Davis, One River, New York, 1996. Davis is primarily an ethnobotanist, and this book – with its magnificent bibliography – is, inter alia, a sort of biography of Richard Evans Schultes

Samuel Escobar, Imágenes de Cristo en el Perú, Lima, 2013 [Images of Christ in Peru]

Samuel Escobar, Protestantismo en el Perú: Guía Bibliográfica y de Fuentes, Lima, 2001 [Protestantism in Peru: Bibliographic Guide and Sources]

Samuel Escobar, Precursores Evangélicos, Lima, 1984 [Evangelical Forerunners]

Paulo Freire, Pedagogy of the Oppressed, New York, 1970

Francisco López de Gómarra, Historia General de las Indias, Zaragoza, 1552. Based on interviews with conquistadores who had returned to Spain.

Ondina González and Justo González, Christianity in Latin America – a History, New York, 2008

Ales Hrdlicka, Disease Medicine and Surgery among American Aborigines, Journal of the American Medical Association, vol. XCIC, 1932.

Wilton Marion Krogman, Medical Practices and Diseases of the Aboriginal American Indians, Ciba Symposia, 1:1, April, 1939.

Weston La Barre, The Aymará Indians of the Lake Titicaca Plateau. American Anthropologist, Memoir, vol. 50, no. 1, part 2, 1948. La Barre was primarily an anthropologist, who collaborated with the famous Harvard ethnobotanist Richard Evans Schultes.

Alfredo Torres Luna, El Problema de la Educación del Aborigen Peruano, Loma, 1940. [The problem of the education of the Peruvian aborigine/native/Indian]

John A. Mackay, Don Miguel de Unamuno; Su personalidad, obra e influencia, Lima, 1919. [Don Miguel de Unamuno: his personality, work and influence]

G. Stewart McIntosh, The Life and Times of John Ritchie, Scotland and Peru, 1878-1952, Tayport, 1988.

James Lachlan MacLeod, The Second Disruption, East Linton, 2000.

John MacPherson, At the Roots of a Nation, the Story of San Andrés School in Lima, Peru, Edinburgh, 1993

Philip Ainsworth Means, The Fall of the Inca Empire and the Spanish Rule in Peru, 1530-1780, New York, 1964

Herbert Money, The Money Memoirs, 3 vols., editor G. Stewart McIntosh,Tayport, 1988

Herbert Money, La Libertad Religiosa en el Perú, Lima, 1965 [Religious Liberty in Peru]

Carlos Monge, HIgh Altitude Disease, Journal of the American Medical Association, 1937.

Dervla Murphy, Eight Feet in the Andes, London, 1983. This book, by an extremely perceptive Irish writer, is primarily the account of a 1, 300 mile walk through the Andes from Cajamarca to Cuzco, roughly following the route of Pizarro in his conquest of Peru. But, tangentially, it very strongly validates many of the perspectives of

Free Church mission work in the mountains of Peru during the 20th century.

William H. Prescott, A History of the Conquest of Peru. A justly famous account, in many editions.

W. Stanley Rycroft [Editor], Indians of the High Andes, Report of the Commission etc. etc. New York, 1946

Moisés Sáenz, The Peruvian Indian, Washington, 1944. Sáenz was a major educationist with a special interest in Indian affairs. A north American (from Mexico), he served eventually as his country's ambassador to Peru.

John H. Sinclair, Protestantism in Latin America: a bibliographical guide, South Pasadena, California, 1976

Brian Stanley, The World Missionary Conference, Edinburgh, 1910, Grand Rapids, MI, 2009.

Alexander Stewart and J. Kennedy Cameron, The Free Church of Scotland 1843-1910, Edinburgh, 1910.

Phylis Thompson, Dawn Beyond the Andes, London, 1955. The book, primarily for children, was published by Regions Beyond Missionary Union, and tells the story of Annie Soper and Rhoda Gould.

Luis Torrejón, Pasos Sobre Fundamentos Solidos, Lima, 2000 [Steps on Solid Foundations]

Harry Tschopik, The Aymará, Handbook of South American Indians, Smithsonian Institution, Washington, and The Aymará of Chucuito, New York, 1951

Harry E. Vanden and Marc Becker, José Carlos Mariátegui – an anthology, New York 2011.

Garcilaso de la Vega, Comentarios Reales de los Incas, Lisbon, 1609. The author was the natural son of a conquistador and a royal Inca mother, who lived in Spain from the age of 21.

Nathan Watchel, The Vision of the Vanquished: the Spanish Conquest of Peru through Indian Eyes, New York, 1977

Francisco de Xerez, Verdadera Relación de la Conquista del Perú: a famous eye-witness account in many editions. [True account of the Conquest of Peru]

POST-GRADUATE THESES

Charles Douglas, MTh thesis, Centre for the Study of Christianity in the Non-Western World, Edinburgh University, 1999. The Importance of Praxis in the Mission of the Church: a case study of the project of education, health and agriculture (PROESA) in the village of Haulqui, Cajamarca, Peru.

William Mitchell, MLitt thesis at St. Andrews University, 1973. Perspectives on folklore and the Quechua people of southern Peru; and PhD thesis at Edinburgh University, 1991, The appropriation of the Quechua language by the church and the christianisation of Peru in the sixteenth and early seventeenth century. Mitchell spent his working life in Bible translation in the Americas.

George Stewart McIntosh. (See above). Master's degree at St. Andrews University in Latin American linguistics and dialectology. And a PhD, at the same university, on Quechuan religious terms.

John Roxborogh, PhD, Aberdeen University, 1978. Thomas

Chalmers and the mission of the Church, with special reference to the rise of the missionary movement in Scotland.

Stanton R. Wilson, Studies in the Life and Work of an Ecumenical Churchman, [ie. John A. Mackay], Unpublished thesis, Princeton Theological Seminary, 1958,1978

FILM STRIP

A Town Called Jesus
In English
Produced by (variously) TEARFUND, tearfund, or TEAR Fund, which is a Christian charity concerned to end global poverty.

SOUND RECORDINGS

Margaret Fraser, later Mrs. Kenneth Mackay, of Achiltibuie and Moyobamba, was sound-taped in 1989 by the distinguished Scottish folklorist and Gaelic singer Margaret Bennet, on behalf of the School of Scottish Studies. The recording is held in the online sound archive of Tobar an Dualchais (Kist o' Riches).

A note on contributors

THE REV. PROFESSOR JOHN KENNEDY CAMERON was born in Easter Ross; his wife came from Gairloch. He was ordained as Free Church minister at Kilbride on the Isle of Arran, and was Moderator of the Free Church General Assembly in 1910-1911. From 1900, for 36 years, he was Clerk to the General Assembly and from 1906 was Professor of Systematic Theology at the Free Church College.

THE REV. RONALD CHRISTIE was raised in Saltcoats, where his father was Free Church Minister. He did an MA at Edinburgh University, and later a B.D. A Master's degree followed at Westminster Seminary, Philadelphia, in the United States. Following his marriage to Morag MacRae, of Plockton, they left for Peru in 1968. They returned from Peru in 1977 and he was subsequently minister in Wick and Govanhill, Glasgow.

THE REV. CHARLES DOUGLAS was brought-up in Musselburgh. After eight years working in the insurance industry he left with his wife for Peru in 1978 as a Free Church missionary. Her father, the Rev. Duncan Beaton, was born in Inverness and had family connections in Lochcarron. The Rev. Douglas returned to Scotland in 1986 to undertake studies for a diploma in Theology at the Free Church

College. His first pastoral charge was on the Isle of Bute. After four years there, he went to Edinburgh University to undertake a Master's degree in Theology. He ran the Free Church bookshop for 19 years.

MARGARET FRASER was born in Dundee and went to St. Andrews University. Her father's brother was Dr. Kenneth Mackay; she was named after Dr. Kenneth's wife, Margaret Fraser of Achiltibuie. She married the Rev. Andrew Fraser in 1974. He was born in Wick and grew up in Plockton and, later, Edinburgh. He did law at Edinburgh University and then theology at the Free Church College. They went to Peru in October, 1974, a few weeks after their marriage.

DR. IAIN FRASER GRIGOR was brought-up in Morar, Lochaber. He attended the universities of Strathclyde and Glasgow and a media *stage* at the CFPJ in Paris. For some time, he worked as a fisherman on the Scottish west coast, and then in newspapers. He has written various books on – to a greater or lesser extent – Scottish themes. Nurse Netta Fraser was his aunt.

ALAN MACKAY of Dunblane studied in Edinburgh and Cardiff, and worked for many years in broadcasting. He contributed media services related to the publication of this book. His great grandfather, W. Murray Mackay, was a noted 19th century Free Church minister in Glasgow. W. Murray Mackay's wife, Christian Sage, was a daughter of the Rev. Donald Sage, eye-witness to the Highland Clearances in Sutherland, and an eminent minister at the time of theDisruption.

JOHN ALEXANDER MACKAY, while engaged in the educational work of the Free Church school in Lima, also held two Chairs at the university of San Marcos – one in philosophy and the other in metaphysics. In 1926, he moved to Montevideo on the other side of South America to work with the YMCA, with a view to evangelising the student corps of the continent. In 1930, he moved to Mexico. Later, he spent 23 years as President of Princeton Theological Seminary.

DR. KENNETH MACKAY was born in Alness and was married to Margaret Fraser of Achiltibuie. They were in Peru as pioneer missionaries of the Free Church of Scotland from the mid-1920s until 1938. He later received an MD from Glasgow University for a study on Kwashiorkor related to parasites from pigs roaming the streets of San Martín.

THE REV. WILLIE MACKAY studied history and geography at the University of St Andrews and then theology at the Free Church College in Edinburgh. He was headmaster of Colegio San Andrés in Lima for 12 years. This book would not have been possible without his contribution: he made available not only Dr. Kenneth Mackay's typescript memoir, but also J. Kennedy Cameron's report to the Mound and the booklet Missionary Enterprise. Dr. Kenneth Mackay was his uncle.

THE REV. JOHN MACPHERSON was unfailingly helpful and encouraging during the production of this book. In 1959 he went out to Peru as a teacher in Colegio San Andrés. From 1975 to 1977, he was Acting Principal of the Lima Evangelical Seminary. He was ordained as a minister in 1974. He was Free Church minister in Dornoch from 1977 to 1988, and headmaster of Colegio San Andrés from 1988 to 1992.

DR. DAVID MILNES was born in 1915. He won a scholarship to study medicine at Cambridge, and on graduation at once entered the Royal Army Medical Corps. His brother, a tank commander, was killed at El Alamein; Dr. Milnes won a Military Cross in the same battle. Hearing of the death from typhus of a young missionary doctor in the southern Andes of Peru, he decided to go there himself. He and his wife Netta Fraser returned to the UK in 1964, where he retrained as a psychiatrist. They were back in Peru from 1974 to 1979, and again from 1985 to 1986.

ALEXANDER RENWICK was a Gaelic-speaker and a former army chaplain in World War One. He spent 17 years at the Free Church college in Lima, and then moved to the British Council in Chile. In 1931, he was Moderator of the General Assembly of the Free Church. He held a Chair in Theology at Edinburgh University. In 1943, he was appointed to the Chair of Church History and Principles at the Free Church College in Edinburgh.

W. STANLEY RYCROFT was a Methodist from Liverpool. After his service in the Royal Flying Corps in World War One, he was an educational missionary in Peru for 18 years, initially with John Alexander Mackay at the Free Church school in Lima, which in time became known as Colegio San Andrés. He also travelled extensively in the Andes. In later years, he held senior Presbyterian positions in the United States.

Appendix 1: Glossary

Aguardiente: home-made alcohol

Aji: capiscum pepper

Alma kachar pariy: sending away the soul (Spanish/Quechua)

Alma waqyah: calling-back of the spirit (Spanish/Quechua)

Altiplano: high plateau

Amuata: Inca functionary; wise teacher (Quechua)

Arriero: mule-driver

Ayllus: co-operative Andean community (Quechua)

Aukis: mountain-spirits (Quechua)

Bestia: beast

Boga: oarsman, ferryman

Brujo: witch-doctor

Burro: donkey

Caldo: broth

Campesino: Andean peasant

Campiña: countryside

Cerdo: piglet

Chacra: small farm

Chalka: very high uncultivable land

Chancaca: unrefined brown sugar

Chicha: beer made with maize

Cholo: half-breed

Chuño: dehydrated potato

Coca: loanword (Quechua)

Colegio: college

Colono: Indian serf

Colporteur: pedlar; distributor of religious tracts (French)

Condor: loanword (Quechua)

Coolans: an Anglicised plural generally meaning puppies but here piglets, from the singular cuilean(Gaelic)

Comunidades: communal farms, Indian communities

Cordillera: mountain range

Cuesta: climb

Curandero: quack doctor; native medicine-man

Cuy: guinea-pig (Quechua)

Direach sin: "just so" (Gaelic) (but the wit does not translate)

Fiambre: food and provisions for a journey

Finca: a farm

Gringo: white foreigner

Guano: loanword (Quechua)

Hacienda: country estate

Halca: the crossing of a mountain height

Huaca or wak'a: venerated object, such as a rock (Quechua)

Huasipunguero: peon who gives service for a piece of land (Quechua)

Humitas: cakes of freshly-ground maize. From humint'a (Quechua)

Inti: Incan sun-god (Quechua)

Kukuchi: spectre, bogeyman (Quechua)

Llama: loanword (Quechua)

Mestizo: cross between Indian and Spaniard

Misti: person of Spanish descent (Quechua)

Montaña: jungle

Muda: magical medical "exchange"

Mulo/mula: mule

Obraje: workshop

Pachamana: Goddess of the earth (Quechua)

Pampas: high prairie grassland (Quechua)

Paqo: spirit-doctor (Quechua)

Patrón: boss, landlord

Peon: farm labourer

Pisco: home-distilled brandy

Poncho: loanword (Quechua)

Pongo: Indian serf; patrón's right to feudal tribute from an Indian

Puma: loanword (Quechua)

Punas: Andean mountain-tops

Quinine: loanword (Quechua)

Quinoa: loanword (Quechua)

Selva: forest, jungle

Serranos: inhabitants of the Sierra

Shapsha: a devil (in southern Peru) (Quechua)

Sierra: mountain range

Soroche: mountain-sickness (from Quechua, suruqch'i)

Supoya: a class of evil spirits (Quechua)

Tambo: mountain shelter

Uma Hampiq: healer of heads, ie. psychiatrist (Quechua)

Upe: gruel of toasted maize

Vicuña: loanword (Quechua)

Yucca: manioc root, cassava

Appendix 2: List of Protestant mission agencies in Peru, at 1946

Amazon Valley Faith Baptist Mission
American Bible Society
Assemblies of God, General Council
British and Foreign Bible Society
Christian and Missionary Alliance
Church of the Nazarene, General Board
Evangelical Union of South America
Free Church of Scotland, Foreign Missions Committee
Holiness Church of California
Independent Board of Presbyterian Foreign Missions
Inland South American Missionary Union
Irish Baptist Foreign Mission
Methodist Church, Board of Missions
Mid-Peruvian Mission
Peruvian Inland Mission
Salvation Army
Seventh Day Adventists, General Conference
Christian Missions in Many Lands
Association of Baptists for World Evangelism

Appendix 3: Photographs of Free Church missionaries in the Andes

From the Monthly Record and From the Frontiers.

June 1925.
J. Calvin Mckay with wife and three children.

May 1927.
Nurse Annabella MacLeod.

June 1929.
Nurse Sarah MacDougall.

November 1929.
Mission Staff, Cajamarca.
Sabbath School, Cajamarca.

March 1930.
Moyobamba School.

September 1930.
Nurses MacLeod and Mackay, Moyobmba.
Nurse MacLeod, Dr. Kenneth Mackay, and Nurse Mackay.

May 1932.
A missionary group at Moyobamba.

June 1932.
Nurse MacMillan, Cajamarca.
Nurse Macdonald, Moyobamba.

June 1933.
Dr. Kenneth Mackay, his wife, three children, Nurse Sarah MacDougall, Nurse Annabella MacLeod.

September 1933.
Miss Christina Mackay.

June 1934.
Flora Matheson.

September 1935.
Flora Matheson and two of Dr. Mackay's children.

December 1935.
The Rev. Murdo Nicolson.

July 1937.
Dr. Harold Lindsay.

January 1938.
Dr. Kenneth Mackay and his hospital staff, Moyobamba; seven people in the photograph.

October 1939.
Rev. Murdo Nicolson and his bride Miss Paterson, from the North of Ireland.

May 1940.
Dr. Harold Lindsay and his bride Flora Matheson.

January 1942.
Photographs relating to the opening of the new church in Moyobamba.

April 1945.
A Cajamarca group: Sarah MacDougall, Rev. Murdo and Mrs. Nicolson, and child.

June 1954.
Nurse Agness Gunn.

October 1987.
A photograph to accompany an obituary for the Rev. Malcolm MacRae.

February 1988.
A photograph to accompany an obituary for Dr. Kenneth Mackay.

April 1988.
A photograph to accompany an obituary for Dr. David Milnes.

1988.
Miss Marie-Christine Lux.

January 1990.
A photograph to accompany an obituary for Mrs. Christina MacDonald (née Mackay).

February 1998.
Miss Christina MacDonald of Edinburgh; photograph taken in 1932. A group photograph which includes: Dr. Kenneth Mackay, Miss Annabella MacLeod (later, Mrs. MacRae), Rev. J. Calvin Mackay, and Mrs. Kenneth Mackay (Margaret Fraser of Achiltibuie) with first child, Eric.

April 1998.
Miss Christina Macdonald (Mackay?) at Moyobamba's "airport", in the early days of aviation.

It is not known if the original negatives or prints are extant.